This Country Must Change

This Country Must Change

Essays on the Necessity of Revolution in the USA

Craig Rosebraugh
Contributing Editor

arissa
media group
PORTLAND • PHOENIX
LOS ANGELES

THIS COUNTRY MUST CHANGE
Essays on the Necessity of Revolution in the USA
Copyright © 2009
Craig Rosebraugh

Arissa Media Group
Tel: (866) 476-0964
info@arissamediagroup.com
www.arissamediagroup.com

Printed and bound in the United States of America.

Library of Congress Control Number: 2009929072
International Standard Book Number: 9780974288475

Cover design by Keri Rosebraugh, www.kerirosebraugh.com.

Arissa Media Group, LLC was formed in 2003 to assist in building a revolutionary consciousness in the United States of America. For more information, bulk requests, catalog listings, submission guidelines, or media inquiries please contact:

Arissa Media Group • Tel: (866) 476-0964
info@arissamediagroup.com • www.arissamediagroup.com

Printed on 100% post consumer waste, FSC certified recycled paper. By using this paper in printing this book, Arissa Media Group saved 16 trees, 12 million BTU's of energy, 1,319 lbs of greenhouse gases, 5,964 gallons of wastewater, and 695 lbs of solid waste. Environmental impact estimates were made using the Environmental Defense Fund Paper Calculator. For more information visit www.papercalculator.org.

Arissa Media Group is a member of Green Press Initiative, which means we meet GPI's environmental criteria and support their efforts to reduce the social and environmental impacts of book publishing. For more information, please visit:
www.greenpressinitiative.org.

DEDICATION

This book is dedicated to all those, past and present, who have struggled against the U.S. oligarchy, against U.S. imperialism, corporate dominance, and especially to those who have recognized and fought against this myth of democracy.

CONTENTS

INTRODUCTION

CRAIG ROSEBRAUGH

Introduction

I first considered this project after noticing the scarcity of literature and other resources available pertaining to the need for a fundamental social and political revolution in the United States. While there are multitudes of books, pamphlets, magazines, and films dedicated to promoting positive change, they almost entirely fall into a reformist category - attempting to modify one or multiple "issues" within the political system rather than confronting the methodology of governing as an entirety.

This lack of resources on the subject of revolution in the United States is problematic, as it reinforces the arbitrary limitations on change that are sanctioned and promoted by the very power structure that is in need of substantial alteration. If the resources are not available to assist in promoting even the discussion of revolution in this country, those desiring change will continue to fall back into the time-tested and failed methods, which have only prolonged the life of a political system that has been unjust since its beginning in 1776.

In the United States, we are instilled with the notions from a very early age that it is our responsibility to do what is right, to promote peace and justice, and to act for the good of others and the world. These values are taught to us by our families, peers, educators, coaches, the government, religion and the corporate media. Without exception, these noble teachings come with one major golden rule - those desiring change must adhere specifically to methods prescribed by the government and reinforced by the media and thus, educators, coaches, religion, family, and peers. The one thing that is not taught to those desiring change in this country is that it is literally impossible to create fundamental political and social change by strictly adhering to only those methods approved by the government. The state-sanctioned means of change, the voting, lobbying and legislation, the rallies, protests and pickets, and other activities that demonstrate one's legal right to object and promote change, have never on their own substantially altered the political structure that has and continues to cause relentless atrocities.

The advances in U.S. society that have been gained - the abolition of slavery, the Suffrage victory, the labor advances, the Civil Rights movement in particular - came about through a variety of strategies and tactics including many that did not fit neatly within the politically approved methods outlined by the government. And yet, while some advances have been made using a diversity of approaches, the governing system that lies at the root of significant "issues" has never been seriously addressed.

In each of the many social and political issues that largely grew out of the awakening period of the 1960s, millions of dollars continue to be spent each year in the U.S. on lobbying and backing political candidates, voting drives, promoting legislation, legal battles, symbolic rallies and protests, media campaigns, and more. Whether for environmental protection, animal welfare, or human rights campaigns, money coming from grants, memberships, fundraisers, and donations is funneled strictly into campaigns that involve only strategies and tactics approved by the very governing body that continues to cause or allow the overwhelming majority of these "issues" to thrive. Yet, there is little to no effort or resources spent on organizing and acting to fundamentally change the political structure itself.

This book is an attempt to assist in enlarging the discussion of the necessity of revolution in the United States. Here, the reader will find essays by twelve prominent activists and authors, all who have demonstrated through their words and actions a commitment to fundamental political and social change within this country. While their backgrounds are diverse, covering a wide range of animal, environmental, and human liberation struggles, they are unified in the realization that what we have done so far as a society has not worked, has not been enough to end the injustice and oppression that is caused by the U.S. government and the corporate/political elite that run the country. They are unified in the understanding that a revolution is needed in the United States and that it is up to all of us to make that occur.

In picking up and opening this book, the reader may notice that the essays contained herein are, with the exception of one, all by male authors. I would like to take a moment to address this problem. In organizing and producing this book, a specific list of activists and authors were approached and asked to contribute. Those considered for publication had all shown a dedication in their lives, through their work and/or writings to fundamental change. Owing to the male dominance pervasive through society, including the often misguided prominence of men as key, important figures in political movements while neglecting crucial female roles and leaders, there were more women activists and authors approached for this project than men. The response was less than even and this project was delayed for one year in an attempt to more evenly provide a balanced approach to this topic. A few people who had agreed to the project, were either unable to get their writings out of prison or had them confiscated by prison authorities. Others, once learning more about the project, became uncomfortable with it promoting revolution as opposed to the safer reformist perspective. Whatever the case may have been, we decided to move forward with the project after waiting a year, even without the balance of the female perspective. That being said, Arissa Media Group is planning a follow-up book that will feature prominent women activists and authors discussing the need for revolution in the United States.

This book is designed to reach two primary audiences - those who are currently involved in social and political struggles and those who have yet to become involved but realize something is wrong in this society. In the former category, it is crucial that current activists rethink their strategies, tactics and focus. What we have done thus far in the United States, has not worked. It has not worked precisely because the political system itself, and its corporate elite have not significantly been challenged and overcome. The longer we fail to realize this, the worse off the environment, animals and people in this country will be. Not to mention the millions around the planet who suffer daily from U.S. imperialist policies. In the latter category, it is important that before you take the first step into attempting to change injustice in this country, you fully analyze what it is you are going to do, why you are going to do it and what are the likely outcomes and barriers. It is important to realize that there is a specific reason that the government, media and significant portions of social change organizations dictate exactly the type of tactics and strategies that are approved for you to utilize. It is important for you to realize that what has been attempted throughout history to stop injustice in this country has not worked. It has not worked precisely because the political structure itself and the ruling corporate elite have not been challenged and overcome. Unless we realize this and act upon it, there is little hope for our future.

I personally would like to thank all of the activists and authors who contributed essays to this book. Your voices are important in assisting to generate the necessary discussion of revolution in this country. Of course, words alone can never change the world, only the actions that words inspire may do so. I hope the reader will find the words contained within these essays as inspirational as I have, and use them to further fuel the fire that ignites change within this country.

CHAPTER ONE

TOWARDS A NEW
AMERIKAN REVOLUTION

JALIL A. MUNTAQIM

JALIL A. MUNTAQIM

This Country Must Change

In 1776, North American's became independent of the British Empire, creating the United States confederation that existed until 1789, after which the United States evolve into a Union. In 1865, the United States enacted the 13th Amendment to end chattel slavery of Afrikans. Approximately three years later, the enactment of the 14th Amendment in 1868, was not only to impose citizenship on Afrikans brought to this country against their will and used as chattel slaves, but also to impose *Federal corporate control* on sovereign states not made part of the Union as a result of the civil war. Naturally, the ending of the civil war and Afrikan chattel slavery resulted in the need to rebuild the economy; thus in 1871 members of the U.S. Congress and the then President of the United States formally incorporated the United States as a for-profit commerce enterprise. The Act to Provide a Government for the District of Columbia, Section 34 of the Forty-First Congress of the United States, Session III, Chapter 61 and 62, enacted on February 21, 1871, states:

> *"The UNITED STATES OF AMERICA is a corporation, whose jurisdiction is applicable only in the ten-mile-square parcel of land known as the District of Columbia and to what ever properties are legally titled to the UNITED STATES, by its registration in the corporate County, State, and federal governments that are **under military power of the UNITED STATES and its creditors.** "*[1](Emphasis added)

The United States, Inc., comprises a 10-mile radius of Washington, D.C., in accordance with Article 1, Section 8, clause 16 & 17 of the U.S. Constitution, and the corporation adopted the U.S. Constitution as its Articles of Incorporation and bylaws. Hence, as early as six years after the ending of chattel slavery, in 1871, the U.S. Corporation formally began the process of forging economic corporate interest as the foundation for building the nation.

It is extremely important to know these historical facts are not taught in schools. The majority of Americans are unaware that the United States is a for-profit corporate commerce enterprise, and this corporation considers Americans as commerce property of a Federal corporation according to the 14th Amendment of its constitution and bylaws. As such, Americans have relinquished their sovereignty as human beings, and have virtually made a contract with a corporate-governing body to expend their rights and lives as they deem necessary to fulfill the corporate interest of the United States, Inc., as wage slaves.[2] Often there are debates about the importance of the Madison and Jefferson papers being the principle architects of both the Declaration of Independence and the Articles of Confederation evolving into the Constitution of the U.S. Corporation. However, what is often neglected in any discussion about these Federalists is their disdain for private banking, the control of the United States, Inc. wealth by a private corporate interest. In fact, in 1802, Thomas Jefferson warned:

> *"If American people ever allow private banks to control the issue of their currency, first by inflation, then by deflation, the banks... will deprive the people of all property until their children wake-up homeless on the continent their fathers conquered... The issuing power should be taken from the banks and restored to the people. To whom it properly belongs."*

James Madison had warned:

> *"History records that the money changers have used every form of abuse, intrigue, deceit, and violent means possible to maintain their control over governments by controlling money and its issuance."*

In 1881, then, President James A. Garfield held: *"Whoever controls the volume of money in any country is absolute master of all industry and commerce."* In his Inaugural Address, Garfield stated:

> *"The chief duty of the National Government in connection with the currency of the country is to coin money and declare its value. Grave doubts have been entertained whether Congress is authorized by the Constitution to make any form of paper money legal tender. The present issue of United States notes has been sustained by the necessities of war; but such paper should depend*

> *for its value and currency upon its convenience in use and its prompt redemption in coin at the will of the holder, and not upon its compulsory circulation. These notes are not money, but promises to pay money. If the holders demand it, the promise should be kept."*

Yet, the United States, Inc., as a capitalist system utilizes the financial institutions and private banking of the Federal Reserve System,[3] which is obligated to fulfill its mandate as established by the March 9, 1933, U.S. Senate, House Joint Resolution (HJR) 192, 73rd Congress, 1st Session, Chapter 1, page 83, 1st paragraph, third sentence that states:

> *"Under the new law the money is issued to the banks in return for Government obligations, bills of exchange, drafts, notes, trade acceptances, and banker's acceptances. The money will be worth 100 cents on the dollar, because it is backed by the **credit of the nation**. It will represent a mortgage on **all the homes and other property of all the people in the nation**. The money so issued will not have one penny of gold coverage behind it, because it is really not needed."* (Emphasis added)

On June 5, 1933, this same Congress at Chapter 48, stated:

> *"The ultimate ownership of all property is in the State; individual so-called "ownership" is only by virtue of Government, i.e., law, amounting to mere "user" and use must be in acceptance with law and subordinate to the necessities of the State."*

This language for all practical purposes implies a socialist notion of government control of property in negation of the espoused democratic ideal about private ownership of property rights. However, as one example, eminent domain, virtually denies the existence of ownership of private property when a member of the plutocracy, and/or corporate entity via the application of state or federal law, decides to take possession of specific property/

real estate despite the 5th Amendment proclaiming this should not be done without just compensation. As further verified by the following quote from the "Civil Servants Year Book, The Organizer" of January 1934, informing:

> *"Capital must protect itself in every way, through combination and through legislation. Debts must be collected and loans and mortgages foreclosed as soon as possible. When through a process of law the common people have lost their homes, they will be more tractable and more easily governed by the strong arm of the law, applied by the central power of wealth, under control of leading financiers. People without homes will not quarrel with their leaders. This is well known among our principal men now engaged in forming an imperialism of capital to govern the world. By dividing the people, we can get them to expand their energies in fighting over questions of no importance to us except as teachers of the common herd. Thus by discreet action we can secure for ourselves what has been generally planned and successfully accomplished."*

Subject to the above, the U.S., is a for-profit corporate enterprise, utilizing a private banking system, the Federal Reserve Bank, to control the wealth and property of the nation, it is not difficult to understand how the housing market is utilized to upend the economy and how easily corporations are able to outsource jobs overseas (NAFTA, CAFTA, GATT, APEC, etc). Although U.S. currency is printed by the Treasury Department, the currency is purchased at cost of printing, procured and distributed by the Federal Reserve Bank.[4]

Thus, Americans do not own real estate property, houses or cars for as long as they have to pay taxes to the government, rather they are leasing such tangible items from the government, the bankers and corporate interests. If an American is delinquent on their payments of taxes, fees, corporate interests, etc., the government will seize their property(s) and assets, impose a fine and possibly incarcerate them depending on the amount of property and taxes that is unpaid. U.S. citizens by virtue of the 14th. Amendment, are considered no more than commerce property, of whom are not to own tangible property, but are duped in the illusion of being able to do so, resulting in permitting the extremely rich and powerful to maintain their quest for capitalist-imperialist global hegemony. For example, on February 17, 1950, Senate hearings held concerning the U.N. and its organization, James P. Warburg testified that: *"We shall have world government, whether or not we like it. The question is only whether world government will be achieved by consent or conquest."*[5]

Since the illusion of democracy disguises the reality of a plutocracy, the rich continue to control the seats of government, and write the legislations that preserve their wealth at the expense of common folk.[6] American's deluded belief of living in a democracy is exacerbated by the ideal of the one man-one vote electoral process. However, again, this ideal was blatantly exposed as fraudulent when the 2000 presidential election was decided by the U.S. Supreme Court *selection* of George W. Bush as president in negation of the popular vote. When consideration is given to the fact the total cost of the 2004 congressional and presidential election was $4 billion, an increase of one billion from the 2000 election, and it is projected the 2008 candidates for the House, Senate and president will double spending to $8 billion dollars to win their elections, one can affirm the reality that the rich rules.[7] In "Towards an American Revolution: Exposing the Constitution and Other Illusions," Jerry Fresia informs, *"Never has a U.S. president been elected by a majority of the nation's adult citizens."*

Given that fact, neither the capitalist economic system or electoral politics benefit the majority of Americans, but rather serve the interest of corporate entities that according to law *are* persons, as Americans are considered commerce property, it is no wonder there is a need for a new American revolution.

REFUTING ELECTORAL POLITICS

What is the Electoral College and why is the one man-one vote not the foundation of this claimed representative democracy? When considering a populace candidate or the popular vote, it must be understood neither is the basis by which U.S. elections are made. The 2000 presidential election spoke volumes of how a candidate can win the popular vote, but lose the election denying the majority of Americans their chosen representative. In that election Al Gore, obtained 50,992,335 votes nationwide, while George W. Bush received only 50,455,156, votes. However, the U.S. Supreme Court awarded Bush the Florida votes, gaining 271 electoral votes to Gores 266 electoral votes. Such aberrations have occurred throughout the history of national elections, including efforts to block the Electoral College selection of a president and vice president.

- In 1824, the House of Representatives awarded the presidency to John Quincy Adams, although he received 38,000 fewer votes than Andrew Jackson did, because neither candidate won a majority of the Electoral College.
- In 1876, Rutherford B. Hayes, with 109,000 votes received nearly unanimous support from small states, a one-vote margin in the Electoral College, while the popular vote went to Samuel J. Tilden, a virulent racist, with 264,000 votes. The Hayes/Tilden compromise resulted in Hayes becoming president, although he lost the popular vote.
- In 1888, Benjamin Harrison lost the popular vote by 95,713, but won the electoral vote by 65, having only the support of six Southern states with 300,000 popular votes, while Grover Cleveland who overwhelmingly had the winning 425,000 popular votes gained from the majority of the country. [8]

Nonetheless, the 2008 election presents the idealism that the electoral process is the means and method to change the fabric of America's socioeconomic, political, domestic and foreign policies. The two principle candidates for U.S. president representing change in the 2008 election were Senators Barack Obama of Illinois and Hillary Rodham Clinton of New York, a mixed race Black man and a white woman, respectively, challenging what has been a white man's domain as offered by all other candidates in the 2008 election. If either of the two were to win the presidency, it would in fact signify a drastic change to the 'ole boy' white man inheritance, but little change in how corporate America operates on either the domestic or the foreign front. Either a Blackman or a white woman U.S. president would present a façade, a symbol of change, while keeping in place the reality of capitalist-imperialist hegemony.

This is the principle contradiction found in electoral

politics when the electorate continues to be bound by the socio-psychological and cultural dynamics of change from the top down hierarchical structural leadership represented in a two-party system. America's two-party system is far from being democratic when considering how the Electoral College functions essentially to negate the one-man, one-vote process and the popular demand for fundamental change. It is especially significant when considering the amount of money infused in a political campaign by corporate donors and wealthy individuals.

"Every four years, on the Tuesday following the first Monday of November, millions of U.S. citizens go to local voting booths to elect, among other officials, the next president and vice president of their country. Their votes will be recorded and counted, and winners will be declared. But the results of the popular vote are not guaranteed to stand because the Electoral College has not cast its vote.

'The Electoral College is a controversial mechanism of presidential elections that was created by the framers of the U.S. Constitution as a compromise for the presidential election process. At the time, some politicians believed a purely popular election was too reckless, while others objected to giving Congress the power to select the president. The compromise was to set up an Electoral College system that allowed voters to vote for electors, who would then cast their votes for candidates, a system described in Article II, Section 1 of the Constitution.

'Each state has a number of electors equal to the number of its U.S. senators (2 in each state) plus the number of its U.S. representatives, which varies according to the states population. Currently, the Electoral College includes 538 electors, 535 for the total number of congressional members, and three who represent Washington, D.C., as allowed by the 23rd Amendment. On the Monday following the second Wednesday in

December, the electors of each state meet in their respective state capitals to officially cast their votes for president and vice president. These votes are then sealed and sent to the president of the Senate, who on January 6 opens and reads the votes in the presence of both houses of Congress. The winner is sworn into office at noon January 20. Most of the time, electors cast their votes for the candidate who has received the most votes in that particular state. However, there have been times when electors have voted contrary to the people's decision, which is entirely legal."[9] (See, 12th Amendment of U.S. Constitution)

With this understanding of the Electoral College, it is noted, general elections are for *electors* and not necessarily for the candidate of choice. The framers of the U.S., Inc. *Constitution* never trusted the American population to choose a president according to popular will. This is particularly important to consider knowing the corporate entity, i.e., U.S. government, operates to ensure that the rich get richer, preserving its plutocratic origins. Hence, expecting fundamental socio-economic and political change via the electoral process from a top-down hierarchical approach, absent a radical grassroots movement demanding fundamental change, is ultimately an exercise in delusion.

THE MASS AND POPULAR MOVEMENT

The United States, Inc. is an imperialist empire of monopoly-capitalist dominion. The country's existence is based upon the domination (colonization) and exploitation of internal (domestic) and external nations. The acquisition of North America by Europeans was by use of force and the genocidal slaughter of Native Americans. The Europeans ability to forge the nation into its present economic and technological condition has been based on hundreds of years of racist exploitation of Afrikans, Asians and Mexicans along with the plunder, colonizing and controlling of national resources, human labor, and institutions of commerce of various Third World countries.

The U.S. corporate empire for a long time has been threatened with the loss of such colonies, as natives of these colonized countries develop national liberation struggles, and fight for their independence. The external colonies' struggle for national liberation causes the empire to seek alternatives in its capacity to continue to acquire enormous profits from cheap labor and the control of valuable raw materials essential for U.S. imperialist development. As these national liberation struggles succeed in their independence movements against foreign occupation and imperialism, the loss of profits from those colonies eventually affects the socio-economic and political condition of U.S. workers and the neo-colonies. This loss of profits leads to devaluation of the U.S. dollar as is currently happening in comparison with Euros, Canadian dollars and Chinese Yuan.

Thus, American products are lost in the world market, as old markets either limit or close their institutions of commerce to American made goods, industry, corporations, etc. The only alternative the U.S. corporate imperialist has to preserve the accumulation of high profits is to cut back the production of American goods at home, importing more than exporting from their oversea operations. They then develop an energy crisis (petroleum, coal, natural gas) to raise manufacturing costs in industries that depend on these resources, raising the prices of manufactured goods or speeding production in stable colonies where labor is cheap, at the same time increasing productivity in the U.S. with low employment. This ultimately leads to inflation in the American economy; products costing more than the limit of standard living wages because U.S. capitalism has cut back worker's employment while raising the prices of products. Such commerce laws and business practices, as NAFTA, CAFTA, GATT, APEC, etc., and the outsourcing of jobs overseas further erodes the U.S., Inc. populace employment market in the name of globalization.[10]

When this situation develops to the point where the American public is unable to buy American products at the inflated prices, the capitalist system develops a recession in attempt to balance the economic disparity of inflation while keeping the economy stable, and without causing the corporate capitalist to lose profits. In this way, the system seeks to allow the American public to purchase products and maintain the system with various stimulus and incentive packages or tax rebates, but this economic condition affects various oppressed nations in the American populace differently.

Because America comprises the neo-colonization of Third World nations, minorities of the American populace are impacted by inflation and recession more harshly than majority of Euro-Americans. The primary reason for this uneven effect of monopoly-capitalist economic affliction on Third World nations, in comparison to the majority of Euro-Americans, is the neo-colonial socio-economic domination of these Third World nations and racist national oppression.

The socio-economic, political condition of racist national oppression on domestic neo-colonial Third World nations by U.S. capitalism-imperialism, along with the continued disfranchisement of poor Euro-Americans by the closing of foreign markets virtually determines the essential aspects of the mass and popular movement within the borders of North America. The class and national divisions in the American population establishes every condition in which the revolution will be tested, molded and developed into a mass movement for the destruction of racist capitalist-imperialism. The class struggle of Euro-Americans, united with the class and national determination of Third World nations in the U.S., Inc. will assure the victory of external colonies' independence movements against U.S. imperialist hegemony.

However, it is necessary that the mass and popular movement in the U.S., Inc. becomes cognizant of its force and power. *The power of the people* is based upon workers of all nationalities developing a political movement against racism and the neo-colonization of oppressed minorities, and for the end of class divisions, exploitation, and ruling class appropriation of profits from workers labor – the end of monopoly-capitalist ownership of the means of production. Once these political determinations have been forged into a struggle for economic and cultural change in the U.S. corporate-government, the character of the revolution will develop a personality towards the collective ownership of the means of production, and each oppressed nationality having the eternal, inalienable human right to determine their own destiny.

In recent years the mass and popular movements have made strides in socialization. The various domestic oppressed nations have developed united actions and mobilizations over such issues as opposing the war in Iraq and Afghanistan, class-war worker support of the miners' strike, the farmers' strike, the auto workers' and teachers' strike, anti-immigration laws and against such repressive bills as House Resolution 1599. Furthermore, such anti-racist and anti-imperialist mobilization as those opposing repressive immigration policies on college campuses and in various ethnic communities, as well as, opposing Zionism of Israel; against fascist regimes in Latin America; fighting for the national independence of Puerto Rico; opposing the regime change and kidnapping of President Jean-Betrand Aristide and the destruction of his Fammi Lavalas Party in Haiti;[11] exposing genocides of Afrikans in Darfur, and the failure to provide essential HIV/AID medication in Afrika and other parts of the world, all provide strength to the entire mass and popular movement ensuring an anti-racist and anti-imperialist perspective within the class struggle of Euro-Americans. In the same way, various domestic national liberation efforts are developing an international perspective in solidarity with the national liberation struggles of external colonies fighting for independence against U.S. corporate imperialism.

At present, the character of the mass and popular movement is that of a struggle for the preservation of democratic rights and equality amongst the various nationalities and sexes. Although this present stage is progressive, the movement has not taken the initiative to call for the end of monopoly-capitalist ruling class control and ownership of the means of production. In fact, today, the mass and popular movement is little different than when Rev. Martin Luther King, Jr. in a speech at Sanford University in April 1967 titled "The Other America", observed:

> *"In a sense, the greatest tragedy of this other America is what it does to little children. Little children in this other America are forced to grow up with clouds of inferiority forming every day in their little mental skies. And as we look at this other America, we see it as an arena of blasted hopes and shattered dreams... 'But we must see that the struggle today is much more difficult. It's more difficult today because we are struggling now for genuine equality. And it's much easier to integrate a lunch counter than it is to guarantee a livable income and a good solid job. It's much easier to guarantee the right to vote than it is to guarantee the right to live in sanitary, decent housing conditions. And so today, we are struggling for something, which says we demand genuine equality... 'And so the result of all of this, we see many problems existing today that*

are growing more difficult. It's something that is often overlooked, but Negroes [New Afrikans] generally live in worse slums today than 20 or 25 years ago. In the North, schools are more segregated today than they were in 1954 when the Supreme Court's decision on desegregation was rendered. Economically, the Negro [New Afrikan] is worse off today than he was 15 and 20 years ago. And so the unemployment rate among whites at one time was about the same as the unemployment rate among Negroes [New Afrikans]. But today the unemployment rate among Negroes [New Afrikans] is twice that of whites. And the average income of the Negro [New Afrikan] is today 50 percent less than Whites... 'Now the other thing that we've got to come to see now that many of us didn't see too well during the last 10 years – that is that racism is still alive in American society and much more wide-spread than we realized. And we must see racism for what it is. It is a myth of the superior and the inferior race. It is the false and tragic notion that one particular group, one particular race is responsible for all of the progress, all of the insights in the total flow of history..."

Over 40 years has past since this speech, and yet, the mass and popular movement finds itself facing a more severe socio-economic and political condition. As example, with rightwing rollback of affirmative action policies, there is a drastic decline in New Afrikan enrollment in colleges, job hiring, promotions and small business contracts. At the same time, welfare to workforce programs have increased the number of poverty stricken single mothers, while Section 8 housing programs are being cut causing an increase in homeless families. The USDA report *Household Food Security in the United States 2004,* informs that 38.2 million Americans live in homes suffering from hunger and food insecurity, including 14 million children. Furthermore, the U.S. Conference of Mayors in the December 2006 report titled *Hunger and Homelessness Survey 2006,* informed that requests for emergency food assistance increased an average of 7 percent. The study found that 48 percent of people requesting emergency food assistance were families with children and that 37 percent of employed adults were requesting such assistance.

Given these general circumstances affecting Americans, the impact on oppressed minorities is exacerbated exponentially by institutional racism. Add to this reality this racist corporate-government imprisons more of its *citizens,* approximately 2.4 million people, than any other industrialized nation. Although Euro-Americans comprise 69 percent of those arrested, institutional racism in the criminal (in)justice system incarcerates New Afrikans in disproportionate numbers. It imprisons New Afrikan men three times more than Euro-Americans and four times more than did apartheid South Africa. While New Afrikans comprise 53 percent of those in prison, they are only 12.5 percent of the entire population. Furthermore, with half of the nation's prison population being New Afrikans, disenfranchising felons has emerged as a modern form of Jim Crow poll tax, effectively suppressing the New Afrikan vote. Today, approximately 6 million people cannot vote due to state and federal laws prohibiting felons from voting. As in a Spring 1964 speech to activists by El Hajj Malik Shabazz:

> *"You and I in America are not faced with a segregationist conspiracy, we're faced with a government conspiracy... it is the government itself, the government of America, that is responsible for the oppression and exploitation and degradation of Black people in this country... This government has failed the Negro."* [New Afrikan][12]

Therefore, to remedy the current situation, it is the responsibility of all progressive and revolutionary organizations and individuals to build the mass and popular movement towards class and national liberation struggle. To establish a theoretical analysis that addresses the masses discontent and disfranchisement beginning from the economic and political crisis of U.S. corporate capitalist-imperialism. This analysis must evolve a political program and national agenda that addresses the problems besetting the oppressed masses. As racism and monopoly-capitalism divides the masses on class and national lines, and further divides each oppressed nation into class divisions, such a program must build the masses struggle for the preservation of democratic rights and direct the popular movement towards the progressive evolution of the revolution.

Thus, the oppressed masses' struggle must be defined in terms of strategy and tactics, with specific goals and objectives to achieve. Each goal must heighten the contradiction between the oppressed masses and bourgeoisie ruling class, and strengthen the criteria from which the struggle for the preservation of democratic rights transforms into an anti-colonial and anti-imperialist movement.

The transformation of the masses' struggle from a defensive posture demanding civil rights into an offensive popular movement for revolutionary change is conditioned on the popular movements being responsive to the heightened oppressive conditions of the crisis of corporate capitalism and globalization. It is when this crisis develops at levels that the masses are unable to maintain a stable livelihood, that Third World people's disfranchisement becomes intolerable, such levels of subsistence being the norm of survival, will the transformation of the popular movement become qualitatively different in form from the civil rights demands for the preservation of democratic rights and equality.

It will be the *demands* of the popular social-democratic movement that will depict the qualitative difference in the overall movement. As example, demands not only for the preservation and restoration of democratic rights and equality, but also for the end of national oppression and neo-colonialism are qualitative. It is when the demands call for the collective ownership by the workers of the means of production – will popular movement take a significant qualitative change and become revolutionary in character.

It is the responsibility of progressive and revolutionary organizations to comprehend the subjective conditions and objective reality of the mass and popular movement. With this understanding, these organizations will be capable of developing national strategies and political programs that accentuate the character of the mass struggle, forging the means for the transformation of the popular movement. The martyred Black Panther Party Field Marshall, George Jackson, advised that:

> *"Consciousness grows in spirals. Growth implies feeding and being fed. We feed consciousness by feeding people, addressing ourselves to*

> *their needs, the basic social needs, working, organizing toward a national left. After the people have created something that they are willing to defend, a wealth of new ideals and autonomous subsistence infrastructure, then they are ready to be brought into "open" conflict with the ruling class and its supporters."*

The subjective conditions are that the oppressed masses' struggle is essentially determined by the socio-economic crisis and the extent of the crisis as it affects their livelihood. The masses struggle for equality between the sexes and the end of racist domination of Third World people are determinative factors of the subjective conditions. Also unemployment, inequality in education, intolerable health care, and deteriorating moral-social values of cultural significance, and lower standards of living because of the socio-economic crisis, all form the basis for the revolutionary transformation towards the creation of a *culture of resistance.*

The objective reality is that the socio-economic crisis tends to polarize issues, classes, and nations as the crisis develops. This two-fold effect is the simultaneous consolidation of both left and rightwing forces, while the divisions between nations and classes become more acute. The oppressor nation of Euro-Americans will be affected most by the leftwing Euro-Americans attempt to divide and eliminate the prospects of continued national oppression by developing the class struggle within the oppressor nation.

Euro-American leftwing forces will have essentially two objectives: 1) To develop the contradiction in the class struggle of the oppressor nation to become antagonistic, and to concentrate the contradiction between oppressor nation classes toward the destruction of private ownership of corporate capitalism; 2) To forge the most progressive elements the oppressor nation classes to support the national liberation struggle of domestic neo-colonies in combating racism and national oppression. Further, to call for the independence of these neo-colonies in support of their fight for autonomy and sovereignty.

In the same vein, Third World leftwing forces must develop an anti-colonial movement that is anti-imperialist in nature, and must recognize the necessity for international solidarity amongst the various Third World nationalities, oppressor nation

Jalil A. Muntaqim

progressive and revolutionaries and their class struggles. The anti-colonial movement also has two aspects to develop: 1) Build the class struggle within the oppressor nations to destroy the perverse colonized mentality within the quasi-class divisions of the oppressed neo-colony. Individuals who have gained influential status in the domestic neo-colony and are recognized as spoke-persons of the neo-colony by the imperialists must become responsive to the aspirations of the national liberation movement; 2) To arouse the Third World populace to confront monopoly-capitalism from an anti-imperialist political perspective. Essentially, they need to build *political decolonization programs* and a *culture of resistance* that broadens the base for raising consciousness and fulfilling the oppressed peoples' needs in the course of building the mass and popular movement.

Once the mass and popular movement gains momentum in its struggle against capitalism-imperialism, and the polarization of the left and rightwing forces has substantially drawn demarcation lines between contending political forces, the masses' struggle will have reached its nodal point, transforming from a democratic civil rights movement into a Human Rights movement of revolutionary significance, with international ramifications. El-Hajj Malik Shabazz in his famous speech "The Ballot or the Bullet" advised:

> *"We need to expand the civil-rights struggle to a high level – to the level of human rights. Whenever you are in a civil-rights struggle, whether you know it or not, you are confining yourself to the jurisdiction of Uncle Sam. No one from the outside world can speak out in your behalf as long as your struggle is a civil-rights struggle."*[13]

The question of Human Rights raises the mass and popular movement to a qualitatively higher level than when it is concerned only with civil-rights; civil-rights are the minimum political objective. The oppressive relationship between the neo-colonies of the Third World nations and capitalist bourgeoisie, and the capitalist bourgeoisie's relationship with the Euro-American oppressor nation, must be challenged and changed since they effect the basis upon which a livelihood can be maintained for all peoples. The relationship of the workers to the means of production must change until the workers gain collective

22

possession of the means of production. Also, the various Third World nations must be able to determine their own destiny, based upon their socio-economic and political aspirations as expressed during the course of the revolution. Therefore, it needs to be argued the question of Human Rights embodies the collective human will to be free from racist, capitalist-imperialist oppression and domination.

To transform the popular and mass movement for the restoration of democratic rights into a mass struggle for Human Rights is a revolutionary concept. The aspirations of the oppressed masses' struggle are detached from the context of allowing the capitalist-imperialist to offer reforms and concessions. Rather, the call for Human Rights strips the capitalist-imperialist of any opportunity to subvert the determination of the masses to control their own lives and destiny, demanding they recognize the inalienable rights of all humanity. The call for Human Rights within the mass and popular movement provides impetus towards international anti-imperialist solidarity. [14]

Once the mass and popular movement has developed a revolutionary character, the means from which progressive and revolutionary organizations can forge the movement will be enhanced greatly. The political program of national organizations in the mass and popular movement will ensure and support the course of the class and national liberation struggle. These political programs must highlight national goals and objectives, accentuating the anti-colonial, anti-capitalist-imperialist demands of popular movement. Such demands as national health care and services, full employment for all workers, the end of national oppression and racism, all of which are civil and human rights issues give credence to the demands for the end of private ownership of the means of production, and the right of Third World nationalities to independence and their own sovereignty. Thus, the *political decolonization programs* of national significance by progressive-revolutionary organizations in the mass and popular movement must change the character of the movement in the direction of the class and national liberation struggle.

It is imperative that these *political decolonization programs* project solutions to the socio-economic and political crisis of corporate-capitalism, and address themselves to specific disfranchised peoples within the class and national liberation struggle. The conditions of disfranchisement and oppression affecting women must be developed thoroughly in a political program of national significance. Distinction must be made between the level of oppression between oppressor nation women and that of oppressed nation women in developing provisions of redress in the masses' struggle. For Third World women, their national condition of oppression must first be addressed on local grass-roots levels, with the establishment of *Third World women community liberation associations*, independent of the oppressor nation's women movement. These Third World women community associations must uphold the demands of the class and national liberation struggle. In this way, national aspirations of Third World women can realize their goals as part of the national liberation struggle and take a leading role in the national liberation struggle.

The conditions of disfranchisement and oppression affecting youth, must be addressed in a national political program. Hereto distinction must be made between youth of the oppressed and oppressor nations, in respects to the nature of their oppression and the criteria for developing a solution in a political program. Essentially, the question of education and unemployment effects all youth, but for the oppressed nations it is imperative that alternative education is established in the Third World communities. Such educational institutions as *community liberation schools* would have the responsibility to develop youth's skills in reading, writing and mathematics, but also to broaden their cultural and political consciousness of their relationship to the class and national liberation struggle. These liberation schools may be responsible for the development of future leaders in the class and national liberation struggle, and to organize youth to be more responsive to the needs of the community. This is especially important as it pertains to youth in street organizations (gangs) targeted by the corporate government with gang injunction, laws characterizing them as terrorist organizations, and such wide police sweeps like *Operation FALCON*.[15] Thereby, an essential part of the curriculum of these schools will be the development of skills for the community's building and preservation. Such skills as plumbing, electrical work, carpentry, as well as printing, typing, and agitation-propaganda, of which is more than obvious considering the aftermath of Hurricane Katrina in New Orleans.

The political program must address the needs of the salaried workers of all nations, especially in the trade unions. Trade unions have the responsibility of confronting the owners of the means of production with the needs of the workers. Also, it is the responsibility of workers to be sure that their trade union representatives develop the issues, which depict their disfranchisement and restore equitable working standards and wages.

Therefore, it is the responsibility of progressives and revolutionaries to move workers and trade union representatives towards the ideals of the revolution. This includes cooperation in ownership of the means of production. The prospects of integrating the trade union revolt in the mass and popular movement depends on the masses arousal (class- consciousness). Such an arousal, through agitation-propaganda and confrontation politics by progressive-revolutionaries must be responsive to concrete conditions of union workers' socio-economic and political instability. The issues in a national agenda will include rising taxes affecting workers, and the tax cut for big business; the demands for greater productivity from the employed, without considering how the unemployed may obtain work; the huge military budget and cut-backs in social service and public education; the imported products flooding U.S. markets because of cheap labor in U.S. external colonies while exports are decreasing; plus, a homelessness and a national health care program, must all be addressed in a national political program. All of this will serve as an impetus to motivate workers to seek change in the economic system evolving a culture of resistance.

The national political program and agenda must demand that the taxes of workers become stable, while big business taxes be used to subsidize social services and public education; that shorter hours be established at wages comparable to living standards, and that the unemployed be able to gain employment meeting the needs of productivity; that a low ceiling be imposed on imports, allowing American consumers to purchase American products, establishing the export quota towards a more equitable trade balance; the establishment of a universal health plan and ending the housing crisis and homelessness to provide housing for low income people. These demands would serve to induce the ultimate demand for the end of corporate capitalist-imperialism, the nationalization and workers ownership and control of the means of production.

Finally, the mass and popular movement must be directed towards understanding the various aspects of the judicial process, the police, court and prisons, and their functions in a corporate capitalist social structure. The demystification of the judicial system provides the mass and popular movement with an understanding of how the masses are controlled, and manipulated by the courts, congress, and legislative bodies of the corporate-government for the benefit of corporate monopoly-capitalists. As poverty begets crime and social revolution, it is imperative that the judicial process be exposed as an instrument of controlling the masses along lines of class divisions and national oppression.

Most U.S., Inc. laws serve the continued morass of national oppression and class exploitation, as the police, courts and prisons preserve this system of domestic monopoly-capitalist domination and prohibit the possibility of revolutionary change. It is imperative the progressive and revolutionary forces expose how the Federal Bureau of Investigation, the Central Intelligence Agency, the National Security Agency, the Department of Defense and the various branches of the military serve to maintain corporate capitalism-imperialism. Thus, it will be exposed how various branches of the judiciary creates laws which undermine equal justices and uphold the existing system of national and class oppression. This should not be a surprise when considering the FBI's memorandum of August 25, 1967 describing the purpose and intent of Cointelpro:

> "...to expose, disrupt, misdirect, discredit, or otherwise neutralize the activities of black nationalist, hate-type organizations and groupings, their leadership, spokesmen, membership, and supporters, and to counter their propensity for violence and civil disorder.

> The pernicious background of such groups, their duplicity, and such publicity will have a neutralizing effect. Efforts of the various groups to consolidate their forces or to recruit new or youthful adherents must be frustrated. No opportunity should be missed to exploit through counterintelligence techniques the organizational and personal conflicts of the leadership of the groups and where possible an effort should be made to capitalize upon existing conflicts between competing Black Nationalist organizations. When an opportunity is apparent to disrupt or neutralize Black Nationalist,

hate-type organizations through cooperation of established local news media contacts or through such contact with sources available to the Seat of Government, in every instance careful attention must be given to the proposal to insure the targeted group is disrupted, ridiculed, or discredited through publicity and not merely publicized.

Intensified attention under this program should be afforded to the activities of such groups as the Student Nonviolent Coordinating Committee, the Southern Christian Leadership Conference, Revolutionary Action Movement, the Deacons for Defense and Justice, Congress of Racial Equality, Nation of Islam. Particular emphasis should be given to extremists who direct the activities and policies of revolutionary or militant groups as Stokely Carmichael, H. "Rap" Brown, Elijah Muhammad, and Maxwell Stanford."

In another internal FBI memorandum of March 9, 1968, it proposed *neutralizing* those who promoted fundamental changes challenging socio-economic conditions confronting poor and oppressed communities. The memorandum specifically encouraged *neutralizing* New Afrikan youths, stating: *"Negro youths and moderates must be made to understand that if they succumb to revolutionary teachings, they will be dead revolutionaries."* The history of domestic civil and human rights violations by the FBI and U.S. military has been hidden from the American population. For example, Americans are unaware of the extent the religious pacifist and civil rights leader, Martin L. King, Jr., was a target of the FBI, other U.S. intelligence agencies and Military Intelligence Group. The U.S. Senate Church Committee Report of 1976, entitled *Intelligence Activities and the Rights of Americans*, informs:

> [T]he "neutralization" program continued until Dr. King's death. As late as March 1968, FBI agents were being instructed to neutralize Dr. King because he might become "a messiah"

who could "unify, and electrify the militant Black Nationalist movement, if he were to abandon his 'obedience' to 'white liberal doctrines' (nonviolence) and embrace Black Nationalism." Steps were taken to subvert the "Poor People's Campaign" which, Dr. King was planning to lead in the spring of 1968. Even after King's death, agents in the field were proposing methods for harassing his widow, and Bureau officials were trying to prevent his birthday from becoming a national holiday."[16]

However, since September 11, 2001, a series of laws has legalized what had been unconstitutional police, FBI and U.S. military domestic activities. In anticipation of U.S. progressive activists opposing this claimed war against terrorism, the federal corporate government has passed new laws broadening the Patriot Act. Specifically, these new laws severely restrict protest, demonstrations and dissent, as for example, the October 17, 2006, signing of the *John Warner Defense Authorization Act of 2007*. In a private Oval Office ceremony, the president signed the bill that permits his office to declare a *public emergency* and station troops anywhere in America, taking control of state-based National Guard units without the consent of the governor or local authorities, in order to *suppress public disorder*. On this same day, the president signed the *Military Commission Act of 2006*, that allows for torture and detention abroad, as Section 1076 entitled *Use of the Armed Forces in Major Public Emergencies*, essentially puts in place the mechanism for the implementation of "martial law" according to Section 333, which states:

> *"...the President may employ the armed forces, including the National Guard, in Federal service, to restore public order and enforce the laws of the United States when, as a result of a natural disaster, epidemic, or other serious public health emergency, terrorist attack or incident, or other condition in any State or possession of the United States, the president determines that domestic violence has occurred to such an extent that the constitutional authorities of the State or possession are incapable of ('refuse' or 'fail'*

in)...."

Most recently, 404 U.S. House Representatives passed HR 1955 titled the *Violent Radicalization and Homegrown Terrorism Prevention Act of 2007*, which in the series of bills has substantiated the means and method for the application of martial law. This latest initiative establishes a crime for the promotion of *ideological terrorism*, and Section 899D creates a *Center of Excellence for the Study of Violent Radicalization and Homegrown Terrorism* in the United States under the auspices Department of Homeland Security. All of these laws severely erode the U.S., Inc. constitution, violate civil and human rights, and project and promote martial law and a fascist police state agenda.

Domestically, the police, courts and prisons are the primary institutions of repressing the aspirations of human rights the mass and popular movement seeks to achieve, prisons being the last rung in the ladder of judicial coercion. Hence, the mass and popular movement must demand the closing and moratorium on prison building, strengthening support for the prison movement, calling for the release of political prisoners of war, an end to torture of captured revolutionaries, the abolition of capital punishment, and for the end of prison slavery as instituted by the 13th Amendment of the U.S., Inc. Constitution. In this way, the judicial process is explained as being inequitable, indicating how most laws serve to suppress the will of the masses' aspirations for freedom, and show how the police, courts and prisons are coercive bureaucracies of corporate monopoly-capitalism. This will ultimately demystify the judicial process and will build a mass and popular consciousness to become fearless in confronting the State.[17]

At this time, the mass and popular movement is factionalized on various issues subject to the socio-economic crisis, and the relationship of the crisis to a particular class or nationality. Such issues include the struggle in the trade union industry, miners, farmers, teachers, social services, and industrial workers' strike, and various civil rights issues, all are of substantial concern to many progressives and revolutionaries in many different ways. However, factionalism tends to drain the masses enthusiasm in struggle, ensuring their participation in struggle only when their livelihood is directly in jeopardy. This reaction to struggle can preserve competitiveness that will serve to maintain divisions between classes and nationalities.

To remedy factionalism, the progressive and revolutionary forces must build national campaigns and mobilizations developing anti-imperialist, anti-colonialist working class solidarity amongst the many progressive elements within the mass and popular movement. It is in revolutionary internationalist solidarity amongst the most progressive-revolutionary forces combating racist, capitalist-imperialism that will provide the impetus for greater unity throughout the entire mass and popular movement.

The mass and popular movement must evolve a national concept of itself, and become mobilized nationally towards specific goals and objectives. This concept should urge the class and national liberation struggle towards confrontation with the socio-economic and political crisis of corporate capitalist-imperialism. The struggle for the preservation and restoration of democratic and civil-rights, must evolve towards a struggle for Human Rights which in turn will take the class and national liberation struggles toward the final and complete destruction of corporate capitalist class exploitation and racist imperialist neo-colonialist oppression.

<u>CONCLUSION</u>

The course of the over all struggle depends on oppressed peoples of all nations and classes recognizing they need to change their thinking about how they are governed. They need to realize they in fact have the power to change the means and methods by which their every day livelihood is obtained through their labor. The *power of the people* first begins by cultivating a theoretical and ideological foundation for political action. Without a revolutionary theory, there cannot be a revolutionary praxis to raise consciousness and inspire the masses to demonstrate and protest for a better future for themselves and their children. During the late 1950s and throughout 1960s, the civil rights and anti-Vietnam war movements succeeded in changing the social fabric of corporate America. There was a culture and a prevailing belief in revolutionary change. In the words of El Hajj Malik Shabazz:

> *"The time we are living in...and... are facing now is not an era where one who is oppressed is looking towards the oppressor to give him some system or form of logic and reason. What is logical to the oppressor is not logical to the*

oppressed, and what is reason to the oppressor is not reason to the oppressed. The black [New Afrikan] *people in this country are beginning to realize that what sounds reasonable to those who exploit us doesn't sound reasonable to us. There just has to be a new system of reason and logic devised by us who are on the bottom, if we want some results in its struggle that is called "Negro Revolution."*

Unfortunately, to reverse the majority of the socioeconomic gains of the social-democratic revolution of the past, the plutocracy employed corporate media and rightwing propaganda throughout the 1980's and 1990's.

This was accomplished by continuing FBI Cointelpro operations destroying leftwing organizations; Reagan era of rightwing validation and George Bush (senior) presidency extending imperialist hegemony; Newt Gingrich's "Contract With America" strategy building a broad-base coalition with evangelical Christians; the influx of CIA procured drugs (heroin from Southeast Asia and Afghanistan and cocaine from Columbia and Peru) devastating oppressed communities with the proliferation of street and drug gangs with it's supportive culture of *"gangster rap"* exploited by the corporate music industry; along with the above mentioned reversals of affirmative action and wholesale incarceration of New Afrikans' and Latinos' young folks, all of which offers a few dynamics that resulted in the defeat of the previous era of struggle.

Furthermore, the September 11, 2001, destruction of the World Trade Center and damage to the Pentagon, the war in Iraq and subsequent war in Afghanistan, has provided the rightwing respite as the jingoist corporate media propaganda incites the American populace to support the rightwing agenda. Such have given them a broader opportunity to persuade the American populace to support the solidification of fascism on the home front and U.S., Inc. imperialist military globalization. All of which identifies the present condition of rightwing nationalistic socio-psychological-cultural influence and control over the American populace.

The above offers insights as to what needs to be done, the when and how is the decision of the oppressed as expressed to the progressive and revolutionary forces. From the masses to the masses is the guiding principle that must be abided by activist, however, it is obvious there is little choice that revolutionary action must be taken to prohibit the onslaught of fascism in America.

In this regard, it is urged that progressive and revolutionary forces seek the means to organize a broad based *National Poor and Oppressed Peoples Convention*, for the specific purpose of developing a revolutionary national agenda. The national agenda would then be the principle socio-economic and political platform by which each participate would return to their respective communities to implement. As a revolutionary national agenda would apply to electoral politics, it would be required this national agenda be the platform for politicians to support in order to campaign and win the votes of the oppressed masses. Where politicians refused to support the national agenda, then if desired to do so, progressives would seek to support their own candidate that will campaign for the revolutionary national agenda and platform. However, it must be understood these campaigns are tactical initiatives challenging the status-quo electoral process to raise consciousness towards the class and national liberation struggle.

The development of community committees, associations, coalitions and fronts will be responsible for the implementation of the revolutionary national agenda. In this way, progressives and revolutionaries will, for the most part be speaking with a unified voice, and this national determination will serve to oppose factionalism and sectarianism in the overall movement. Of course, this is not a national strategy or panacea for all of the problems besetting the building of a mass and popular movement. However, it is proposed that such be organized particularly when considering past efforts of the Black Panther Party to accomplish a similar mission.

In November 1970, the BPP planned to convene the People's Revolutionary Constitutional Convention at Howard University, which preceded the September 5, 1970, Revolutionary People's Plenary Session at Temple University attended by 10,000 activists. Unfortunately, the convention was not held due to FBI Cointelpro intervention, and subsequent interfering with the principle BPP leaders, and disrupting their ability to organize the convention. Nonetheless, a successful *National Poor and Oppressed People's Convention*, today, would certainly challenge present day rightwing fascist politics, and inspire poor and oppressed peoples across the country to begin the process of taking control of their lives in a mass and popular movement.

(Footnotes)

[1] Since April 15, 1861, every succeeding so-called President has issued an Executive Order proclaiming a national emergency virtually extending federal military powers and control of the United States, Inc. The introduction to Senate Report 93-549 (93rd Congress, 1st Session, 1973), states in part: "A majority of the people of the United States have lived all of their lives under emergency rule... And, in the United States, actions taken by the Government in times of great crisis have - from, at least, the Civil War - in important ways, shaped the present phenomenon of a permanent state of national emergency." See, also, November 14, 1994, Executive Order No. 12938, by then so-called President William Jefferson Clinton, where he states: "...Therefore, in accordance with Section 202(d) of the National Emergencies Act (50 U.S.C. 1622(d), I am continuing the national emergency declared in Executive Order No. 12938."

[2] Pursuant to Title 28 U.S.C. 3002 (15) (a), the United States is a Federal Corporation. Title 28 U.S.C. 3002 (15) (3), further informs that all departments of the U.S., are part of the corporation. The Commerce Department acquires birth certificates via county and state governments, which contractually, makes these live births ultimately commerce property of the U.S. Corporation, with a monetary value attached to each certificate.

[3] On November 22, 1910, Paul Warburg, Nelson W. Aldrich, then the powerful Chairman of the Senate Finance Committee, and a group of bankers secretly met on Jekyll Island, Florida, conspired and planned for the development of a central banking system. In 1913, Congress passed the Federal Reserve Act establishing the Federal Reserve System. Title 31 U.S.C. Section 462 (392) states: "All Federal Reserve Notes and circulating Notes of Federal Reserve Banks and National Banking Associations heretofore or hereafter issued, shall be legal tender for all debts public and private." However, the "fiat money" distributed contradicts and negates the U.S., Inc. Constitution, Article 1, Section 10, that states: "No State shall make any Thing but Gold and Silver Coin a legal tender in payment of debts."

[4] It must be understood the U.S. dollar (fiat money) is a promissory note, backed by nothing other than the credit of the nation, amounting to nothing more than an I.O.U. This was forward by the 73rd Congress of March 9, 1933, holding that: "...it (the new currency) will be worth 100 cents on the dollar and will represent the *credit* of *their* nation. It will represent a mortgage on all the homes and property *of the people* of the nation."

[5] Paul Warburg was a chief protagonist for the passage of the Federal Reserve Act, who in 1913 testified before the House Banking and Currency Committee identified himself: "I am a member of the banking house of Kuhn, Loeb Company. I came over to this country in 1902, having been born and educated in the banking business in Hamburg, Germany, and studied banking in London and Paris, and have gone all over the world. In the Panic of 1907, the first suggestion I made was let us get a national clearing house. The Aldrich Plan contains some things that are simply fundamental rules of banking. Your aim in this plan [the Federal Reserve Act] must be the same centralizing of reserves, mobilizing commercial credit, and getting an elastic note issue."[The Secrets of the Federal Reserve, by Eustace Mullins, p.21] Paul Warburg was also a representative of the House of Rothschild banking cartel of Europe.

[6] Research the Trilateral Commission, Council for Foreign Relations and the Bildenberg Group. Then, Chairman David Rockefeller, in 1991, described Bildenberg Group's purpose: "We are grateful to the Washington Post, the New York Times, Time magazine, and other great publications whose directors have attended our meetings and respected their promises of discretion for almost forty years... It would have been impossible for us to develop our plan for the world if we had been subject to the bright lights of publicity during these years. But the world is now more sophisticated and prepared to march towards a world government which will never again know war but only peace and prosperity for the whole of humanity."

[7] Figures according to www.opensecrets.org

[8] See: THE ELECTORAL COLLEGE, by William C. Kimberling, Deputy Director, FEC Office of Election Administration, [Revised May 1992]

[9] Quoted from: "How the Electoral College Works" by Kevin Bonsor, http://people.howstuffworks.com/electoral-college.htm/printable.

[10] Today, the U.S., Inc., is bankrupt, according to U.S. Treasury report of 2006, it has a federal debt of more than $5 trillion, while Saudi Arabia, Japan, and China governments and corporate investors either control or highly influence major U.S. banking and properties, having purchased close to 100% of that debt. That's $3 trillion borrowed from the Saudis, the Chinese, the Japanese and others. The Arabs of the Gulf nations took $252 billion in 2005 for OPEC's oil – and put back $311 billion by purchasing U.S. Treasury bills Latin America borrowed $227 billion at high interest – while lending the U.S. $379 billion at low interest. Americans bought $243 billion in products from China – while China holds nearly a trillion dollars ($800 million) in reserve to buy up the U.S. See, also, January 20, 2008, New York Times article: "Overseas Investors Buying U.S. Holdings at Record Pace – Weak Dollar Lures Foreigners, Reigniting Debate" byline Peter S. Goodman and Louise Story.

[11] To learn more about the U.S., Inc. involvement in the February 29, 2004, kidnapping of President Aristide out of Haiti, read: "An Unbroken Agony", by Randall Robinson, published by Basic Civitas Books.

[12] Twelve Point Program of the Revolutionary Action Movement, 1964.

[13] Malcolm X, "The Ballot or the Bullet," Malcolm X Speaks [New York: Grove Press, 1965].

[14] On December 10, 1948, the General Assembly of the United Nations adopted and proclaimed the Universal Declaration of Human Rights. Following this historic act the Assembly called upon all Member countries to publicize the text of the Declaration and "to cause it to be disseminated, displayed, read and expounded principally in schools and other educational institutions, without distinction based on the political status of countries or territories."

[15] An article, "Operation FALCON and the Looming Police State", by Mike Whitney who won a 2008 Project Censored Award, discusses how the Justice Department has been running exercises to implement a police state as already provided by the Reagon administration's 1988 "national security emergency" Executive Order 12656.

[16] For more information on Martin L. King, Jr., being a U.S. government and military target read: *The COINTELPRO Papers: Documents from the FBI's Secret Wars Against the Dissent in the United States* (Boston; South End, 1990), by Ward Churchill; *Whiteout: The CIA, Drugs and the Press* (Versco, NY 1999) by Alexander Cockburn; *An Act of State: The Execution of Martin Luther King*, by William F. Pepper (2003).

[17] In 1998, two specific organizations were formed for this specific purpose, the Jericho Amnesty Movement and Critical Resistance, and both continues to be a source of information and resistance exposing the overall criminal (in)justice system. Check: www.thejerichomovement.com and www.critical resistance.org. The Jericho Amnesty Movement has also called for the reopening of Cointelpro hearings, on behalf of approximately 100 Cointelpro victims, U.S. political prisoners languishing in prison for 30 to 40 years.

ABOUT THE AUTHOR

Anthony Bottom/Jalil Abdul Muntaqim was born October 18, 1951, in Oakland, California, the first of four in his family. His elementary school years were spent in San Francisco. In junior high school, he obtained a summer scholarship to attend a high school chemistry course, and while in high school, an advanced college math and engineering program. During the civil rights movement, he participated in NAACP youth organizing and was one of many who engaged in street riots against racism and police brutality in San Francisco. In high school, he became a leading member of the Black Student Union. Because of his ability to articulate issues confronting Black students, Jalil often toured San Jose, California, in what was called "speak outs" with the BSU Chairman of San Jose State and City College. He had become a member of the *House of Umoja*, a cultural-nationalist affiliate of Ron Karenga's *United Slaves* organization.

At age 16½, on April 6, 1968, two nights after the assassination of Martin Luther King, Jr. the BSU Chair of San Jose State and City College, Jalil and a couple of high school students were arrested in a car and charged with possession of high-powered rifles and Molotov cocktails. Black high school students picketed and demonstrated in front of San Jose City Hall demanding their release from detention. After the assassination of Rev. King, Jalil began to believe a more militant response to national oppression and racism was necessary, and began to look towards the Black Panther Party for Self-Defense for leadership. He affiliated with the BPP when he was 18 years old. Having moved back to San Francisco from San Jose, Jalil was recruited into the Black underground by elementary school friends who had since become Panthers. Less than two months from his twentieth birthday, on August 28, 1971, Jalil was captured along with Albert *Nuh* Washington in a midnight shoot-out with San Francisco police. It has been alleged that Jalil and Nuh attempted to assassinate a S.F. police sergeant in retaliation for the August 21, 1971, assassination of BPP Field Marshal George Jackson.

Jalil, subsequently was charged with a host of revolutionary underground activities, including the assassination of NYC police officers for which he is currently serving a life sentence. When arrested in 1971, he was a high school graduate and employed as a social worker for the California State Employment Office. Having been imprisoned since 1971, Jalil is one of the ten longest held Black political prisoners in the world (on April 28, 2000, Nuh died of cancer in prison).

While imprisoned in San Quentin in 1975-77, Jalil was able to organize the first national prison petition campaign to the United Nations. He established the first revolutionary prisoners national newspaper called *Arm the Spirit*, and organized the first Black August demonstration in front of San Quentin. From his prison cell, Jalil with the support of another BLA prisoner of war, Sundiata Acoli, organized the first march to the United Nations calling for recognition of U.S. political prisoners, as well as the first demonstration in front of Harlem State Office Building calling for the recognition of U.S. political prisoners.

Since being in New York State prisons, Jalil wrote and submitted a legislative bill for prisoners with life sentences to receive good time off of their minimum sentences. This bill was introduced to the NY State Assembly Committee on Corrections. Jalil has filed numerous lawsuits on behalf of prisoners civil and human rights challenging the prison system's way of doing business. In addition, he has received awards of appreciation from Jaycee's, NAACP and Project Build prison chapters for his active participation and leadership, and two commendations for preventing prison riots.

After many years of being denied the opportunity to attend college because he had been designated a Central Monitoring Case (CMC) security classification, in 1994, Jalil graduated from SUNY-New Paltz with a BS in Psychology and a BA in Sociology. He is a founding member of the New Afrikan Liberation Front (NALF), and continuingly working to develop a National Prisoners' Afrikans Studies Project (NPASP). In 1998, he initiated the international mobilization, *Spring Break '98 Jericho March on the White House and U.S. Embassies to Demand Amnesty for U.S. Political Prisoners*. Approximately 6,000 activists marched and rallied at the White House calling for the amnesty of U.S. political prisoners, resulting in building the Jericho Amnesty Movement. Over the years, he has written and had published several political booklets and essays, including an unpublished novel and teleplay. His most recent book, a compilation of prison writings is *"We Are Our Own Liberators"*, being reprinted by Arissa Media Group.

In New York State, Jalil appeared before the parole board in 2002, 2004, and 2006, each time denied and held to reappear in two years. On April 4, 2007, Jalil was extradited from N.Y.S. prison in Auburn and sent to San Francisco pursuant to a felony complaint. Along with seven other alleged former members of the Black Panther Party, he was charged with the assault on Ingleside Police Station and killing of a police sergeant on August 28, 1971. The case of the *S.F. 8* is a persistent nefarious and egregious corporate-government attack on the legacy of the Black Panther Party. As the result of these new charges, he is now being held at San Francisco County Jail in an isolation unit on 23-hour lockdown. He states: *"The United States does not recognize the existence of political prisoners. To do so would give credence to the fact of the level of repression and oppression that exists in the United States. The corporate-government would have to recognize the fact that people resist racist oppression in the U.S. Inc., and therefore legitimize the existence of not only the individuals who are incarcerated or have been captured, but also legitimize those movements of which they are part."*

For more information on Jalil check:
www.freejalil.com and www.thejerichomovement.com

CHAPTER TWO

WEAVING MULTIPLE STRATEGIES FOR SUCCESS

JEFF LUERS

JEFF LUERS

Governments of the world were first warned about the dangers of global warming in the late 1980s. The Intergovernmental Panel on Climate Change published its first report on climate change in 1990. In 1995, the United Nations summarized, "the balance of evidence suggests that there is a discernible human influence on global climate."[1]

The evidence provided by scientists was so overwhelming that it led to the Kyoto Protocol, a worldwide treaty to reduce carbon dioxide and other greenhouse emissions to 1990 levels. Though ratified by all other member countries of the United Nations, the U.S. and Australia refused to participate.

While global warming and climate change issues have been the center of increased public debate and media attention throughout Western Europe and Canada since the turn of the century, American awareness of the risks posed by global warming has lagged far behind. This is due in large part to an insidious strategy by the Bush Administration to censor documents on global warming and sow skepticism among the American media and public.

It is one thing to dispute a scientific finding with peer-reviewed analysis. It is quite another to censor or alter findings in order to further strengthen one's political or economic position.

On September 26, 2006, a report in the journal, *Nature,* exposed the censorship occurring at the hands of Bush appointees, prompting a group of democratic senators to call for an investigation.

Researchers at the National Oceanic and Atmospheric Administration (NOAA) accused Bush appointees to the NOAA of dismissing possible connections between the intensity and frequency of hurricanes and global warming. The researchers also accused the NOAA of censoring scientists who believe there is such a link.

Bush appointees at the NOAA prevented noted NOAA scientist Tom Knutson from talking to reporters in 2005 because he had published studies linking global warming and hurricane strength. The department of commerce requested that Knutson share his views on global warming in an interview with CNBC.[2] The request was denied and a NOAA scientist who disputed this hurricane-warming connection was chosen to conduct the interview in Knutson's place.

Scientists at the NOAA are not the only ones who have cried foul. James Hansen, director of NASA's Goddard Institute for Space Studies also said that he had been censored by the Bush Administration for speaking out about global warming and climate change. In 2006, the *Independent* (U.K.) reported that the Bush Administration was trying to censor Hansen's call for immediate cuts in greenhouse gas emissions.

Hansen stated, "Communicating with the public is essential because public concern is possibly the only thing capable of overcoming the special interests that have obfuscated the topic."[3]

Following an investigation into the matter of political interference by the Bush Administration, the House Committee on Oversight and Government Reform held hearings in March 2007. As part of the hearing, the White House Council on Environmental Quality was made to produce more than eight boxes of papers that Democrats said showed strong indications of political interference. Democrats, themselves, produced hundreds of pages of legal depositions, exhibits, and email exchanges between administration officials. The evidence was overwhelming and disturbing. Officials with no scientific training were editing and often rewriting reports on global warming in order to align them with administration policy.

One flagrant example was demonstrated in a report by the U.S. National Research Council who had concluded, "greenhouse gases are accumulating in the atmosphere as a result of human activities causing surface air temperatures to rise and subsurface ocean temperatures to rise."[4]

Philip Cooney, Chief of Staff at the Council on Environmental Quality, rewrote the above statement to read, "some activities emit greenhouse gases that directly or indirectly may affect the balance of incoming and outgoing radiation, thereby potentially affecting climate on regional and global scales."[5]

Cooney, a former oil lobbyist, came to the White House in 2001. Before joining the Bush Administration, Cooney spent more than fifteen years with the American Petroleum Institute as their "climate team leader." During the hearing, Cooney denied that he had any loyalty to the oil industry or that he attempted to create doubt about climate change. Resigning from the White House in 2005, Cooney now works for ExxonMobil Corporation (the company that has offered grants to scientists who will dispute global warming).

Through writing research reports and controlling what

scientists could say about their work, the Bush Administration purposely misled the public about global warming and climate change. These manipulations of public trust only served corporate interests. By ensuring that the public only heard distorted messages about climate change that emphasized or exaggerated doubt around the dangers of global warming, the White House was able to defuse calls for action to limit greenhouse emissions.

The federal government isn't the only institution colluding to allow corporations to profit at a cost to the public. Several states have undercharged their major polluters by up to $50 million, according to a March 2007 report by the nonprofit Environmental Integrity Project.

The Environmental Protection Agency (EPA) requires that states pay nearly $40 million per ton of noxious emissions of sulfur dioxide, nitrogen oxide, and smog forming volatile organic compounds. These emissions are byproducts of power plants, refineries, chemical plants and incinerators. While states do bear the majority burden of enforcing the law, monitoring emissions, inspecting facilities, and collecting fees, the EPA oversees the process and has a duty to ensure these responsibilities are met.

In March 2007, the news agency, *Reuters*, reported that at least eighteen states collected fees below the federal minimum.[6] More than a dozen states collected millions less than they should have. Among them were states with heavy oil or coal interests; Florida, which collected $4.5 million below the minimum standard, North Carolina, with $5.4 million less, Texas, at $5.6 million below the mark, and Louisiana, topping the chart at $9.8 million below the federal minimum.[7]

Under guidance from the Bush Administration, the EPA also refused to regulate greenhouse emissions from cars or power plants. Bush maintained that the EPA lacked the authority to do so. The Administration, agreeing with automakers, and apparently standing by its policy of not recognizing global warming, claimed that carbon dioxide is not a pollutant as defined by the Clean Air Act.

In April 2007, the U.S. Supreme Court disagreed, ruling in one of its most important environmental decisions in years, that the EPA has the authority to regulate greenhouse emissions from automobiles. The decision, a strong rebuke to Bush's Climate Policy, sets the stage for other regulatory lawsuits to move forward, including a challenge to the EPA's failure to regulate carbon emissions from power plants.

In a statement the day after the Court's decision, Bush stated that he took the ruling very seriously. However, he affixed two conditions to any EPA regulation of carbon dioxide that would markedly reduce the regulation's effectiveness. Bush said that no regulatory program should limit economic growth, nor should any benefit to the atmosphere be offset by emissions from China, India, or other developing countries.

Bush appears to believe that while the U.S. has contributed more greenhouse emissions than any other country, we are not obligated to reduce our emissions. And true to form, Bush continued to ignore any evidence that contradicted his position on climate change.

The Stern Review, one of the most comprehensive assessments of the economic impacts of climate change, published in 2006, strongly presented a case for limiting greenhouse gases now in order to mitigate severe impacts on the world economy in the future. The 700-page report, compiled by Sir Nicholas Stern, chief of the British Government Economic Service and former chief economist of the World Bank, evaluated a body of scientific studies on global warming and climate change from an economic perspective.

The report first examined the evidence in terms of the economic impacts of climate change itself. Then it explored the economics of stabilizing greenhouse gases in the atmosphere. The report concluded that, "the benefits of strong, early action considerably outweigh the costs."[8] The evidence confirms that taking action now to cap greenhouse emissions must be viewed as an investment made to avoid the serious risks of major disruption to economic and social activity later in this century.

The White House Council on Environmental Quality - the same council that censored global warming reports - dismissed the report when it was published as just "another contribution" to "an abundance of economic analyses" on climate change.[9] This translates into "our policies don't recognize the existence or threat of global warming."

In yet another calculated move to install business-friendly conservatives in powerful government positions, Bush, with the Senate on its spring break, appointed Susan Dudley as Director of the Office of Information and Regulatory Affairs at the White House Office of Management and Budget. By using a recess appointment, Bush enabled Dudley to serve without Senate confirmation until the 110th Congress adjourns. Bush utilized recess appointments more than 100 times, often to avoid Senate opposition to his appointments.

Dudley, who has gone on record as opposing government regulation in favor of market regulation, opposed the EPA's proposal for stricter limits on arsenic in drinking water. She argued that the EPA's cost-benefit analysis overvalued some lives, particularly the elderly. In Congressional testimony, Dudley has stated that it would be more cost-effective for the government to initiate a pollution warning system, so sensitive individuals can stay indoors on smoggy days, rather than for the government to order polluters to clean up emissions.[10]

Bush's own proposals for cleaner fuels also revealed his bias toward oil and coal industries. Among them, he has proposed liquefying coal as a fuel for automobiles, a process that would actually result in greater emissions of greenhouse gases.

Despite his own lip service recognizing the serious problem of global warming, the Bush Administration cut funding for climate change budgets by 20% in 2006. Far from limiting greenhouse emissions, the Bush Administration's policy put the country on track to increase U.S. emissions by 19% by 2020 (an increase of nearly one-fifth of 2000 levels), despite urgent calls from leading scientists at home and abroad to drastically and immediately curb all greenhouse emissions.

•

The Nobel Prize winning Intergovernmental Panel on Climate Change (IPCC) was established in 1988 by the World Meteorological Organization and the United Nations Environmental Program. The Panel is made up of more than 2,500 expert scientific reviewers and includes more than 800 contributing authors and 450 lead authors from 130 countries.

The IPCC review process is a consensus-based, three-tiered procedure. To start, existing literature and published studies on climate change are gathered, materials ranging from species extinction to glacial melt and famine. This material is then reviewed by the panel's experts. Governmental representatives and more experts from each participating country then review the documents. Finally, all of the governments involved review the final summaries developed by the IPCC and must sign off on them before they become the official stance of the IPCC.

The result is that the IPCC assessments are the most

thoroughly peer reviewed science documents in human history, making the IPCC the most authoritative voice on global warming and climate change in the world. So when the IPCC states that we must take immediate action to curb greenhouse gases and address threats posed by global warming or face catastrophic consequences, it is in all of our best interests to heed their advice.

Our government knows this, in fact the United States is a member of the IPCC. The Bush Administration had access to all of the best information science had to offer on human-caused climate change. Yet, with all of this information at its disposal, the Bush Administration proceeded to cover up and censor any American document that acknowledged climate change as a human-caused event or even a threat to the American public.

At the risk of sounding trite and cliché, one can only assume the reason for such duplicity is that acknowledging and addressing global warming could be bad for profits. Never mind that the Stern Review very authoritatively underlined that addressing climate change now will save billions of dollars in the future.

While it is tempting to hope that the Obama Adninistration will take the immediate and necessary steps to address this crisis, let us not forget that oil and gas interests, along with other powerful industry groups, donate heavily to both Republican and Democratic candidates. That fact is underscored by the lack of legislation coming out of the House or Senate to address global warming and the watered down attempts at forcing industry compliance with national goals.

By far, one of the largest problems facing the American public is the lack of easily accessible information about today's pertinent topics. The government holds a monopoly on the means of communication. The information released by the government gets parroted by the media to the general public. There is no review process. Case in point is the now infamous *weapons of mass destruction* used as a pretext for the Iraq War.

Corporate media is powerful. Just take a moment to think about just how much the media shapes our lives. As the accepted voice of credible information, media outlets are able to shape opinions ranging from politics to fashion.

And big media is big business. Contrary to what many believe, media profits are not solely derived by subscriptions. A very large percentage of media profits are made by the sales of advertising space to major corporations. Of course, the more subscriptions or viewers, the more that can be charged for advertising space.

Now, if your profits are derived from corporate advertisements, such as those paid for by British Petroleum, Occidental Oil, or Chevron about their environmental stewardship, how likely are you to point out that these companies have spent nearly as much on advertising their green shift as they have spent on investing in green technologies (which is to say the perception of being green is worth more than the reality)? How likely are you to print or air stories that might illuminate a cover up or denial of global warming? In fact, how likely are you to even suggest a link between these industries and global warming?

The lies and the disinformation came from the top and were manipulated to be accepted as truth. The American public was duped by those responsible for our well being, our government. We were then misled by those who hold the time honored tradition of telling the truth, the press. Even today, with nearly every rational American aware of the causes and consequences of global warming, many corporate media outlets continue to insert skepticism about the fundamental nature of climate change into their reports. Of course, this skepticism about whether global warming is human caused, or even real, naturally is claimed to be fair and balanced reporting.

It is no secret that America is in a state of turmoil. Public discontent with government is at an all time high. More young people are starting to take an active role in current affairs and political campaigns. This could be the signal that much new fundamental change is about to occur. However, it isn't just change at the highest levels that is needed. A change in the American consciousness is also needed. Placing a vote is not the end of our responsibility, indeed it is just the start. Those in power are there because we put them there, whether they are elected officials or businesses we have built by buying their products. The powerful are only powerful so long as we choose them to be.

Learning the truth is not the same as acting on it. To make change, we must create it. To create change, we must demand it.

American history is full of examples of those individuals who struggled to progressively change America. From John Brown and Harriet Tubman, to the struggle for the eight-hour work day.

From the Suffragettes to the Civil Rights Movement. American history has been shaped by ordinary citizens who recognized their responsibility and need to act.

This generation has proven no different. While the boiling point issues have changed, the determination to struggle against injustice has not.

For years, environmentalists have been waging a determined battle against the Bush Administration and environmentally devastating business practices. These individuals and groups have ranged from non-profits and grass roots activism lobbying to create change and helping to raise public awareness to college and high school youth engaged in acts of protest and civil disobedience. This growing dissent has been met with single-minded heavy-handedness, from accusations at the highest levels questioning the integrity and patriotism of the dissenters to outright intimidation.

While the people and actions I am about to discuss are by far the most controversial of them all, I choose them because of a dangerous precedent the government recently set, and the fact that the media and therefore the majority of the American public bought into it.

The Earth Liberation Front (ELF), a loosely knit group of radical environmental activists, has been engaged in acts of sabotage and arson in the U.S. for over a decade. This organization, which in truth is nothing more than a guiding list of principles anyone can follow, has used these acts of property destruction in an effort to raise public awareness about environmental destruction, while simultaneously trying to slow said destruction and punish those responsible for it.

These acts of vandalism and arson have been dubbed "eco-terrorism" by the government and hence picked up by the media. The federal government has long considered these acts, and most notably the ELF, as the number one domestic terrorist threat in America.

In December of 2005, after years of fruitless effort, the F.B.I. finally broke the cell of one of the most prolific ELF cells in America. In the aftermath, nineteen people were indicted, sixteen arrested, and the others considered fugitives.

On January 20, 2006, before many of those arrested had ever been arraigned, then Attorney General Alberto Gonzales, along with F.B.I. Director Robert Mueller, held a media conference in Washington, D.C. to announce the arrests and to brand those arrested as "domestic terrorists." The media picked up story and ran with it as headlines across the nation read, "America's most wanted domestic terrorists captured." Few media outlets ever questioned if the accused' crimes rose to the level of terrorism.

All individuals were convicted of various acts of vandalism or arson. Of those, seven were convicted of the terrorism enhancement.

It is important to note that the judge, when finding the seven guilty of the terrorism enhancement, stated that she did so not because of their crimes, but rather because of their motivation. Specifically, Judge Aiken stated that because the crimes were committed with the goal of creating social change or retaliating against the government for perceived bad acts, such crimes were by law terrorism. In other words, the physical crimes they were convicted of were arson, vandalism, and sabotage. The crime of terrorism, however, was not a physical crime but a thought crime.

While the government and media have labeled these individuals terrorists and these types of activities terrorism, this label does not in fact make it so, no more than Britain's labeling of the Boston Tea Party as terrorism and the subsequent newspaper headlines that made Samuel Adams a terrorist.

•

As noted, the government holds a monopoly on the means of communication. It can advance false definitions of terrorism to the media, who parrot it to the American public. Effectively, they have the ability to erase the possibility of the public asking, "What policies have created these grievances and are these extreme actions in any way legitimized by those policies?"

"Terrorism" then, is not just a word, it is a weapon, which the government has used to demoralize and malign eco-activists. By branding dissent as terrorism, the government deflects attention away from the fact that their policies and unwavering support for the corporate agenda are directly responsible for today's environmental crisis.

The Bush Administration proposed immigration changes to grant refugee status to people who have engaged in terrorist activities in furtherance of U.S. foreign policy. No doubt, the State Department refers to these individuals as "freedom fighters" or some equally benign term. Meanwhile, the very same government that endorses and supports acts of murder abroad condemns acts of property destruction here at home as "acts of terrorism."

Clearly, it isn't violence that the government finds objectionable. Rather, it is how that violence is directed and the philosophy behind it. However, beyond just the government label of "eco-terrorism," many activists on both the left and the right have distinguished these acts as terrorism, even drawing comparisons to the anti-abortion movement. This claim is easily countered. Anti-abortion advocates have used violence, including murder, to subjugate women and force their own moral dogma on the civilian population. It is a self-serving, self-righteous cause.

Radical eco-activists, on the other hand, have used violence as a means to challenge corporate and state activity responsible for dangerous pollution, climate change, and mass distinction - problems that all of humanity has a stake in.

Others have put forth the notion that sabotage or arson do more harm than good, that only passive "non-violent" resistance can succeed in creating change. These proponents of non-violence often tout Gandhi and Martin Luther King, Jr. as examples of the power and success of nonviolence. The problems with this argument are multiple. First, while Gandhi is the best known resister of the British Raj, he was only one of many leaders and his tactics comprised only part of the Indian Revolution. Another, though less well known, leader was Subbas Chandra Bose who organized armed opposition against the British. Where Gandhi did succeed was in tarnishing the British image around the world. Pictures of British soldiers beating and killing Indians peacefully opposed to the foreign occupation and rule of their land lowered the world's opinion of the British. This type of passive resistance would never have worked with Hitler or Stalin, however, and it did not work against the English closer to home, when the Irish struggled for their sovereignty. The Irish ultimately had to resort to true acts of terrorism against England in order to gain independence.

Here in the States, King also used non-violence as a successful component of the civil rights movement. However, to attribute success solely to his efforts is to dismiss the enormous contributions of Malcolm X, the Black Panther Party and other militant Black leaders. King himself stated that he was only effective as long as there was a shadow of an armed black man standing behind him.

I am in no way attempting to dismiss or disregard the

good that non-violent resistance has accomplished. I am only demonstrating that it is but one facet of struggle, and like any tactic, must be molded to its circumstances. Any one tactic alone cannot by itself prove successful.

It is true that education and ethical debate are powerful tools for raising public awareness. In fact, public awareness about the dangers of global warming or human suffering is the only way to create meaningful and lasting change. The power of education has been demonstrated by Al Gore's documentary, *An Inconvenient Truth*. Through his film, Gore was able to put climate change into the hearts and minds of the American public.

However, education and debate can only sway reasonable people whose problem is that they are unaware, and not that they just don't care. Corporations and governments cannot claim that they are unaware. They have had access to all of the best facts and data that science has to offer. With all of this information at their disposal and instead of acting in proactive ways to solve the problems, both governments and corporations have used every tool at their disposal to conceal and cover up this information, and proceed with business as usual. These entities, and their agents, have institutional and monetary biases against limiting pollution that no amount of persuasion or education is likely to change. These institutions have been confronted with unquestionable evidence that has implicated their activities and practices as creating a global environmental crisis. Yet, they stubbornly and criminally refuse to change.

As humanity becomes increasingly threatened with irreversible harm as a result of industry and government malfeasance, one becomes invested with the inherent right of resistance to that which would harm him or his home. Yet, resistance in this case is legitimized by more than just an abstract theory of self-preservation. Human conscience also allows for and often necessitates that one challenge injustice.

When faced with the degree our own government has colluded to cover up global warming, dismantle the endangered species act, give industry loopholes around the Clean Air and Clean Water Acts, and in general put corporation interests before the interests of its own people, the use of extreme direct action, such as sabotage or arson, against government and corporate institutions or their agents is justified.

But let us not kid ourselves about the severity of extreme direct action. The tactic of property destruction is not non-violent.

It is true that the violence is not directed against life. Yet, property destruction, particularly arson, can create a level of fear and insecurity in those targeted. They may feel intimidated or coerced. They may even feel victimized. It is not a tactic that should be romanticized or taken lightly.

Sabotage and political arson are only tools. Outside of targeting a specific company until it is forced out of business, they will not and cannot create social change. Only a change in the social consciousness and thinking can do that.

Outside of specific campaigns such as protecting a forest, extreme direct action has been most commonly used as a way to eat into corporate profits. While many will point out that it is insurance companies that absorb the costs, one must consider the cumulative effects of a specific company and/or industry being targeted again and again.

After the first arson at Romania Chevrolet, a second one caused $1 million in damages. Romania, eventually, went out of business. While it would have been better, and more productive, to directly target General Motors, the targeting of SUVs at dealerships across the country led to increased insurance rates nationwide, as more and more fell prey to midnight saboteurs.

There is also the psychological role that extreme direct action plays. Once a company has been hit it knows that it is not immune. It has a target on its back. The company knows that its policies and practices are being watched. The action will likely open the company up to increased public scrutiny. The action has also served notice that there are consequences to putting profit before environmental and public health.

Obviously, the use of extreme direct action opens one up to the possibility of doing time and being labeled a criminal or even a terrorist. However, sometimes the line between right and legal gets blurred. Under Hitler, it was clearly illegal to oppose the internment of Jews, though opposition was still morally right. Today, radical eco-activists are compelled to disobey the law in an effort to protect our environment from incredibly destructive industries and government collusion.

Like the numerous successful social justice movements that have come before, only the successful weaving of multiple strategies will lead to success. The combined efforts of education, non-violent protest, and militant resistance is the only method by which to both raise public awareness and confront those responsible for ongoing injustices.

Bibliography
Rosebraugh, C., *Burning rage of a dying planet*, Lantern Books, 2004.
Best, S., Nocella II, A., Eds., *Terrorists or Freedom Fighters*, Lantern Books, 2004.

Endnotes
[1] "End of Nature"
[2] Evans, B., "NOAA accused of blocking climate report," *Asheville Global Report* 403, 2006.
[3] Buncombe, A., "Bush tried to gag environmental expert," *Independent UK*, reprinted in *AGR* 368, 2006.
[4] Gaouette, N., "Congressional hearing heats up over changes to climate report," *LATimes.com*, March 20, 2007.
[5] Ibid.
[6] "States undercharge polluters," *Reuters AGR* 426, 2007.
[7] Ibid.
[8] Stern, N., "Stern Review: The Economics of Climate Change," 2006.
[9] Evans, B., "Failure to manage global warming would cripple world economy," AGR 408, 2006.
[10] Havemann, J., "Bush bypasses Senate with three appointments," *LA Times*, reprinted in the *Register Guard*, April 5, 2007.

ABOUT THE AUTHOR

In June 2001, Jeff was convicted of the arson of three trucks at the Joe Romania Chevrolet dealership and attempted arson at the Tyree Oil Company, a Unocal 76 Company. Both actions occurred in Eugene, Oregon.

The stated purpose of the Romania action was to raise awareness of the dangers of global warming, problems today we are all too aware of.

Jeff was sentenced to 22 years, 8 months in prison. However, in February 2007, this sentence was thrown out by the Oregon Court of Appeals. On February 28, 2008, Jeff was re-sentenced to 10 years. Having been incarcerated since June 2000, his sentence is almost served.

During his imprisonment Jeff has remained active in the struggle for social and environmental justice.

Please visit his website, www.freejeffluers.org, or write to: Friends of Jeffrey Free Luers, P.O. Box 3, Eugene, OR 97440 for more information on how to get involved with activism or to contribute to Jeff's support campaign.

CHAPTER THREE

CHANGE WE JUST CAN'T BELIEVE IN

BILL DUNNE

BILL DUNNE

This Country Must Change

Change is the universal constant, the only universal constant. Change is always happening, the relationships between things are always changing. Change ebbs and flows, sometimes lurching quickly and massively, sometimes oozing glacially and in fine detail. Change is happening here and now, not only as some physics construct out in the cosmos or an abstraction from a far-flung war zone. Change is felt by everyone all the time – present tense, first person economic, political, social, and environmental change in the cities and towns and countryside of the United States.

There is no guarantee, however, that we, the people, will like the change or that it will be positive. Few like the economic changes of these recessionary times brought on by capitalists playing casino with the country's finances. While recent political change may seem attractive after the dark and stormy long night of the Bush regime, the unfortunate reality is that they are superficial and cosmetic; the political system remains firmly in the hands of imperial capital's pair of political parties. Segregation by wealth, race, education, et cetera in U.S. society is growing, and the divisions are becoming more rigid and exclusive. Poverty and inequalities are rising as income disparities and social disconnection worsen. U.S. corporations still plunder the naturality here and abroad, and climate change becomes an ever more inconvenient truth.

On the other hand, there is no reason that change must be despicable, that it cannot be progressive. Some people like the changes mentioned above; verily, people caused them because they desired the results. Similarly, people could have made them otherwise. The point is that change is not some immutable force of nature or some mystical storm of which we are fated to be victims. Change, in the sociological sense, is the stream of our collective lives whose depth, breadth, turbulence, speed, direction, and viscosity we, the people, can control. We cannot afford to just "ride with the tide, go with the flow". We, the people, have to channel the inevitability of change such that we can have a change "to form a more perfect union, establish justice,...promote the general welfare, and...secure liberty to ourselves and our posterity". In other words, we must make the change revolutionary.

The necessity for the revolutionary change we so desperately need in the U.S. is the same necessity that has existed since the dawn of the industrial revolution, but more urgent and immediate. Revolutionary change is a class war first and foremost and is already happening in this country. Indeed, it never ceases. It was already in motion when the bourgeois, rich, slave holding, property owning, male, white elite revered as the country's founders wrested turf from the British empire and the Native American Nations. The struggle between bourgeois and proletarian has since waxed and waned throughout the country's history. The result has been some net gain for our, proletarian, side of the barricade—but not lately and not resolving the class contradiction.

Transformation in the context of the contradiction, in the field of struggle, is now telling us that we must drive change toward full resolution lest the contradiction be resolved in favor of the adversary (bourgeois imperial capitalist) class. We must throw off the ruling class's hegemony and replace it with a revolutionary socialist paradigm. Success will launch a social confluence of the US's diverse populations in which all people will have the greatest possible freedom to develop their full human potential. Failure could condemn generations to come to a subsistence of exploitation and oppression in service to a new aristocracy of wealth and power built on technological control.

Change is. *What change* is up to us. A brief look at the economic, political, social, and environmental landscapes that characterize US' late imperial capitalism—the here and now—shows why not mere change but a revolutionary change is imperative.

ECONOMIC EXPLOITATION AND PRIVATION

The United States is the richest country in the world. That statement begs a host of questions. Why, then, are so many of its citizens living in poverty? Why are so many U.S. residents living in constant fear of losing the job upon which depends their and their families' tenuous access to such basics as adequate food, clothing, and shelter? Why are so many U.S. Americans denied access to adequate health care? Given more or less continuous economic growth, why have real wages for everyone in the U.S. but a small elite been declining for decades? What accounts for the growing income disparity between that small elite and the huge majority of people in the U.S.? Answering these and other questions clearly shows the economic necessity for not just change in the U.S., but revolutionary change.

This Country Must Change

The short answer to questions about why so many people's lives are so lacking in the most materially wealthy country in history is the capitalist economic system that afflicts the U.S. Understanding its basic features makes this clear.

Capitalism's underlying theory is that people with money will invest it in economic enterprise, such physical capital as factories and equipment, the means of producing goods and services. These capitalists then buy labor and other inputs for as little as possible from other people who then actually use the means of production to create goods and services. The owners of the means of production then own the goods and service that others produced, which they try to sell in the market for as much as they can.

If the capitalists were astute, the market rewards them with fat profits—i.e., pays much more for the products than they cost to produce. They then reinvest these profits in expansion of the old or in different enterprises. Frequently, they borrow the money for this investment in the expectation of profit, speculating they will make more than enough to pay it off. This expands the economy and creates more jobs and wealth, some of which trickles down to the lowly workers who own no means of production but whose labor produces the profitable goods and services. If the capitalists were not astute, the market punishes them with loss of their capital, they go out of business and their workers lose their jobs. This results in the efficient allocation of resources: the astute get more money on the notion they will repeat their success, and the inept are prevented from repeating their failures. And everyone is entirely free to be a capitalist on those terms. Well, that's the theory.

The actuality is that the probability of anyone becoming a capitalist is exceedingly small without the necessary connections and opportunities and money. All but a small minority of people are frozen out of the capitalist class and its economic machinations. They may be allowed—indeed, forced—to play the capitalist game in small ways like buying small amounts of stocks and bonds or operating a small business, though always at the mercy of the market. But given the education, jobs, and opportunities to accumulate enough financial capital and knowledge available to that vast majority, they are mostly doomed to selling their labor to survive.

Moreover, "old money" and denizens of exclusive universities, elite society, corporate boardrooms, big business associations, et cetera, have more than technical expertise and business acumen; they have the network of connections and privileged information that permits them to form a barricade to market power. Established interests use economic power to smash or swallow smaller or weaker competition. The real world is thus increasingly an oligopoly of a few major interests too big to fail that control the economy as wealth is concentrated in ever fewer hands.

Worse than the exclusivity of the pinnacles wherein dwell the economic mighty is capitalism's socialization of production—and risk, contrary to capitalist mythology—and privatization of profit. A lot of people contribute to production—workers in the legal, emergency response, transportation, utility, education, and financial sectors all contribute to each factory's output in addition to the factory's workers themselves. But the product becomes the sole property of the owner of the means of production—the capitalist, who might never even see the product or its production process. S/he keeps the surplus value of labor—the value of labor's output beyond what s/he paid for overhead, materials, and labor. Multiplied by millions of workers, that is a lot of swag in capital's bag.

Capitalism does not explain why of all the contributors, only the capitalist gets a share of the profits—does not explain why production and risk are socialized but profit is privatized. All of the contributors risk their inputs. Workers additionally risk the entire potential for future sale of their labor, which is lost in whole or in part if they are injured or killed on the job. In today's U.S. capitalism, the big capitalists do not even risk their inputs, as the recent public bailouts of many private financial institutions and other businesses attest. Yet it is purportedly the risk of punishment in the marketplace that justifies the capitalists appropriating the entire production.

The combination of privatization of the profits of social production and exclusivity mean capitalists accumulate enormous financial resources. This financial capital must be constantly reinvested because holding actual money produces nothing and thus no profit; it may be lent and so earn interest, at best comparable to normal profit, but not economic profit, the holy grail of capitalism. Money needs to be exchanged for physical capital, means of production, and the resulting goods and services must be sold. Not only must they be sold, they must be sold at as great a profit as possible for capitalists to prosper. Hence, the fact that the exchange value of a given good or service is greater that its cost of production does not mean under capitalism that there is an extra increment of additional wealth available to feed the hungry or tend the sick; that would not be profitable. Indeed, the capitalist could not tolerate such use of the surplus as it would tend to bring the price of the good or service down. Capitalism prefers full store shelves and packed warehouses in the face of poverty to full absorption of the social production by society absent sufficient profit.

This capitalist organization of economic activity has disastrous consequences for society. Capitalism creates two antagonistic classes in society whose interests are diametrically opposed—the small minority owners of capital and the large majority who have only their labor to sell. Capitalism is anti-democratic, skewing political process in favor of wealth. Capitalism distorts production toward military and luxury products that serve the needs of few people but raise the price and availability of essential goods and services for everyone. Capitalism inherently includes cycles of boom and bust from the privations of which the rich are insulated but that inflict severe hardship on poor and working people. Capitalism fosters imperialism and militarism and raises the likelihood of war.

Capital's and labor's interests are irreconcilably opposed because, at base, capital wants to pay labor as little as possible and labor wants capital to pay it the full value of its labor. Capital knows that every cent paid in compensation for labor is a cent less profit it gets; labor knows that every cent of profit is a cent of value it created it is not getting. Control of this surplus value determines which class is the ruling class. In addition, capitalists' and workers' lives are characterized by an essential difference: capitalists live off the labor of others while workers live off the sale of their labor. This gives rise to the great social divide in US society, elite claims that it is a classless society notwithstanding: capitalist (ruling) class and working (ruled) class—bourgeoisie and proletariat. However one may want to subdivide these two classes, they remain the fundamental division of U.S. society and, indeed, all capitalist society.

Nor is it merely direct wages and benefits capital recognizes as compensation and seeks to drive down. Less obvious compensation it opposes include health, safety, and environmental—indeed, any—regulation of business. Regulation costs businesses money—transfers wealth to workers by improving their safety, health, security, environment, et cetera—and thus reduces profit. So do other, tax-supported, services like schools and hospitals. Capital opposes them all, except where they serve its interests, because it sees the taxes as transfer payments from it to the poor who need but can't pay for the services.

Production for profit also distorts the mix of goods and services the economy produces away from that which would provide the greatest benefit for the greatest number of people. Corporations use the political muscle of their money to insure guaranteed large profits on military projects as well as a lot of military spending to absorb excess production. The trouble is that military spending does not contribute to economic growth. What does, for example, a tank do? It sits around, rusts and wastes a lot of fuel and ammunition in practice and tempts the ruling class to use it as an instrument of oppression in expensive imperialist adventures. A tractor, on the other hand, tills a field that grows food, creating jobs for farmers, mechanics, grain handlers, bakers, retailers, and filling empty bellies.

Luxury goods similarly waste a lot of resources but serve only a few—often at the cost of major pollution. A business jet, for instance, does nothing but occupy a few skilled people and burn mass quantities of fuel for nothing more than to ferry a few fat cats who are too good to mingle with the hoi polloi on an Airbus, let alone a road bus. So it also goes with opulent offices, palatial estates, yachts, cars, jewelry, and a host of high end goods and services a worker will only ever see on VH-1.

This military and luxury excess absorbs a lot of material and labor and productive capacity. That reduces the amount available for producing food, housing, health care, education, and even down-market consumer goods, thus raising the prices of all those necessities. Capitalists don't care about the higher prices because they already buy higher end versions of necessities and can afford it, anyway.

Also inherent in capitalism is what is known as the business cycle to capitalists and boom and bust to people whose lives are thrown into disarray by it. Capitalists increase production (and cut costs, like labor) to maximize profit. They then have to invest the resulting money capital in yet more production for yet more profit because greed is good in the capitalist system and growth protects the capitalist from being overtaken by bigger or more agile competitors. Speculators contribute to this inflation of productive assets and production by borrowing against anticipated profits, often with no or overvalued collateral. In essence, they gamble on what and how much will sell.

Eventually, selling more of the product becomes too difficult because available markets for those products have become saturated. Inventories of unsold products begin to rise. Production starts to decline in the face of rising inventories, causing investments in productive capacity to lose their ability to provide an adequate return (profit). Capitalists don't want to pay workers as production slows and productivity declines, so people are thrown out of work. They then have less money to buy products, aggravating their downturn. The return on capital assets declines as does their value.

Since most of these capital assets are bought on credit in the expectation of inflated returns, the speculators dump them as fast as they can before their value falls below the debt incurred to buy them. Many of their gambles turn out to be wrong and they lose—as with the recent housing crash that rippled through the U.S. economy and precipitated a worldwide bust. Other capitalists are stampeded into following suit, causing stock (representing equity/ownership stake in physical capital) values to crash. Lenders refuse to lend, afraid that collateral will lose value and borrowers will not make enough to either service the debt (pay interest) or pay back principal. Buying and production slow even more. Some capitalists have to retrench, downsize, cut back, lay off. Others go bankrupt.

While the bourgeoisie may lament the loss of paper assets and the reshuffling of seats on corporate boards in such busts, its members rarely suffer any lack of access to necessities or even more dislocation because their greater financial resources insulate them. Suffering is the proletarian portion to the extent the system forces workers to live paycheck to paycheck and then without a paycheck.

Capitalism's insatiable demand for new sources of raw materials and cheap labor as well as new markets in which to unload its surplus production stimulates imperialism. In the old days, "gunboat diplomacy" was the norm of empire wherein the ruling classes—monarchist aristocrats and then bourgeoisie—of industrialized countries sent their surplus labor as troops and bureaucrats to conquer and occupy less developed areas so their capitalists could exploit the resources and labor there. Eventually, the exploited and oppressed people of most of the colonies got hip to the fact they were being robbed instead of having the benefits of "civilization" bestowed on them, and they kicked their colonial rulers out.

Next came neo-imperialism in which the imperialists returned and either imposed or bought local ruling classes in resource rich but development poor areas to serve the same function: protect the capitalists' exploitation of resources and labor with military and "development" aid supplied by imperial governments. Sometimes neo-imperialist tactics are inadequate to secure the desired access to resources and/or labor, and the iron fist comes out of the velvet glove as capitalism reverts to military invasion, conquest, and occupation—as in Iraq.

As the foraging illustrates, so many people in the U.S. live in privation and poverty and precariously because the capitalist economic system denies them the opportunity to consistently and securely make a living wage. Concentrating wealth and power in the unaccountable hands of the small minority elite subjects the majority to the rule of that class, the bourgeois class. The ruling class exploits the great majority working and poor proletarian class and oppresses its members if they resist that exploitation. As a result, although most U.S. Americans work hard, they can never be secure in their employment. Given the adversarial relationship between capital and labor, bourgeoisie and proletariat, there is constant downward pressure on wages and other forms of compensation. Hence, even where working people can keep themselves above the poverty line, they are still too frequently unable to afford living standards that include levels of nutrition, housing, health care, and education that should be considered human rights for everyone.

Under U.S. capitalism, these conditions have been worsening and can only continue to worsen as blood and treasure are squandered on imperial adventures and bailing fat cats out of financial trouble of their own making. As industrial competition from the rest of the world increases, imperial capital will be forced to cut living standards in the U.S. to further depress the lifestyles of the working class. Those cuts will not come out of the bourgeoisie's end of the economic equation—unless we change it, revolutionize it.

This glimpse of the U.S. economic system shows that it cannot and is not intended to fulfill the greatest portion of the needs possible for the greatest number of people. In fact, it is intended to satisfy only the minimum number of needs that will reproduce labor—keep as many people as necessary working at high enough productivity to maximize profit, regardless of the consequences to those working. Keeping an immense pool of un and under employed labor depresses the cost of labor, and the threat of unemployment and poverty makes workers more tractable to autocratic bosses. And what good is a threat without occasional enforcement?

Hence, poverty and privation are kept real and job and economic security are not. Since much healthcare is provided through employers, its denial is another threat to keep labor in line. Many people are not paid enough to purchase health insurance on their own; they must rely on employers reducing the cost with economies of scale. Plus, healthcare is expensive and, however provided, amounts to additional compensation for labor. While capitalists may be able to profit from providing healthcare, they can profit more by not providing it. Similarly with education: outside of fee-for-service, education amounts to compensation for labor—and of a particularly dangerous kind. Lawyers and engineers, for example, for whom there is no place in the economy are more likely to realize that it is not their fault, be angry about it, and know or learn how to do something about it than someone without a high school education.

These circumstances illustrate why, despite decades of economic growth, real wages for all but the economic elite have been declining. Capital has used its economic power and the political influence it buys to chisel away at labor's share of the social wealth workers produced. And that is the source of the growing crevasse between the incomes and wealth of the ruling elite and the working majority—the bourgeoisie and proletariat.

POLITICAL DISENFRANCHISMENT AND CONTROL

The United States claims to be the land of the free. Such a political claim also raises a rash of questions, many of them similar to those raised by the U.S.'s wealth in juxtaposition to the privation of its people. What does the freedom US rulers are constantly insisting characterizes U.S. culture really mean? How does such a country incarcerate proportionally more of its people than any other? What does the democracy those leaders are touting mean in a country where the last president lost the popular election? Can all U.S. interests be respected in a system with only two narrowly separated parties, especially considering the diversity of the U.S. population? Why is the U.S. so reviled abroad if it is so busily exporting freedom and democracy? Answers to these questions show that in order for the US to truly be the land of the free, massive change—yeah, revolutionary change—is necessary.

The answer to the foregoing and other political questions about why there is so little liberty or justice in the land of the free is the same as that to the economic questions looked at from another angle: the capitalist political system that afflicts the U.S. The type of freedom it claims is not absolute freedom as in "do what thou wilt" or even broad freedom as in freedom from poverty, disease, ignorance, exploitation, oppression. It is, instead, the freedom to buy and sell, to accumulate and manipulate property, to compete with and profit from others. Other freedoms retained by USians are incidental to and circumscribed by that limited license. The social contract is between rivals and adversaries with few guarantees for the unsuccessful or economically small and weak. Such a system makes capitalists the ruling class.

With capitalists the ruling class, there is no real democracy in the U.S. U.S. residents not disenfranchised completely by virtue of a felony conviction or no formal citizenship have a little bit of political democracy: they can choose one of the two ruling class party candidates for virtually any major post, vote for a protest candidate with no chance of actually winning, or not vote. The Democratic and Republican (capitalized only to avoid insult to little d democrats and little r republicans) party machinery, not the voters, select the two candidates. They are picked based in large part on their record in playing ball with capitalist interests and perceived ability to advance those interests as well as ability to raise money (one dollar, one vote rather than one person one vote, and signifying acceptability to those with many dollars). Having a choice of one of two whose difference is not that great to enact and enforce crucial public policy is not much democracy—and it is only not much political democracy.

U.S. Americans enjoy all but no economic democracy. For the vast majority of USians, their job is the most important element of their lives because it is through that job that they support themselves and their families. All but a vanishing few businesses, however, are autocracies in which it is the bosses' way or the highway. Workers have little input into their work schedules, what is produced, the conditions under which it is produced, or the compensation for their labor. Nor do people get to vote on the conduct of business through government, except in a very limited indirect way.

Social democracy is also lacking in the U.S. In a society driven by property and wealth, there are endless gradations of "status" even within the two sides of the class contradiction. People are segregated by economic status. Mixed income "hoods" are exceedingly rare. Social organizations such as membership associations and clubs are also formed on the basis of economics, education, location, and other exclusions. Laws proscribe various forms of discrimination—but not others, allowing virtually anyone to be excluded from the social functions where many political important decisions are made.

But, but, but! How can this be in the land of the free? 'Tis because the ruling class's financial power determines political outcomes in the U.S. Corporate interests and individuals made wealthy by them finance the Democratic and Republican parties. People without the right connections cannot penetrate the ranks of these parties in any meaningful way. These parties are supposed to represent the entire political spectrum with Democrats on the left and Republicans on the right. Both, however, are staunchly capitalist parties, the Democrats slightly more "liberal" and the Republicans slightly more "conservative", and both are to the right of center. Candidates from one or the other are the only ones with any real chance to get elected to significant positions. No other party can compete with the money and opportunities and other resources—which translate as the organizational capacity—the capitalists give them. That means there is little political room for minor parties, and those parties operate in invisibility outside the media spotlight they can't afford, regardless of how many people they individually or collectively represent in program and practice.

The two parties throw up candidates for any office worth contesting. Poor and working people are, except in extraordinary circumstances, excluded from running for office. They have to work for or hustle a living, which doesn't leave much time or money to campaign. Even with a lot of volunteers from, say, a union or other group, getting the word out requires paying for transportation, staging events, media, etc. The really big and unavoidable expenses are media. In this day and age, there is no possibility for an unknown candidate to get enough name recognition to win a major election without extensive exposure in radio, publications, internet, billboards, and especially television. The mainstream parties have massive warchests with which to finance their anointed candidates, which they funnel from the ruling class to minimize the visibility of the fact that U.S. politics is a pay to play game. A candidate thus must make him or herself desirable to one of the two parties to obtain enough money and organizational support to mount a viable campaign or must accept an also ran (or couldn't run) status.

Nor does the ruling class really care whether the Democrat or Republican wins. Both U.S. mainstream parties support what is generally characterized as the "conservative" agenda, virtually unquestioned support for: military and police; deregulation of business; curtailing social welfare spending; limiting education expansion despite singing its praises; impeding labor organization; lower taxes for the rich; accumulation of gross disparities in wealth, among other things. Democrats might up a little more pay and benefits to minimize privation unrest and, incidentally, support the businesses in which needy people will spend the money. Republicans might pander to reactionaries and religious zealots by pushing militarism and school prayer. But each does all it can to promote the interests of capitalism and the owning class and neither is going to do anything that undermines those interests.

Perhaps the most dangerous weapon in the U.S. political system of class control is the media, the ruling class's means of generating public opinion. In a country in whose political mythology freedom of speech is held sacrosanct, there is remarkably little freedom of political speech. Why? Because "the press is free to him what owns one" [sic] and only to him or her. The radical left speaker or publisher, for example, does not have big capital, so s/he cannot afford transmitters and presses and web servers and offices and staff to disseminate his or her information widely. Without capitalization, such a media outlet even has difficulty gathering diverse and timely information, being unable to hire and support researchers, reporters, video and audio crews, et cetera. That makes it less competitive with glitzy corporate outlets in the amount of the audience it can reach. Indeed, that reality makes it difficult for alternative media voices to stay around long at all. That also lets the kept media dismiss alternatives that present views radically different than theirs as the lunatic fringe or over the edge.

The information mainstream media given to USians reflects the interests of capital. The media uses that information to condition the public's perceptions of events and thus their conclusions about them. Authors, reporters, pundits, and other content producers are "naturally selected" by the system. Content providers know what gets disseminated and arrange their product accordingly. If editors—who also know what superiors like—approve, the story goes out and the producers get kudos and opportunities to work on bigger, more important projects. If not, the story dies and its journalists get brickbats and don't increase their reach. Egregious or chronic offenders of status quo sensibilities may disappear from the mainstream entirely.

Look, for instance, at the picture of the U.S. political landscape the media servants of capitalism convey. The first and perhaps biggest whopper is that the U.S. system is classless. Rare is the mainstream story that mentions class distinction as a fact or compares the circumstances of wealthy capitalists and struggling workers in those terms. Class appears almost exclusively in laments over the plight of the "middle" class, as if all U.S. people are middle class and only an insignificant number belong to the other two classes "middle" at minimum implies. In fact, polls suggest that a large majority of U.S. residents think they are exactly that. Where did they get that impression? It is clearly not the case. The misimpression is no accident.

The media also propagates the myth that business is the source of all good things in society, and business people—especially the big ones—are exalted paragons of virtue to whom we must look for leadership. Politicians, however, are venal and corrupt. This projection is turned up and down depending on ruling class' needs to either use politicians or keep them subservient. Union leaders are greedy and uncouth. Environmentalists are crazed tree huggers or trust-fund elitists who don't know squat about needing a job. Another antidemocratic media distortion is its incessant message that it is too stormy and cold outside to venture personally into the marketplace of ideas. The consequent isolation limits the extent to which people will get a view of the political landscape different than the media's.

The ruling class manipulates and controls public opinion and the political system this way because the government is its executive tool. Government is a way to gain access to mountains of capital and a giant market. It also makes the laws and regulations that enable big capitalists to socialize production while privatizing profit, marginalize labor and challenges to work and property relations, legalize business and financial practices that benefit capital, and to protect themselves from the consequences of their actions. It made all the financial depredations that led to the current economic crisis possible and is bailing out its capitalist architects without requiring criminal liability or restitution or even major restructuring. Such economic disasters can simply be blamed on the last crop of politicians and bureaucrats and alleged to be solved with a new crop. Meanwhile, such wealth is lost and, though less, distributed upward relatively.

The U.S. political system also makes it easier for the ruling class to take the country to war. War at home is waged against the working class in its revolutionary potential. The war on "crime". The war on drugs. The war on terrorism. The war on the working class. None of these attacks addresses the cause of the problems the ruling class exaggerates to justify maintaining an apparatus or repression against and amongst the population. It needs this apparatus to protect its property and the work and production relations that make it the ruling class—especially in times of economic upheaval.

No alternatives to criminalization and repression as the only response to crime and rebellion—or their causes—are even entertained. If crime and illegality and rebellion are merely the expected sociological responses to poor, butchered half-lives lived in squalid poverty inherent in subsistence under late US capitalism for too many U.S. residents, there should be sociological medicine and therapy for them. But the political system says there is none but repression. The ruling class wants and admits no cure because it must justify the apparatus or repression.

One of the fronts in the war at home, therefore, is using the criminal "justice" system to define as criminal the only routes out of various sorts of ghettoes. Many people cannot and will not and do not accept as their lot the ghetto life—a concatenation of non-living wage, dead-end jobs interspersed with periods of unemployment clinging sometimes unsuccessfully to the bottom of a ragged social safety net—be it urban or rural. Sure, a few people may pull themselves out of the lumpen proletariat in the approved manner, but the probability of that happening is exceedingly small, given crumbling, under-financed, trouble-plagued, overcrowded schools, absent and uneducated parents, poor nutrition and health care, sub-standard housing, poverty, and insecurity that characterize lumpen lives. Hence, drug use and sales, collectivization in gangs, and redistribution of wealth in various unsanctioned ways with their more immediate returns are attractive to many people in poor and oppressed communities.

Politicians and the media seize on this activity, associate it with the worst atrocities committed by the more vicious predators (except for U.S. war crimes), and define it rather than capitalist and government policies as the root of all evil in poor and oppressed communities—and, indeed, the society at large. Yet the system allows a certain amount of crime to pay precisely to attract the dissatisfied, rebellious, and capable—the people who would be community organizers, political activists, union leaders, and guerilla commanders in other circumstances (and maybe are already). The apparatus then tars and feathers them with the crime and criminal labels and consigns them to far-off prisons.

The U.S. maintains the largest gulag archipelago in the world, imprisoning a higher proportion of its citizens than any other, even the countries of the so-called "axis of evil" or the former "evil empire". Who is consigned to this chain of prisons and why are quintessentially political decisions. Now the archipelago is populated mostly by petty criminals and perpetrators of illegalities (not all illegalities are crimes and not all crimes are illegal), some two and a half million—almost one percent of the population and a grossly higher proportion of U.S. racial minorities. If imperial capital was suddenly confronted with an internal threat to its status quo, such a system could swallow another 100,000 people without a burp. And if that were not enough, it could release half the current population—small-time drug traffickers and property offenders, not that it has any problem with grotesque overcrowding—without political consequences significant to capital interests.

Removing so many people from poor and oppressed communities also serves a preemptive function. It saps the vitality of those communities by depriving them of mothers, fathers, brothers, sisters, friends, neighbors, workers, and teachers. Many such people have energy and acumen and inclination that could be channeled into addressing social and political problems. Strengthening communities thusly, however, would raise for the ruling class the specter of resistance. Justice does not prevail in relegating people to the dark concrete corners of the U.S.'s endless complex of prisons, given their purpose and the vast disparity between the apparatus and individual defendants and even their communities. But the gulags and criminalization and removal from conflict zones for as long as necessary are effective in diverting and containing the potential (and actuality!) for political unrest and resistance in communities that have so much to gain thereby.

Nor is the warfare the U.S. political system facilitates limited to class war at home. Imperial war spends the lives and wealth of U.S. residents to conquer resources, markets and attendant profits and to otherwise make the world's climates favorable for business. Controlling the national legislature, ruling class politicians make impassioned speeches about, for example, weapons of mass destruction and mushroom clouds and terrorists and the axes of evil who wield them without rebuttal or opposition. They do so notwithstanding the absence of evidence for such claims on patriarchic implication that they have secret or superior knowledge. That provides the cover for all of them to vote to initiate war.

The fawning media duly reports the impassioned speeches as statements of fact, and fails to display, trivializes, or disparages voices of dissent as less than serious and/or unpatriotic. The invasion or support for military action by a proxy is passed as if there is no possible alternative—to applause from a public media that is programmed to glorify the military and believe the politicians. By the time the official and media misrepresentations are discovered, it is too late to change course, the system says, and too often it is. So it also goes with lesser imperialist actions such as basing policies, military "maneuvers", and support for client regimes—saber rattling short of actual wielding to demonstrate the dangers of "threatening" U.S. interests.

The U.S. political system with its capitalist ruling class, the foregoing shows, can only be characterized as a dictatorship of the bourgeoisie. The working class—proletariat—has virtually no power to demand anything within it. The best we, the people, can expect from this system is what members of the ruling class might think is necessary to make the majority of the U.S. population, off whose labor they live, believe in a certain political mythology in which anyone can be president, CEO, and rich. In that mythology, everyone in the U.S. is equal and the U.S. is a classless society. All the people democratically elect—on the basis of one person, one vote—precisely the political representatives they want and need, which representatives act altruistically without fear or favor in the best interests of their constituents and the country. Justice prevails in all things, and the military and police selflessly serve and protect the populace from threats foreign and domestic. The reality is exactly the opposite.

That reality reveals the answers to our questions. The

freedom U.S. rulers claim is freedom to exploit and oppress. The ruling minority lives large off the labor of the big majority and maintains a military, police, and prisons apparatus of repression for those who might resist such victimization. The democracy the ruling class so often attaches to the freedom it exports on bayonets is really just a fragment of political democracy that exists more in appearance than in actuality. There is ever less economic and social democracy. Disenfranchisement of the proletariat by the bourgeoisie is masked by the appearance of all three. There is less difference between the two parties that control the U.S. political system than there is within some of the parties few can see in their shadow. The Republicans and Democrats only represent a narrow slice of political opinion—and intend no more. Only people hoodwinked, duped, and socially conditioned could accept such a system as true "freedom and democracy". That's why it must be imposed on people not long subjected to the US media's conditioning at gunpoint. And everyone reviles people who would impose thusly.

SOCIAL MANIPULATION AND DISLOCATION

The United States purports to be a melting pot wherein people from across the spectrum of economic conditions, national origins, cultural traditions, religious persuasions, political perspectives, racial heritages, and gender orientations interact in a social blender to produce a classless, egalitarian land of opportunity characterized by freedom and democracy. The trouble with this popular social mythology is that, like the United States' economic and political mythologies, it raises many uncomfortable questions. Why is the society so segregated and unequal according to income? Why then do sexism and racism persist in a society in which a white woman and a black man can duke it out for major party presidential candidacy in the mainstream political arena and the black man beat an old white male who didn't have a chance against either in the presidential election? Why do people take refuge in and cling to racial ethnic, religious, gender and other "identities" instead of assimilating— "melting"—into a larger and supposedly better national culture? Why are so many people increasingly forced into an underclass of ignorance within the economic underclass? The answers to these questions demonstrate a social need for revolutionary change.

Stratification by income is inherent in capitalist economics, as was explored earlier, but segregation and social inequality are not, at least in U.S. mythology. There is no reason why neighborhoods and even whole cities and regions could not be economically integrated. Verily, that would be more democratic and conducive to the melting pot. It would also be more economically and environmentally efficient. Low, middle, and upper income housing projects could all be located in the same urban complexes or suburbs. Manufacturing facilities, office space, and executive suites could all be located in the same parts of towns and cities. All USians could live and work in proximity of each other and enjoy a more diverse yet common cultural and social ambience as well as having a more mutual experience of living and working conditions. They could interact with each other more directly and evolve a more common national culture in which economic status would not be such a determining factor of people's ability to achieve their full human potential.

Unfortunately, social segregation, like economic segregation, is unavoidable under the U.S. capitalist paradigm. Capitalism needs this social segregation to both hide the extent of the inequality and help maintain the fiction that the economically successful are somehow special and entitled to a bigger cut of the social wealth. Plus, the ruling class needs to prevent its executive arm from becoming too sympathetic to the working and exploited class, with whom many of the executive class members have more in common than the ruling class. Perhaps largest in ruling class perceptions is having learned from history that physical removal from the exploited and oppressed makes it easier to defend against insurrection.

This segregation also allows the bourgeoisie to represent and feel that they are "better" than people who cannot afford to life in bourgeois communities, frequent bourgeois workplaces, and have access to bourgeois social and cultural institutions. Being "better" allows the bourgeoisie to see the proletariat as not fully human and to objectify its members. Bourgeois superiority is predicated on the mystique that class members have some unique combination of traits that enables them to provide service to society so sublime as to be worth hundreds of times the compensation of the average toiler.

The bourgeois entitlement also enshrines the notion that people's personal value and thus call on social resources is determined in dollars—not in their character or deeds, but in how much money they can get. Thus, for example, emergency medical technicians, who save lives despite the risks of high speed responses, not to mention infectious diseases, are worth less than persons who destroy lives, neighborhoods, towns by moving factories to places they can pollute more and/or pay less or by foreclosing on aged victims of predatory loans. So it goes with other occupations such as teacher, musician, janitor, home health care provider, baker, electrician, construction worker—all of whom bring pleasure and comfort to people via hard work. Compare their paltry pay and social position versus that of bankers, arbitrageurs, speculators, defense contractors, corporate lobbyists—people who redistribute wealth upward regardless of the pain that might cause. A corollary to the notion that people can and should be valued in dollars is that the needy are needy not because the bourgeoisie don't pay them a living wage but because they are incompetent or slackers.

The segregation of bourgeois capitalist and proletarian worker also sets up the condition for a range of separations and segregations by economic class—bourgeoisie petit bourgeoisie, executive class, labor aristocracy, working class, lumpen, and other graduations. The economic differentiation, in turn, encourages other social divisions as well, such as by race, religion, ethnicity, et cetera. It legitimizes—indeed, lionizes—the notion of differentiation, division, and divergence outside of the strictly economic. All these segregations, affirmed by bourgeois concepts of personal value, create a hierarchical society and virtual caste system, propaganda about equality and democracy notwithstanding.

The ruling class created, promotes, and aggravates these divisions in practice despite its official theoretical line, "We're all Americans, equal and united." The ruling class exploits the division by pitting the groups against each other competitively instead of fostering cooperation. Thus, it becomes less likely that the groups will realize their commonality and combine in resistance to their collective expropriation by the bourgeois ruling class. Rather, they will more than likely harden the lines between themselves.

The media advances this segregated character of U.S. society. It shamelessly touts competition as the only path to social progress, readily divides society into groups with hard lines between them, and constantly pushes the social hierarchy as if it were a natural law like gravity. From news to entertainment, to arts to education, it conveys the impression that the executive class has everything under control (and keeps the ruling class out of the limelight). It pushes the notion that people are inherently competitive, that everything can be slotted into some competitive group, and that the poor and oppressed are just losers in the competition through some fault of their own.

Mainstream media news misrepresents this U.S. reality, to put it mildly. The Iraq War was launched on lies. So was, for that matter, the current recession as well as other socio-economic disasters. A completely false picture of reality, however, would soon lose the ruling class and its media credibility and thus effectiveness. As important, the lower socio-economic strata who operate the system on which bourgeois profit and power is predicated would make wrong choices in their work that could ultimately crash the system if their picture of the world is a complete fantasy. Accordingly, the misrepresentation more commonly takes the form of half-truths, omissions, spin, et cetera, which lead people to conclude that bourgeois prescriptions are correct for everyone.

As in the economic and political realms, the ruling class uses the media to mold public opinion about social issues. All of the mainstream sources claim objectivity, but they don't practice it. How can a TV news story about immigration in which the news readers prattle on over a banner footline "BROKEN BORDERS" be objective? How can giving patently unequal sides, like environmentalists versus strip miners and clear cutters, equal coverage as if they were morally or on any other basis equivalent be objective? Indeed, how can news be objective when the very language is biased as in the Israelis always being "allies" and the Palestinians always "terrorists"? "Bipartisanship" is sold as a great thing concession must be made to achieve when people voted massively for the advertized social program of one party and in broad opposition to that of the other? Reports say banks and their rich and influential stockholders and executives must be bailed out of the consequences of their bad decisions. But they never explain why workers don't get bailed out of the layoffs and other losses stemming from those same decisions. Et cetera. Et cetera. Ad nauseam. Whatever the news story, it is laid out in the light most beneficial to the ruling class.

Nor is news the only way the ruling class uses the media to manipulate society. Another is the mass propaganda of entertainment programming. To the extent sports, movies, serial dramas, comedies, celebrity shows and other programming ever criticize aspects of ruling class behavior, it is only in a way representative of disagreements within the ruling class—disagreements and the solutions for which rarely threaten the status quo. Capitalists are generally portrayed as fine and upstanding paragons of virtue who are the source of all good for the people around them—jobs, pay, economic development, good government, et cetera—and society in general. They are only punished—and then often merely circumstantially—for deviating from the capitalist ideal. Their henchpeople, minions, and lackeys in the apparatus of repression are always selfless defenders of truth, justice, and the U.S. American Way. Amongst them, we might occasionally find a few bad apples, but never a systemic problem despite myriad corruption and brutality scandals. And the system, the system's voice says, always straightens things out, smiting the evildoers.

Bad guys are usually proletarians and always not merely perpetrators of illegality but evil, nasty and just plain bad people. No real exploration of circumstances that drive people to crime or entrap them in it—or of the fact that all illegalities are not crimes and all crimes are not illegal—is provided. The United States of America, right or wrong, is another frequent fiction, as difficult as it may be to wrap the flag around every imperialist adventure and atrocity so the empire's storm troopers can be held up as heroes and heroines who can do no wrong. Fictional entertainment also aids and abets the news in painting the picture that the world beyond the front window is a scary, dangerous place best left to "official" entities who are here to help.

Sports, entertainment, poetics, and even religion in which "stars" figure so prominently create a celebrity culture that is a major distraction from what's really going on. People are attracted with various thrills to watch a bunch of flashy performers chase balls, play fantasy rolls, create scandals, and bloviate on TV. They know names and claims to fame and frequently a lot more about sundry glitterati with little sundry beyond the glitter. But they infrequently know even the name of a single CEO or major stockholder or lobbyist of a Fortune 500 company. Why? Because there are no legions of paparazzi chasing these magnates. The ruling class prefers to operate on the down low and conduct the business of exploitation and oppression in the darkness outside the spotlight and under the radar. The paparazzi and pundits and producers and editors know their lines. So the people get the Wizard of Oz instead of the man (or woman) behind the curtain.

The razzle-dazzle of fantasy media distracts people not

only from what's going on, but from what's not going on. The media celebrity culture disparages education as the province of nerds and puritanical scolds. This is a deliberate effort to make education less attractive to people on the lower end of the socio-economic continuum. If people are ambivalent about education, failure to fulfill election cycles' hyperbolic promises about a glorious education renaissance go without political consequences. Limiting education for the systemically poor and oppressed is the best way to keep them "in their place". It inhibits the proletariat from learning of its plight, that it can do something about it, and how to do it. The bourgeoisie also wants to protect its sons and daughters from competition for the diminishing number of good jobs. With a shortage of knowledgeable people in a community to turn off the video game, the sports, the celebrity culture, and encourage learning and accomplishment in the real worlds, poorer communities are disproportionately victimized by the anti-education propaganda and the substitutes for education.

Perhaps the most socially egregious media abuse is fear of mongering. In addition to its political consequences touched upon earlier, engendering fear is socially destructive. Most of the message coming via radio, TV, print, movies, et cetera is that it is a hard and dangerous world out there full of terrorists and psychopaths and criminals and "foreigners" and other predators. All of them are lurking in the freedom-hating shadows, slavering over the prospect of pouncing on anyone foolish enough to leave the security and comfort and familiarity of home or workplace for no other reason than the lurkers are evil and nasty.

The result is to minimize real social consciousness and replace it with an abstraction of social connection—to isolate people from class brethren and sistren. Thus isolated, people no longer know their neighbors and don't get their information about the world from social interaction and direct experience. They must relate to the world—and form their opinions about it and what should be done in it—through the ruling class's media: if it wasn't reported, it didn't happen; the way it is shown, it is.

To the extent people retain social connections beyond their individual families, they tend to do so according to their segregations the ruling class both foisted on and inveigled them to adopt: gender, race, religion, orientation, ethnicity, et cetera, et cetera. In a competitive environment, it is easy for the ruling class to draw the lines around them harder and sharper and create situations (and propaganda) to maintain and aggravate those divisions while mouthing a "Can't we all just get along?" and "We're all Americans" pretense. It is so easy to make the exploited and oppressed groups appear to be the source of each other's problems: affirmative action beneficiaries taking "our" jobs; illegal immigrants violating "our" borders and threatening our security; welfare queens stealing money and social services; religious fanatics making us insecure; "foreigners" luring "our" jobs overseas and diluting "our" culture; blacks being criminals and gangsters; whites being oppressors and privileged devils; greedy workers fueling inflation (or business bankruptcies) with unreasonable wage and benefit demands (but never greedy bosses or owners with excess profits and bonuses), et cetera.

These artificial separations have, like all things, an economic base. Were it not for the economic power of the ruling class and the economic stratification of U.S. society, the presently hot-button separations would be no more issues than those between people from different U.S. states or carpenters and masons. Without the material benefit of discrimination (division to exploit and oppress for perceived benefit), discrimination would lose its incentive. Without the profit and attendant disparities in wealth, there would be no power to discriminate to any real end. So, for example, without the motive of more surplus value, there would be no reason to employ, say, a Chinese worker to produce goods for export to the U.S. rather than a U.S. one to produce domestic goods. Without that profit, it would be difficult for profiteers to discriminate because they would lack the capital power—and the potential victims would have their surplus value with which to resist attempts to exploit and oppress.

Unfortunately, the long tenure of capitalism in the U.S. has led to the institutionalization of many of these segregations, most notably racism, sexism, and homophobia. The ruling class is working on the xenophobia, having apparently decided the "give me your tired, your poor" era is over. The long tenure of the social separations has given them a life of their own divorced from both incentive and power to discriminate. People have been practicing these artificial divisions so long they have become ingrained in some U.S. residents with varying virulence. Most such people cannot articulate why they must continue to discriminate against or, worse, seek supremacy over other groups for no other reason than their different appearance. Nor can people who advocate keeping women "in their place" or homophobia give any real reason why. Discriminators are generally reduced to idiocies like, "Well, that's how I was brought up." or "God said so." Such people continue these irrational discriminations even where it is contrary to their material interests. Other people discriminate unconsciously as a result of social conditioning prior to learning that discrimination based on people's inherent characteristics is improper for being unjust, a failure of class solidarity, oppressive, and an impediment to the truly free and democratic society in which they want to live.

Fortunately, the trajectory of racism ·is in the right direction. Getting to the point at which deliberate and offensive racism as well as unconscious and defensive racism are minority attitudes has been a long process of struggle and education against the continuing efforts of the ruling class to maintain these social divisions as tools of manipulation and control. The ruling class created racism and xenophobia over hundreds and even thousands of years to get peasant and proletarian armies to do their bidding against other rulers' peasant and proletarian armies. Resistance to racism and xenophobia by its victims and other opponents has forced ruling classes into a continual, albeit uneven, retreat from these oppressions' most virulent forms. But that has not stopped the ruling class form using so valuable a tool of social control. The trajectories of sexism and homophobia have been similar: they have long been used to further ruling class interests, but resistance to them has eroded the extent of the oppression and its usefulness.

True social equality, however, though growing in perception and in fact, remains elusive. The reasons for this dissonance are disparities in power and that divide and rule is still a useful—indeed indispensible—tactic for the bourgeoisie and their interests. So business and government (guided by the men and women behind the curtain) create enmity between groups—groups who may already harbor suspicious of each other based on both real and imagined, personal and historical experience.

What, for example, could be more natural than affirmative action and even quotas to redress the long denial of equal access to the labor market and thus to the possibility of economic equality for minority groups? Yet, business, reluctant to accept any regulation of its conduct, aided by its lackeys in government and media, managed to implement it only to the extent they could not avoid and in a way that created new radical divisions in U.S. society. The implementation was cast in light of forcing integration down people's throats rather than a communal breaking of bread. It made the question between workers: "Why are you taking our jobs?" The real question between workers and bosses: "Why aren't there enough jobs?"

So it goes with immigration: the focus is on "broken borders" and the problems associated with immigration with scant attention to the benefits of immigration and of normalizing it, that all U.S. residents are descended from immigrants or are immigrants themselves, that U.S. business and business models and government business policies are responsible for most of the immigration. So it goes with civil rights for gay and lesbian people: capital promotes inane religious prejudices to a par with the right of consenting adults to do with each other what they desire. Similar prejudices are promoted against women in which capital tries to reduce them to objects and property even as it exploits their labor. Et cetera. Et cetera.

All this fomenting of divisions by the ruling class prevents U.S. society from ever approaching the melting pot culture common to all USians so heavily advertized in popular mythology. Instead, the ruling class maintenance and manipulation of social divisions and the hard socio-economic landscape characterized by dog-eat-dog competition for scarce resources pushes people to retreat into narrow identities. Everyone is some kind of nasty, so that becomes a focal point, a label, an identifier—and a self-identifier. People cling to the exaggerated visions of identities as both an explanation of their plights and an escape from them. White supremacy. Black power. "Honor" killings. Don't ask, don't tell. Sweet baby Jesus versus bitter economic reality. Et cetera.

Everyone is forced to struggle against everyone else to snatch as big a piece as possible of life's necessities (because enough is rarely available). Every social, racial, gender, cultural, religious identity must struggle against every other for its people to hack out a socio-economic space in a less than zero-sum game. Struggle, fight, compete rather than render mutual aid, work together, cooperate. Associations of all kinds become ossified and the identities cannot change to the point at which a circle-the-wagons mentality makes them just another oppressor of their constituents. Yet another struggle becomes preserving and exaggerating the sharp distinctions between identities.

All the cultures of the past, to be frank, have elements that suck. They were characterized by sexism, racism, acquisitiveness, xenophobia, homophobia, militarism, hierarchy, and/or a range of other negative subsidiaries. Yet the ruling class promotes these social separations. Culture, though, which the real source of separation between people rather biology, is not, should not, and cannot be absolute, rigid, and unchanging. Yet the ruling class pretends not only that it is, but that it must be. Cultures are not worth preserving in and of themselves, but only to the extent they serve the people who practice them better than other practices. Yet the ruling class does not want the people better served, for that would disserve it. Accordingly, U.S. society is increasingly becoming a contest of identities and their members on the basis of hard, stereotypical lines across which only enmity can fly—and a contest only for some small relief from their exploitation and oppression, from the enemy identity.

On top of income inequality and political disenfranchisement, the result of the ruling class's social manipulation and control answers the questions raised by the dissonance between U.S. social mythology and reality. US society is segregated and unequal on the basis of income so the ruling class can protect the figment that it is entitled to its excess, to promote the propriety of stratification, segregation, and hierarchy, and promote exploitable divisions of society. Sexism, racism, and homophobia and other artificial bases for discrimination and oppression allow the ruling class to divide and rule, to insure that we, the people, can't threaten the status quo because we're too busy trying to pluralize the already plural. Accordingly, the ruling class does what it can to aggravate divisions while appearing to reject them. Ignorance contrived by the ruling class contributes to the effectiveness of the control tactics used against poor and oppressed people and also inhibits their ability to resist. All of those answers expose the face that the U.S. has a society and culture that may be superficially attractive but, in reality, makes U.S. residents live lives of isolation, competition, fear, anger, insecurity, and dissatisfaction.

ENVIRONMENTAL PILLAGE AND PLUNDER

Right next to the national anthem in nationalistic songs taught to U.S. school children is "America, the Beautiful", which at least in part is a paean to an exquisite natural endowment and a stewardship that would preserve that beauty. Somewhere, however, the song's environmental sentiment has been lost in rampant capitalism and cultural contamination. Now its rendition no longer extols the U.S. naturality but raises questions about the stewardship. Why have "purple mountains majesties" given way to mountain top removal strip mining and clear cut forests? Why have "spacious skies" been replaced with smoggy skies? Why have "shining seas" been supplanted by cesspools strewn with "dead zones", poisonous algae blooms, destroyed fisheries, oil slicks, and hazardous medical waste that sloshes up on public beaches? And why is it that poor and working and disenfranchised communities suffer disproportionately the consequences of this environmental rapacity? The answers show that on this count, too, not just change, but revolutionary change is demanded not only by a cherished national image, but by health and justice as well.

Environmentally, capitalism is the definition of disaster. Business necessity to maximize profit and therefore to minimize cost leads capitalism to count environmental damage as an "externality", something outside the cost of production. This results in needlessly destructive agricultural practices and rapacious extraction of resources from the body of mother earth. Another result is pouring massive amounts of pollutants into the air, water and land. Urban sprawl uglifies the landscape as endless fast everything outlets spread like fungus across vast tracts of open space in a blind quest for a few dollars more. This and escalating "infrastructure" damage to the naturality diminishes the quality of life and sickens and kills thousands of poor and working people each year.

Carbon dioxide and other greenhouse gasses trap heat in the atmosphere and thus change the average weather—climate. The U.S. is not the only offender in this, but it is the worst, particularly per capita. Climate is, at base, driven by temperature fluctuations in the atmosphere. Changing the pattern of these fluctuations by adding heat to the system changes the risks of fires, floods, storms, as well as altering crop and livestock distributions. Melting ice raises sea levels and aggravates the heat problem by decreasing albedo. Consequently, many people who formerly lived in harmony with their environments can no longer do so due to global warming—not to mention direct deforestation, mining, and pollution changes to their climates and environments. As a further result, some of them are pushed into poverty, migration, and sometimes war.

The discharge of greenhouse gasses—and the refusal to remedy it—derives from the drive for profit. Pollution costs money, but that cost can be converted to another form and externalized, i.e. imposed on someone outside of the production process. The cost of handling greenhouse gasses is imposed on the whole world by just vomiting the gasses into the atmosphere. But the products and profits are privatized, kept by the producers. So it goes with a myriad of other forms of pollution.

Sulfur and nitrogen oxides contribute to acid rain, which damages forests and kills microorganisms at the base of the food chain. Mercury and other heavy metals are lofted long distances and fall out of the air in unexpected places to contaminate the food chain and ultimately sicken people, diminishing lives and escalating public health costs. Chlorofluorocarbons deplete the ozone at high altitudes, exposing humanity to dangerous levels of solar radiation, while ozone and particulates spewed at ground level cause thousands of premature deaths annually. Et cetera. Et cetera. Ad nauseam. Again, the explanation is capitalism's efforts to externalize the costs of minimizing, neutralizing, and controlling industrial emissions.

The capitalist environmental equation also victimizes the land and the water. Dumping mass tons of myriad manufacturing byproducts straight into the rivers, lakes, oceans, or even on the ground in landfills or just anywhere is cheaper than recycling or reprocessing them into less toxic forms. For this reason, stories of chemical contaminants leaking into food and water supplies and elsewhere and causing disease, not to mention injuring other species and their habitats, abound. When corporations are busted as the sources of these contaminants, they deny, defy, lie, stonewall, and set legions of lawyers to their defense. Even when they can't avoid responsibility, they try to wriggle out of shouldering it in every conceivable way. And all for a few dollars more.

Nor is pollution with production byproducts the whole story. Direct environmental destruction is rampant. Lumber companies "buy" lands or lumber rights or gain access to national forests via political machinations and clear cut them, leaving the landscape a wasteland like a no man's land in a titanic battle or the surface of a dead planet. Fishing fleets do essentially the same thing to the oceans with drag and drift nets that tear up the sea floors beyond their ability to readily recover, kill multitudes of non-food creatures, and strip the waters so clean that whole fisheries die, in addition to other depredations. Meat producers slash and burn rain forests to graze cattle for a few years til the soil is so depleted it won't even grow grass. In the process, they cause more greenhouse emissions than the entire world's cars, trucks, busses, planes, ships and trains combined. Mining companies dig miles into the earth and blow whole tops off mountains, filling valleys with tailings, debris, and mineral contamination. Whole ecosystems—flora, fauna, land, water, even communities that had previously lived harmoniously with their surroundings—are destroyed in the process. And these illustrations are only the head of the zit. Behind it all is the hunt for mo', mo', mo' money—and faster.

Cultural pollution engendered by capitalism's incessant and insatiable drive to produce and sell more regardless of the products' utility also wreaks ecological havoc that adversely affects quality of life. Vast tracts of urban sprawl of cheaply built fast-food joints, vehicle service pit stops, discount retailers, big box stores with acres of parking lot, merchandise depots and warehouses, honky-tonks, sagging strip malls selling endless bric-a-brac and other detritus of overproduction metastasize like cancers. Such wasted space has a short commercial life and eventually becomes urban and suburban blight without contributing anything really necessary or significant to culture or society. But they are demanded by the capitalist imperative to grow or die, to chain everyone—and the naturality—to production and consumption of whatever.

Capitalism's social programming conditions people that the good life is consuming as much as possible even if living it kills them. And it does as they chase this cultural imperative through an asphalt and plastic maze of pirates, jokers, clowns, colonels, and malevolent children who lure them to sit passively and gorge on unhealthy food, guzzle the wrong stuff, and pursue intellectually barren to mindless entertainments. Wandering through the maze, they are induced to buy junky consumer goods of minimal to negative utility and durability. For this they bind themselves to the production wheel, working more to consume more, laboring under a ruling class zeitgeist that they can never consume enough to be adequate. An environment damaged thusly is not merely a physical threat, but a social and emotional one as well.

Environmental destruction diminishes all people's lives in the U.S. In addition to the broad liabilities of climate change and acid rain, strip mining and clear cutting, oil spills and ocean dumping, urban sprawl and unhealthy material relations, there are direct and personal detractions of ecological degradation. Aside from the aesthetic sadness a destroyed forest, stripped mountain ecosystem, ruined shoreline engenders, the society is sicker.

Asthma, particularly in urban areas, is on the rise, as is diabetes. Cancer is a specter casting an ever bigger shadow across the land. Many maladies of unknown etiology seem to come with no other common factor than the coming of industries and their chemicals. Particulates cause thousands of premature deaths each year—more than any drug, yet there is no war on particulate emissions. Cardio vascular disease has become the biggest killer in industrial societies. Ever more studies link ever more illness to environmental factors related to products themselves, not merely their byproducts—outgassing and leaching from manufactured goods, heavy metal poisoning, noise, electromagnetic radiation, et cetera. Salutary outdoor activities are curtailed by smog and commerce and the time absorbed by consumption and work to support it. Moreover, all the time spent on consuming, much of which is passive and sedentary, and working to support big consumption habits leaves little time to develop the knowledge and skills conducive to rewarding social relations—and the relations themselves. Physical, psychological, and emotional suffering are thus the wages of synthesizing capitalism and the environment.

Environmental classism and racism are also profit driven: even where technology exists to avoid pollution and clean it up where it exists, using it is often a cost that can't be recouped in the market. Urban ghettoes tend to be located near production facilities and thus pollution sources because land is cheap and housing undesirable for those reasons and because poor and working people cannot afford to live far from potential jobs. Such ghettoes tend to be populated disproportionately by members of racial minorities because their compensation is even less than labor's average and they thus have fewer options. As a result of corporate decisions to externalize pollution and other commercial damage costs, working and minority people disparately—and needlessly—bear the negative health and quality of life consequences of environmental destruction. And poor and minority people lack the money and therefore legal and political muscle to protect themselves from such "externalization".

The incompatibility of the cultural mythology of "America, the Beautiful" and capitalist production and consumption culture is the answer to where all the purple mountains majesties, spacious skies, and shining seas have gone. They have all been purchased and paved and converted to mountains of tawdry consumer products, spacious parking lots for endless cars attracted to sky's the limit credit, and seas of profit for capitalists. We need a more compatible culture before the extant one kills us.

WE CANNOT MERELY BELIEVE IN CHANGE

Any people wanting to be free cannot merely believe in change or accept change they can only believe in. We, the people of the United States, are no exception. Change is happening all around us all of the time, and right here in the U.S. as much as anywhere else. Just believing in change and that it will be an improvement on the shabby reality to which we, the people, have been relegated is that the ruling class and its metaphysicians would have us do. They want us to be content with our lot (not rebel) and seek not material goods (not demand enough pay to do so) and to let work set us free (so the profits will set them free). What we should want, however, is freedom from the bourgeoisie's shabby reality. It cannot be fixed. It must be replaced.

The reign of U.S. imperial capital is a disaster not only for the people of the U.S., but for the rest of the world's people as well. It concentrates wealth and power and control of our lives in the hands of a small and unaccountable power elite—bourgeoisie, ruling class, exploiters. The people in that class do not share the same consciousness of human rights to the basic necessities of life we, the people of the U.S.—proletariat, working class, producers—share.

"They" run a system that allows them to live in opulent excess while everyone outside their executive class lives in insecurity, material insufficiency, squalor, poverty, and/or at risk from environmental pollution. They pit class sistren and brethren against each other in a class war at home and wars of imperial conquest abroad to preserve and enhance their power. They use that power and the attendant resources to isolate people into competitive identity groups who regard each other with at least suspicion and too often malice. They sow rigidity and dissension within the groups to maintain the class-debilitating division so the groups lose their refuge and resistance potential. They destroy the environment on which we all depend and impose the consequences thereof on us—and use wealth we produce to insulate themselves from those consequences in fancy neighborhoods. They disenfranchise us with placebo versions of freedom and democracy that contain little freedom and no real democracy. Thus, we can't cure what ails us from the ballot box. They own the editor's box. "They" gotta go.

We, the people, must dissolve the bonds that bind us to the exploiting and oppressing class under and in defense of our own class. It is only in this way that we can form a more perfect union—indeed, any union at all. We can do this. We have the numbers. We cannot, however, merely believe this change will come—especially not now with technology telling us the numbers might not all always be enough.

If not now, when?
If not you, who?

ABOUT THE AUTHOR

Bill Dunne was arrested on October 14, 1979 after the attempted liberation of Artie Ray Dufur from a Seattle jail. Both Dunne and Dufur were a part of the San Francisco-based WellSprings Communion revolutionary group and Dufur had traveled to Canada in search of land for the collective to practice the art of making revolution. On his way back into the United States, Dufur got into an altercation with a border guard, ending with the border guard being fatally shot. While in custody in the King County Jail in Seattle, Dufur was liberated by an armed group that included Dunne. In the ensuing struggle, Dunne was arrested and charged with conspiracy to rescue a federal prisoner, possession of an automatic weapon, car theft and three bank expropriations. Dufur was also recaptured. Dunne was sentenced to 90 years in prison in 1980, in addition to another 15 years to run consecutively as a result of an attempted self-emancipation in 1983.

As a political prisoner, Dunne has continued to be involved advocating behind bars for the disadvantaged as an author and outspoken voice for justice. Bill may be contacted at:

Bill Dunne
#10916-086
USP Big Sandy
P.O. Box 2068
Inez, KY 41224

CHAPTER FOUR

The Master Race Revolutionary

Deck Chairs, Sinking Ships, and the Human Reich

Peter Young

PETER YOUNG

This Country Must Change

Cowardice asks the question: Is it safe? Expediency asks the question: Is it politic? Vanity asks the question: Is it popular? But conscience asks the question: Is it right? And there comes a time when one must take a position that is neither safe, nor politic, nor popular, but one must take it simply because it is right. - **Martin Luther King, Jr.**

Convulsions are induced with each push of the button. Electrodes run to her temples and flesh burns. When her captor gets the information he seeks, the shocks will stop – for a time. It is of no matter if the data is inapplicable to his mission, or wholly inaccurate - he has a job to do. His alliances lift this ritual from "torture" to a righteous cause. The captive will soon die, and if her captor didn't give the information he wanted, there are more up the hall who will. And the war carries on.

Instinctually filed away as a scene from Guantanamo Bay, in fact lifted from the research protocol of a U.S. laboratory. The victim: a non-human primate. A scene to be repeated ad infinitum until the demise of the Human Reich, and the execution of the only revolution worthy of the title: that which brings liberty for all.

***

Masked saboteurs bring a sledgehammer down on devices used to electrocute pigeons. A vivisector awakes at midnight to find his Mercedes in flames. Trucks used by a tree removal company hired to vacate tree-sitters have their tires slashed. Strikes against the many tentacles of oppression, carried out by revolutionaries who accept humans as one part of a larger struggle, one to bring liberation to all life.

You can't stop an idea whose time has come.

***

The holding of our species' interests as supreme: an ideological plague called speciesism. A foundational belief system maintaining humankind's position as slavemaster over all life on earth. A prejudice in every way analogous to sexism, racism, and

93

every social inequity of our time. Yet there is no injustice whose roots are so deep, so pervasive, and with so many victims as the hierarchy of humans over non-humans.

The False Revolutionary limits the annual victim count to:
Iraqi deaths: 91,000+
Murders by police: 300 to 1000
U.S. Prisoners: 2,300,000
…and so on.

Halting this injustice is not revolution, only patchwork pretense. The only just revolution will bring freedom for the whole of our system's victims:

Chickens: 9,500,000,000
Pigs: 100,000,000
Animals in laboratories: 70,000,000

Each one written out of the equation, victims of omission, a "single issue" relegated to the secondary status while we settle larger issues of which our species is the sole beneficiary. Reshuffling of the current arrangement of one species on this earth is not peace, justice, or revolution; only the convincing illusion of such.

These victims, human and non, are to find permanent relief in nothing short of a revolution in the United States. Still we find one set devalued to secondary status; one told their freedom will have to wait; and only one murdered in the most callous ways, their flesh consumed by those who scream "revolution". Exactly whose revolution is implicit: the Master (Human) Race.

I, Supreme: Formulaic Revolution and the Politics of Denial

To scream justice for some and not all is the imposter's revolution, the charlatan's demand seeking freedom for themselves built on the blood of a billion others. We have successfully packaged a superficial rearranging of relationships within one species as revolution, and ignored the whole of injustice. For anything ignoring the bulk of suffering and oppression to be packaged as revolution is shameful; the domain of the reformist and self serving.

This is the Master Race mentality. From neo-conservatives to anarchists, we find the assigning of arbitrary measures of value to sentient life, never questioning the hierarchy of worth itself. Purporting to lead us to freedom, they lead us only to freedom for the few on the backs of the many. Some give lip service to equality, while holding actions done in non-human's behalf in lower value than those with rewards solely reaped by the species to which they belong. The tongue communicates equality, the actions betray the mentality of the self-identified Master Race.

The true revolutionary acknowledges the totality of injustice and the root of all oppression: a belief that any life holds more value than another.

Dominant culture places humans above all else, and excuses all cruel whims carried out in the name of our own. Progressive culture makes token attempts to keep up appearances of consistency, with fashionable pretense of outrage over the killing of field buffalo or hunting of whales, turning a convenient blind eye to the carnage of the slaughterhouse and egg farm – in this way repackaging dominant culture's showcasing of token non-human causes deemed worth of outrage (dogs/cats traded for buffalo/wolves) with the "edgy" flair of an "alternative" species. Again, the politics of feeling good win over the politics of doing good.

Prevailing revolutionary culture serves its adherents an irresistibly conscience-soothing checklist program. Critically, gestures such as mass bike rides and controlled-circulation publishing are accepted and pushed as driving forces to a better world – anything that moves us in the right direction so long as human interests are central, and the presuppositions of our Master Race mentality are intact.

Many who want a new world do take the necessary step of veganism and acknowledgement of our species most egregious cruelties. And even among them do we find our culture's force-fed concept of a hierarchy of suffering – Iraqi children near the top, worthy of the most attention; rats in laboratories near the bottom, never to be spoken of and unworthy of mention. Focusing our efforts on the Master (Human) Race becomes revolution, while extending it to all life becomes a "single issue". The blood spills, and we live under the illusion of accomplishment. The Human Reich continues its 17,000 year reign.

Indeed many of those who act in the name of human

centered issues do so with an aggregate analysis of injustice. Acting in service to all life can just as easily take the form of indigenous defense of corporate invasion as net sabotage of underwater fish farms. Resistance assumes many forms. Yet only few act to win the freedom of others with an eye on the true scope of planetary suffering. Few progress past cultural assumptions to achieve total dismantling of speciesist belief in a Master Race. When the cow longs for freedom with the same intensity as the sweatshop worker, how few act in a way consistent with this truth.

Even apologists for the maintenance of the anthropocentric revolution are unable to turn a blind eye to the liberation of non-humans. Crops grown for animals raised for food consumes nearly half of the U.S. water supply and 80% of its agricultural land. Animals raised for food in the U.S. consume 90% of the soy crop, 80% of the corn crop, and 70% of its grain, while every 3 seconds a child dies of starvation somewhere in the world. There is no human liberation without liberation for all.

An appeal of the False Revolution is the palatability of its scale. We all love winnable battles: ending the Iraq war, creating a sweatshop-free garment industry. The scale of ten billion lives, each with the same will to live as you or I, the same entitlement to this world and its pleasures and pains, is of crippling scale. Fear of challenge of an incomprehensible scale is not an excuse for creating a "just" world in which the rivers flow with blood. We should fear freedom for one species at the expense of billions of non-human slaves more.

The old guard cries "first things first", a paradoxal implication that liberating all is inconsistent with liberating the few; that respect for all life is inconsistent with concern for racism, sexism, and all social inequities. In fact there is nothing less consistent with the cry of "equality" than crying it from a mouth that is the graveyard for a thousand animals, and working towards this "equality" in an ideological framework which annually claims ten billion lives as its victims.

The change that we desperately seek – for health care, education, just yield for labor – becomes a thoughtless Band Aid on a sea of blood when it ignores the larger part of injustice. Justice denied one is justice for none. When we move towards the new dawn, will we do so carrying the same artificial constructs and hierarchal relationships, just with "better wages" (at the slaughterhouse) and "community run" fur farms?

To an End, However Impolite

Every top member of the Bush administration has direct links to corporate interests. Activists like Eric McDavid are marked as subversives and sentenced to 20 years for mere discussion ("conspiracy") of illegal activity. Ten billion sentient creatures are killed each year for the taste of their flesh and perceived medical value. The human prisoner population tops 2 million. Alternative energy developments to avert last minute ecological collapse are suppressed. Hardwired for exploitation and decline, this empire demands not reshuffling but revolution.

In all of us, a voice that screams for revolution. We are the married men of middle america who have never known risk in our entire lives. The inner city woman serving life for defending against a home invasion by police. The factory workers questioning the forces that confine us to a soft-celled prison 40 hours a week. The pig, living its entire life in a metal crate, never knowing the sun or companionship of another creature.

In the face of this, the cry for reform is the cry for a pacifier. The promise of "change" stifles the prisoner of an unjust drug war from taking back his freedom over waiting for it to be given. The empty hope of change brings passivity to the man staring across the fields of his youth as they are laid to ruin by bulldozers. These false promises are the placaters that bring appeasement when we most need revolt. We must defy mere "change", for the very reason that we need change.

And this revolution must begin here. The United States has unleashed the most egregious advancements in control, confinement, and torture that have spread virulently across the planet and brought it to crisis. Nanotechnology, with uneclipsed implications for control, came in larger part from U.S. laboratories. Genetic engineering, the first technology to be truly irreversible once unleashed, was the product of U.S. research. Most factory farming practices – now with single farms confining over 1,000,000 animals – have U.S. origins. Beyond our perpetually murderous political system, the United States is the host to a supremely influential research apparatus. Coupled with corporate influence in the world marketplace, the United States is ground zero for global suffering and ecological devastation. In naming a head to the beast, the United States is most worthy of the mark.

Why revolution? A revolution because conspiracy charges see people never caught with a gram of drugs serving life sentences based on mere testimony while the prison population tops 2 million. Revolution because 9.5 billion chickens are butchered alive each year to satisfy an acquired taste for their flesh. Revolution because the constitution has been voided and our last line of defense from the most abusive forms of power with it. Those who have not accepted the necessity of revolution would do well to ask themselves: how bad does it have to get?

In fact it is not a question of revolution, but whose revolution. They have revolutionized our relationship to non-humans and the earth. They have revolutionized our once harmonious relationship with each other to introduce fabricated divides such as race and class. The very way we represent this reality in our heads has been revolutionized, with enforced priorital convulsion, and making that which makes us feel most alive things to fear. Their revolution is not a static monolith in a state of conclusion. It is in a state of advance, a continued revolution in the direction that serves them. When we feel accomplishment from a Myspace bulletin, or allow another legal example of Constitutional erosion to neutralize us into silence; we have been made a foot soldier in their revolution. We are all participants in revolution, the only question is: for whose side.

From the Root: The Politics of Revolutionary Anti-Speciesism

Let me say it openly: we are surrounded by an enterprise of degradation, cruelty, and killing which rivals anything the Third Reich was capable of, indeed dwarfs it, in that ours is an enterprise without end, self-regenerating, bringing rabbits, rats, poultry, livestock ceaselessly into the world for the purpose of killing them. --J. M. Coetzee

Revolution worthy of the claim uproots the fundamental cause of the horrors from which we seek to liberate ourselves. This root is the belief in one form of life as more valid than another. The dominant revolutionary paradigm targets singular manifestations of that belief (sexism, capitalism) leaving the root issue unresolved, and worse yet - unmentioned. To strike merely at a symptom of injustice is to be complicit in all injustice.

For all human bloodshed has at its root callousness towards all creatures. At each meal, we reinforce the violence within our species by dining on the product of violence against another. When there is no peace in the slaughterhouse, there is no peace. The revolution that addresses one branch of suffering while ignoring the rest is a pseudo-revolution without foresight or conscience.

For a mirror to our own atrocities, we can find a no more analogous comparison than that of human slavery in the U.S. The ideological framework which gave it birth – a hierarchy of worth among sentient life, arbitrarily decided upon by the Master Race (species) for its sole benefit – creates in its image a relationship between the oppressed and oppressor, one which mirrors that between humans and non-humans. There is direct lineage from the first enslavement of non-humans to the first human slaves; with the domestication of animals segueing seamlessly and effortlessly to human slavery. As Karl Jacoby writes, human slavery is "little more than the extension of domestication to humans."

The dominant revolutionary paradigm offers selective justice, a fashionable outlet for personal biases of which form of life one deems most worthy of liberty. Thus we have anti-capitalists wearing the skins of capitalism's most abundant victims, and activists working against sexism consuming embryos for which a billion non-human females lived their lives in caged darkness. Only in living by one ethic, one that encompasses all life, will any of us truly be free. Violence breeds violence, and we reap what we sow.

Synthetic Justice and Applied Schizophrenia

With power comes responsibility. If non-humans are simply here for us to use, then so are the bars of the prisons which confine our friends, so is the napalm used to burn children in war time, and so too are women and non-whites our resources to exploit.

And if non-humans are simply here for us to use, then so are the crowbars we take to the doors of their prison cells night after night to free the victims of this human supremacy complex; so are the hammers taken to their laboratory torture devices; and so are our hearts which know injustice in all its forms – not just those currently in vogue.

And so we now face the next phase in mankind's evolution. Analogous to the continued evolution in our relationships to other races, we move towards the inevitable obsolescence of the speciesist revolutionary: The climate change conference catered with the secretions of factory farmed animals. The environmentalist revering the lives of wolves but not cows. The schizophrenic champion of "freedom" and "justice" who denies it to the larger segment of victimhood at breakfast, lunch, and dinner. Laying aside our collective self-importance, we move towards a submission to the interests of true justice, and lay to waste those blueprints to change which leave the bulk of all life as its silent victims.

We must redefine relationship to animals if we are to redefine relationship with ourselves. Can our culture's presuppositions, re-appropriated towards our own ends, ever lead us anywhere but to a recreation of the same oppression with different victims?

The War Within: Counterrevolutionary Psy-ops and the Structure of Belief

Between us and this world for which all life cries out are the bars of an invisible cage, a seamless fabric of interwoven lies. Revolution begins with obliterating the foundation of falsehood. Without the humility to accept that everything we've been told is a lie, the gears of oppression that are in motion will stay in motion.

Achieving the clarity of vision required to accept the necessity of revolution demands a rearrangement of conditioned belief, yet only in part. When the larger part of the conditioned belief remains intact, the world we wish for remains forever out of reach. The first enemy that must be defeated is the willfully maintained enemy of false belief. The prisons taunting us in the distance are ones of concrete and steel. The one we live in is a prison of ignorance and fear. A prison built on limiting belief, implicit threats, and artificial distinction.

Your worth is in your wealth.
This earth exists for the benefit of human beings.
Revolution follows information.

Our map of reality has been distorted so serve the interests of those who feed on power and blood. And in our failure to restore congruency, we reap the consequences:

Wasted lives chasing the illusory "American Dream".

Ecological collapse by 2025.

A generation of "informed" and internet addicted revolutionaries.

This is the power of beliefs. Revolution begins by ceasing to ask if a belief is objectively true, and asking if it is useful. Beliefs that serve as obstacles ("I could never survive prison") give structural support to the status quo and are impediments to progress. In the dismantling of our limiting beliefs, we know freedom for the first time. Freedom for ourselves, so that others may know it too.

Paralysis By Analysis:
The Myth of Consequence

"Whenever justice is uncertain and police spying and terror are at work, human beings fall into isolation, which, of course, is the aim and purpose of the dictator state, since it is based on the greatest possible accumulation of depotentiated social units."- Carl Jung

Wedging the gap between this world and one worth living in, implicit threats weaving a prison as strong as concrete and steel. And the implicit threat with a deterrent effect eclipsing all else: the specter of consequence.

The fear of prison exists seemingly as the sole domain of activists acting outside the law. In fact, its most sinister work is done in the psyches of the rest of us, affecting every facet of every movement. Vague and unfocused, the fear is the leash, with police in our heads maintaining a filter of fear governing all actions. Participation in extralegal activity is not requisite for the specter to take hold. The mere unspecified threat of police contact in any course of activism is the trigger deterring the smallest of actions, from the entirely legal to the benign infraction level video-taping of factory farms, and beyond.

Through the dominant lens, revolution is a dangerous landscape, with the threat of prison haunting us all at each step. Objective surveying of the facts reveals something else. Over a thousand Animal Liberation Front actions in North America since 1979 have resulted in less than 30 arrests, with only a handful resulting in any substantive prison time. Analysis of most of the few cases for which prison was the consequence reveals a small list of errors avoided with the application of care and caution. Others have pointed out you have a better chance of dying in a car crash en route to the grocery store – an activity carried out every day without thought – than being arrested for actions in defense of the earth or its inhabitants.

It takes no more skill to liberate a chicken from a factory farm than it does to sneak into a movie. One exposes themselves to potentially greater legal consequences carrying a forged ID to get into a club than trespassing in a laboratory basement at midnight. And one is more likely to be caught doing a "beer run" than emptying a mink farm. We stand confronted with the decision: To what extent is prison a credible threat, and to what extent is it merely an effective psychological back door out of working for the world we dream of?

It is this climate of fear, predicated on false and limiting beliefs, which has induced the examples of paralysis and inaction I encounter daily. PETA employees afraid to let me (the "ex con / PR liability") in their home for fear of a consequence never explained. Activists confessing in private a paralysis by the implicit threats of the vaguely worded Animal Enterprise Terrorism Act, too fearful to attend even a protest. Being caught in the crossfire of criticism of blind and ignorant believers in the false dichotomy of "direct action" vs. "peaceful protest", an arbitrary and non-existent division, which serves only the oppressor.

Forcing the last of us into submission, phantom threats of "having our name on file", criminal records, government surveillance, and vague concerns over impediments to career advancement – all of which lack basis in actual consequence - which plague most and limit us to the status of hopeful revolutionaries in a perpetual state of willful bondage.

Resistance Culture and the Fetishization of Group Theory

It is the most disempowering of beliefs: blind faith in strength in numbers. Strength in numbers keeps the would-be rioter looking to her left and right before storming the barricade. It means another night at home for the neighbor of a veal slaughterhouse, toying with a lighter as she looks out the window, remaining forever in wait for a local animal protection group to form before taking action. It has the would-be saboteur waiting for the tomorrow that never comes, because "there isn't anyone to work with."

There is no strength in numbers when our blind faith in its authority cripples us into inaction. The individual can incite, raze, and infiltrate. She can write the communiqué that will change the world and publicize covertly confiscated government documents that will do the same. The world's most successful jewel thief had one rule: "Always work alone."

War On Illusion and Advanced Psywarfare

"Make the lie big, make it simple, keep saying it,
and eventually they will believe it"
— **Adolph Hitler**

To confront our future, we must confront the artificial distinctions that obstruct our view. Having won ground in progressive culture on the hierarchal falsehoods of race and nationality, we move forward to uproot those lies thriving in an even more advanced state of growth. Chief among them: the cultural construct of the human/animal divide.

Like the human constructs of race and nationality before it, the species line is the next Great Artificial Divide. Entirely without basis, we have internalized a line with ourselves on one side, and every other victim of injustice on the other. We announce the twin issues of "human rights" and "animal rights", as two sides of the line, while the line itself is never questioned. Even the bold assertion that both fights are "equal" in importance asserts the myth that the distinction is legitimate, and the Master Race mentality is reinforced to live another day.

103

Peter Young

Demolition as a Creative Impulse

The revolution begins with a process of dismantling. Moving into the fray with a conditioned belief system intact brings hopes of a seamless transition to revolutionary, and guarantees the recreation of the same injustice in different forms.

To serve the truth we must defy the lies. Chains drop when a woman decides change is worth more than a career and stays home to plan her part in creating a better world; when an under-construction vivarium is reduced to dust, giving its future victims a temporary reprieve; and when one person surrenders blind faith in the illusion of an indistinct "critical mass" to decide today what steps they will take towards being the spark to start the prairie fire that will cleanse the world.

Jugular Veins, Exit Strategy and Ratios of Effort to Yield

Achieving a dismantling of false beliefs, we are staged for a phase shift to the flesh and blood front, where the machinery of death must too be dismantled.

Today more lives are taken daily in the onslaught of the Master Race mentality than at any point in history. Our many years of protest against and resistance to human targeted wars (ostensibly such – as their victim count is inevitably more non-human than human), non-human animal exploitation, and environmental devastation; have not only failed to stop them, they have left us with more victims of each than when we began. The question then is why we are more focused on the process than the product; and when does fetishizing of the means yield to devotion to results. Revolution is our "culture" when our interests are focused on the means. It is our mission when our service is to results.

We have more victims in this war on innocent life than at any time in history. The death count has been on the exponential incline since the birth of civilization. The United States Constitution, with its protections we hold as being our savior, has offered a substantial safeguard against civil liberties abuses, but nothing in the way of preventing actual suffering. The false promises of freedom of assembly, freedom of the press, and free

104

speech have delivered us nothing but a death count unprecedented in human history. The bare math confronts us with the need for an escalation we have yet to deliver.

The Necessity Defense: In Defense of Necessity

The formula has been followed. Our "freedom of assembly" and "freedom of speech" have been exercised beyond all reason. This blueprint of "freedom to petition" and "peaceful protest" has pacified us while those in power have continued their assault of kindred life forms and our earth. We have given them what they ask of us: polite discourse, literature publishing, and symbolic protest. And the death count rises.

In fact in those rare instances when entirely lawful exercise of constitutional freedoms offer an immediate and direct threat to injustice; the response has been constitutional circumvention, criminal charges, and prison. The Stop Huntington Animal Cruelty campaign, seeking to close the Huntington Life Sciences laboratory by making its employees and shareholders accountable, exercised their "freedom of speech" by advertising via the internet their personal information, including home addresses and telephone numbers. Over 400 companies severed ties with HLS as a result, forcing it to the brink of bankruptcy. This effective use of once protected speech led to the use of obscure and little used "interstate stalking" charges for six defendants and sentences of up to 6 years in prison. Rod Coronado answered a question at a lecture on how he constructed an incendiary device to torch a mink research laboratory, and also found prison as a consequence. If exercising "free speech" changed anything, they would make it illegal. And they have.

In this damned if you do, damned if you don't climate; the message is clear: They are coming for us either way. Operate effectively on the radar and guarantee consequences from forces with resources we can never match. Operate effectively off the radar and the chances of consequences drop close to nothing.

The spirit of justice is subservient to a higher law, which calls for freedom for all and disregards the interests of those who have disregarded the interests of others. When property denied to one brings liberation to a thousand, then an act of great service to the earth has been carried out, and we have achieved the truest form of justice.

We all want change, and we all want someone else to cast

the first stone. Clandestine activity communiqués are plentiful with calls to action, pleas for uprising to eradicate oppression with gloves and crowbars, attempts to incite the public to carry out extensional self-defense against the most egregious cruelties of our culture. Resistance follows a snowball effect, making crucial evidence that we act as a part of something much larger than ourselves. If for every direct blow to the infrastructure and instruments of injustice there were two others inspired, there would be no effective killing machine by the year's end.

With knowledge comes responsibility. Among the only redeeming benefits to the unparalleled information overload under which we are buried in this age of the internet and Xerox machine is that the excuse of ignorance has been removed. If we are not directly downwind – or down the block - from any of the modern day Auschwitz's which dot our landscape, their corporate headquarters, or the homes of those at their helm, their whereabouts are no longer kept secret from us in this "information age". The responsibility of knowledge is to confront the obligations that come with it.

In the debate of revolution versus reform, an objective survey of the state of our planet demands the question: How bad must it be? At over 100 species going extinct each day, must it be 200? If ten billion animals do not make the case, must it be 15? Staring soberly at the scope of this injustice, we find that patience isn't virtuous but criminal.

A true revolution is for us, and them. A true revolution brings freedom to the totality of life. This death machine is one with gears, machinery open for assault, each facet exposed with its unique vulnerabilities. Education with some, eradication of specific buildings with others. Fearing injustice more than comfort will deliver us to a world worth living in. With an eye on results, we move from the course that makes us feel good to that with yield. Releasing our sentimental grip on feel-good activism, the mirage of change is slowly replaced by the thing itself, and feeling good merges with progress, not the illusion of such.

The Element of Distraction

No sense killing us if we pacify ourselves. To accomplish this, a collection of distractions and neutralizers rendering any revolutionary movement useless and unthreatening. The packaging of intoxication as "rebellion" is among the most savvy of ploys, keeping generation after generation of subversives inebriated, docile, and impotent. The internet, packaged as salvation for the new generation of verbose revolutionaries who count only syllables in their arsenal, offers information overload and the illusion of efficacy through the endless shuffling of electronic impulses in one giant, closed loop; as though injustice ever took place in cyberspace. And cliché protest rituals further the misdirection of energy away from the weaknesses of this machine and ushering it right into the gutter. Everyone goes home drunk, informed, and "active", and the gears of oppression grind on.

To bring us forth to victory we must prepare ourselves for what is ahead. This is no less crucial for the progressive class than any other. We carry with us an internalized sense of entitlement (unrestricted "food" choices, boorish intoxicant indulgence), attachment to guaranteed outcomes (cruise ship vacations, paychecks), risk aversion (parental appeasement, exaggerated "security culture"), and servitude to physical comfort (hotels, dining culture) – only marginally less true of resistance culture than the rest. From this platform, those who count themselves as revolutionaries take on this killing machine only to the extent our entitlements, comforts and sensibilities remain undisturbed. The line is drawn at intruding upon convenience, social incentive, or comfort; presupposing that the successful revolution can be won without sacrificing each. We wish to take on the riskiest endeavor in human history without ever having taken a risk in our entire lives.

Innocent lives and the earth itself are under attack. The masses sit in perpetual drugged bliss of television and the internet. Activists stand huddled in a dark corner, debating gender pronouns and the white privilege implications of bus pass forgery, indulging ourselves in the greatest leisure activity of the progressive class: critique.

We find at its origin the fundamental faith in words as an inevitable precursor to action. Out of sight from our privileged distance is the more accurate understanding of action as something borne of immediate necessity. In confronting the privilege of distance, we can assess the merits of our various paths on grounds of efficacy over merely our emotional response to them. Not being under the axe or in the crosshairs gives rise to exorbitant debate: the most indulgent privilege of the unpersecuted.

Illusion of time to spare gives rise to this revolution of

the verbose, to inflated promises of feel-good activism. "Direct action" literature over direct action, "insurrectional anarchism" over insurrection. It might be asked: what is action without theory and critique as its foundation? Yet is there not more merit to critique built on experience over the buffer of the classroom? Must theory always be a prerequisite for action in the 3-D realm, or must our theory be the product of our action? Our inefficacy is built on the faith of words before tangible results, as though there were time to spare; and that theory without holes is requisite for making an advance, not the product of it. The critique based ghettos of cultural anarchism and political music scenes must give way to their action based successors. As it stands, we suffocate on zines, and the world suffocates from neglect.

From Obstacle to Opportunity: Deflection, Circumvention, Reversal

Our weapons are limitless. In our toolbox, a collection of resources uneclipsed in all of human history. So deep are we in resources they obscure our eyes, with which we might see their potential. Yet everywhere there are those who have stripped their lives of distractions, and moved to capitalize on the tools that are the byproducts of our human privilege. Press releases are used to bring spotlights on injustice even the corporate media cannot ignore. Portable fire escape ladders are lowered from rooftops to physically access bottlenecks of injustice. Satellite images are surveyed for telltale structural forms giving physical location to once abstract injustice. Their GPS devices are attached to vehicles, revealing movements of those who thrive on their sinister work being carried out in secrecy.

On the front of resources and physical might, we can never win. Our weapons are circumvention, invisibility, clarity of vision, and justness of purpose.

Their obstacles become our opportunities. In the art of circumvention, those things packaged as obstacles become their weaknesses. Behind our sugar coated world of cheerleaders and talking mannequins, we can look to the history books for the volumes of stories offered as lessons on their dictates being turned against them – to their greater detriment than had they never been imposed.

Legal campaigns against the Coulston Foundation

primate research lab in New Mexico were futile, failing to have substantive relief to the animals they held captive. The facility existed far from public view in the New Mexico desert, making even the barely symbolic gesture of public protest useless. Prescribed outlets – government watchdog agencies and sanctioned protest – proved to be barriers, not channels, to justice. Anonymous saboteurs entered the property under the cover of darkness and burned one building to the ground. The laboratory soon closed forever. Buffers in place did not serve their intended deterrent function as a pressure release, and this torture apparatus was brought to its abrupt end.

With the technology we fear comes blind faith in its power – a truth to be exploited on both sides. The nighttime saboteur tracked via embedded cell phone GPS devices mails it to Arizona for the weekend to carry out a nighttime raid of a transgenic mice breeding facility – serving not just the cause of establishing innocence in a courtroom, but deterring suspicion entirely. The laboratory which installs a state of the art security system fires the security guard, and the anti-speciesist who has read the manual and studied its flaws suddenly finds herself in a much better position to enter undetected than with the presence of a guard. In this way, there is opportunity in high tech surveillance, when it brings their attention one direction while you operate in another. We see opportunities, never obstacles.

This reversal is carried out to great effect in every struggle and on every day. Concerned people respond to inefficacy of prescribed protest and act outside the law to achieve progress against those with no regard for life. Looking at the increased high profile use of informants and snitches in social justice movements, there are those who do not respond with more despair but with better tactics, reformatting their work to be carried out alone. Activists are sent to prison, and when their cases are publicized the effect for many is not fear, but galvanization translating to clandestine actions carried out in their name. They send one of ours to prison, the slack is picked up threefold by inspired activists who respond with raids. The opposition yields a net loss as it suffers more blows against their machine than were ever carried out by the fallen liberator.

It is either momentum reversal or defeat, tactical ju jitsu or the end of all life. We cannot win this on the playing field of resources or legal standing. Only by capitalizing on their obstacles do we take their power and make it ours.

Rebirth

There is not a lot on the line. There is everything on the line. Time is short for the earth, and there is none at all for the thousands of lives taken every second in wars, human prisons, slaughterhouses, and farms. If we're not going for the throat, they are coming for ours. And they already are – at a rate of millions a day.

Praise to the truest of revolutionaries, who with their every move act in the interest of *all* life, moving forward to liberation for all.

Swift death to false revolution. Ascent to that which brings freedom for all. We spit back anything else as the siren's song of illusory justice. Staring into our destiny unmediated by the filters of false belief, we confront the totality of injustice and fight for nothing less than Total Liberation. Only with the clarity of this expanded consciousness will we see a world worthy of being called free.

"You cannot stop an idea whose time has come".

ABOUT THE AUTHOR

Peter Young is a former political prisoner and the first ever prosecuted for "Animal Enterprise Terrorism". After a two week wave of overnight raids which saw the release of over 8,000 mink from 6 fur farms, he was indicted by a grand jury on multiple criminal counts. He spent the next 7 years wanted as a federal fugitive and subject of an FBI manhunt before being apprehended in 2005. Young pled guilty to a conspiracy role in mink liberations at six farms and was sentenced to two years in prison. He was released in 2007.

Today as a speaker, Peter has spoken at over 100 universities and events since his release from prison, speaking on the subjects of direct action, activist repression, and animal liberation theory and praxis.

He has joined with veteran activists to form the Voice of the Voiceless Fund – a fundraising vehicle and support fund assisting in the legal and living expenses of those imprisoned for acting outside the law in defense of non-human animals. To date the fund has contributed over $10,000 to prisoners such as Eric McDavid (http://supporteric.org), the Alex Hall & BJ Viehl (www.supportbjandalex.com) and the AETA 4 (www.aeta4.org)

Young oversees www.voiceofthevoiceless.org, bringing attention to under-exposed tactics, news, and media. The site features interviews, analysis, and hard to find printed material; "to arm others for effectively resisting the ongoing war against all life."

He is currently writing a book documenting his personal history in, and broader history of, the animal liberation movement.

Peter Young can be contacted at:
peteryoung@voiceofthevoiceless.org

CHAPTER FIVE

REIFICATION

AN IMPEDIMENT TO SOCIAL CHANGE

RONALD KUYKENDALL

RONALD KUYKENDALL

A change in the political administration of government, i.e., change in what groups of politicians temporarily are in power, does not necessarily lead to a radical overturning of the existing social order. What is at issue here is not an administration but a socio-political system. Simply changing one political (party) faction for another has little effect, because political (party) factions represent the fundamental class interests of the existing socio-political system. Therefore, it is the socio-political system that must be transformed. And, there are many reasons that would substantiate the necessity for a radical social transformation within the United States, not least among these reasons would include the problematic and oppressive effects of capitalism which is responsible for a wide array of social problems and social pathologies, e.g., structural poverty, exploitation, social and political inequality, the perpetuation of racism and sexism, and environmental disrespect among other social ills. But endemic to the capitalist system is also the conversion of social relations, i.e., the relations between people, into commodity relations. In other words, social relations have been reduced to economic relations in which social interaction has become a relation between things instead of a relation between people; it is the dehumanization of social relations. This process is referred to as *reification* which is a significant obstacle to achieving radical social transformation.

Reification as a concept refers to thingification, i.e., the transformation of ideas and abstractions into independent concrete things that affect human behavior. It also refers to the transformation of human beings and human relations into thing-like beings and relations. In other words, reification is the personification of things and the thingification of human properties, relations, and actions. The history of the concept of reification began with Karl Marx. However, the concept of reification was implicit in the philosophy of Georg Hegel. Hegel explained history as the self-realization of Spirit, mind, or God. Starting with Spirit as pure thought, Spirit unfolds itself to become conscious of itself as Spirit. Spirit then objectifies itself in nature and through the human mind as self-conscious being achieves consciousness of itself as Spirit. This process involves overcoming Spirit's "alienation" from itself, which occurs when Spirit as a knowing mind confronts a world that appears objective, as other than Spirit. Knowing as recognition destroys the illusory otherness of the objective world and recognizes it as actually subjective. The process terminates with "absolute knowledge,"

Spirit having recognized the whole of creation is Spirit. The history of the world is therefore essentially thought. Such is the argument of Hegel which was interrogated and exposed by Ludwig Feuerbach through his critique of Hegel and expounded in *The Essence of Christianity* which asserted that religion is projection and a form of alienation that is set-up to dominate the individual. Marx recognized the revolutionary implications of Feuerbach's critique and made it "one of the ingredients of his materialist conception of history" (Bottomore 1983, p. 171). Consequently, Marx constructed the basic elements of a theory of reification which was later expanded by Georg Luckács who demonstrated that the totality of human existence is a reified existence. Hence, Feuerbach, Marx, and Luckács demystify social reality by explaining the effects of reification on social existence—specifically social relations—its contribution to social problems, and the need to change this condition.

Feuerbach's significance and contribution to an understanding of reification was his discovery and application of "transformational criticisms" to Hegelian philosophy, his recognition of religion as self-estrangement, i.e., self-alienation, and his insight into how reified ideas become independent agents capable of acting on human behavior. Feuerbach, through his critical approach to the study of Hegel, discovered that the mystery of Hegel was his personification of the Absolute, God, or Spirit and his treatment of abstract concepts like thought as agents, and therefore, through what Feuerbach called "transformation criticism" the social reality of Hegel's philosophy could be discovered by transposing subject and predicate in Hegel's principal propositions, i.e., by inverting the subject and predicate the proper understanding is restored. Therefore, instead of starting with the "thought" of God, as Hegel did, and hence thinking as an agent out of which emerges being, this can be transposed into thinking as an activity of existing humans in which thought comes out of being, not being out of thought. By reading Hegel's proposition backward, Feuerbach believed he had arrived at the correct understanding.

It is from this understanding that Feuerbach recognized religion as self-estrangement, i.e., self-alienation. Instead of asserting that Spirit or God is estranged from humanity, as Hegel did, Feuerbach saw this in reverse, i.e., God as self-alienated humanity. God thus becomes a projected, idealized image of the human and so humanity becomes estranged from itself, i.e., self-alienation. According to Feuerbach (1989/1854): "What man calls Absolute Being, his God, is his own being" (p. 25), in other words, the individual being of humanity becomes the object of thought as another being, and hence to Feuerbach, "the Divine Being is nothing other than the being of man himself, or rather, the being of man abstracted from the limits of the individual man or real, corporeal man, and objectified, i.e., contemplated and worshipped as another being, as being distinguished from his own" (p. 25).

Feuerbach also believed the origin of this objectification of human being begins in imagination and feeling, i.e., a longing for a reality that can grant self-value, miracle, and immortality. Through imagination the feelings and emotions are stirred; what is painful to the feelings is set aside; and, it drapes the abstracted real world in sensuous imagery. But to Feuerbach this is deception; it cheats reason; it screens contradictions and sets aside limits; it confuses the abstract with the concrete; it takes the characteristics of human consciousness and unifies them in a divine being. In other words, the human alienates self when it objectifies its nature in the Divine (Harvey 2008).

Therefore, by way of his "transformational criticism" and the recognition of religion as self-estrangement, Feuerbach understood Hegelian philosophy as reification. Whereby Hegel used a mystery to explain a mystery, Feuerbach demystified Hegel through his transformational criticism. This recognition allowed Feuerbach to identify a connection between alienation and reification in the form of projection, i.e., by attributing the characteristics of human consciousness onto a divine being the human alienates self, and the alienated self as the divine being— an abstraction—is confused with the concrete, i.e., it is taken to be real, and so an idea conjured up in the human imagination is thingified, given human characteristics, and is believed to be independent and capable of acting on human behavior.

Karl Marx would use the intellectual innovation of "transformational criticism," or what he described as "turning Hegel on his head," as the main ingredient for his materialist conception of history and applied it to other spheres than religion. Marx would establish the basis for reification not in religion but in human economic life, i.e., human productive activities—specifically capitalist production. The human history of production becomes the history of human estrangement. However, unlike Feuerbach who attributed the reifying attributes of religion to imagination and feeling and which he believed could be overcome by recognizing in humanity what has been projected on to God, Marx understood self-estrangement as an institutional reality which requires a real revolution in order to escape, i.e., a collective act of repossessing the externalized social power given to institutions.

In the *Economic and Philosophic Manuscripts of 1844* Marx discussed the process of the estrangement of labor. Labor as a productive activity creates objects, things, materials which confront the worker as something alien and independent of the worker. This is the objectification of labor: "The alienation of the worker in his product means not only that his labor becomes an object, assumes an *external* existence, but that it exists *outside him*, independently, as something alien to him, and that it becomes a power of its own confronting him; it means that the life which he has conferred on the object confronts him as something hostile and alien," i.e., the objects created by the worker do not belong to the worker nor does the worker have control over the object (Tucker 1978, p. 72).

But the worker is not only alienated from the objects of production; the worker is also alienated in the very activity of labor. Labor which is performed as a means to satisfy needs external to labor "is therefore not voluntary, but coerced; it is *forced labour*" (Tucker 1978, p. 74). In other words, labor is performed not to satisfy the needs of the laborer but rather to satisfy the needs of someone else. In this situation labor does not belong to the worker but to someone else and so constitutes a loss of self, i.e., self-estrangement. Hence, the laborer is estranged from the product of labor and estranged from the activity of labor. This estrangement further leads to "*the estrangement of man from man*," i.e., the estrangement of human relationships (Tucker 1978, p. 77).

But to whom do the product of labor and the activity of labor belong if not to the laborer? According to Marx: "The *alien* being to whom labour and the produce of labour belongs, in whose service labour is done and for whose benefit the produce of labour is provided, can only be *man* himself," i.e., another human being other than the worker—the owner of the means of production (Tucker 1978, p. 78). And so the position of the worker towards this other human being, like towards the object and activity of labor, is as "master of this object, someone alien, hostile, powerful, and independent of" the laborer, someone for whom the activity of labor is "performed in the service, under the dominion, the coercion and yoke of another man" (Tucker 1978, p. 78). Thus, the result and consequences of alienated labor is private property which is on the one hand "the *product* of alienated labour, and that secondly it is the *means* by which labour alienates itself, *the realization of this alienation*" (Tucker 1978, p. 79). Therefore, the laborer, by way of alienation, projects onto the objects created by labor, the activity of labor, and the person who owns the product of labor power and control over both labor and its product. This is reification.

However, it is in *Capital* that Marx draws out the process of reification through his explanation of the secret of commodities. Commodities as products are exchangeable. In exchange a definite quantity of one product changes places with a definite quantity of another. Because commodities exchange with each other in definite quantitative proportions each commodity can be thought of as containing a certain value. This value can be abstracted in the form of money which is independent of any particular product. Hence, the relation between producers, i.e., the labor of private individuals or groups of individuals, is reduced to impersonal and uncontrollable market forces, and though the producers' world is created by other people, they see themselves as existing in a world of things—commodities, i.e., the world of labor is enveloped in commodity production—the very core and purpose of labor; the laborer's primary relationship is to these commodities; commodities are all that matter. Consequently, social relations between people are reduced to commodity relations, i.e., relations between things. This confusion of the relations between people with relations between things is the fundamental contradiction of commodity production, i.e., the *fetishism of commodities*: the process by which the products of human labor come to appear as an independent and uncontrolled reality apart from other people who have created them. In other words, the product takes on a life of its own as though independent of human will.

Under the spell of commodity fetishism, commodity production appears as a social relation, existing not between people, but between the products of labor. The social relationship appears between commodities in terms of the ratio at which these things exchange with each other rather than in terms of the labor embodied in them. This conceals the relationship between producers; the relations connecting laborers are not social relations between individuals, but material relations between persons and social relations between things. In other words, the relation between things conceals the relation between people, i.e., the human element involved in commodity production. Hence, the economic forms of capitalism conceal the underlying social relations; it establishes a dichotomy between appearance and reality.

The *fetishism* of commodity fetishism is where material objects have certain characteristics conferred on them in virtue of the prevailing social relations, and take on the appearance that such characteristics belong to them by nature—but they are not natural properties; they are social. Their characteristics constitute real powers, uncontrolled by, indeed holding sway over, human beings. The illusion of fetishism stems from conflation of social characteristics and its material shapes. This gives rise to illusions concerning the natural provenance of these powers, i.e., powers which render people subject to the dominion of things. What happens here is a distortion of perception. Consequently, an imaginary power is bestowed on the commodity which then influences and controls human behavior (Bottomore 1983).

Therefore, by way of the capitalist productive process Marx concluded that the laborer becomes estranged from the objects of production and the activity of production, and then projects onto these objects and the owners of these objects power and control. Consequently, the whole process of commodity production is reification, i.e., the objects of production are transformed into a thing which has become independent of its maker and governs the life of labor, but also in this process human beings are transformed into thing-like beings, i.e., commodities. Hence, the whole process is akin to humanizing things and dehumanizing humans.

Georg Lukács in *History and Class Consciousness* (1971) devotes an entire chapter to reification—"Reification and the Consciousness of the Proletariat." In it Lukács extends the Marxist analysis of reification to demonstrate how commodity production influences the total society, i.e., "the problem of commodities must not be considered in isolation or even regarded as the central problem in economics, but as the central, structural problem of capitalist society in all its aspects" (p. 83). For Lukács, the nature of commodity-structure is demonstrated by the following: "Its basis is that a relation between people takes on the character of a thing and thus acquires a 'phantom objectivity,' an autonomy that seems so strictly rational and all-embracing as to conceal every trace of its fundamental nature: the relation between people" (p. 83). Hence, human relations in general have become thingified. Consequently, contra Feuerbach and Marx, Lukács understands the resolution to be awareness, i.e., consciousness of the contradiction in order to disrupt the process of reification.

Once the commodity becomes a ubiquitous disposition within the whole society, i.e., the total arrangement of society is the commodity-structure, "the reification produced by commodity relations assume decisive importance" (p. 86). Now the subjugation of human consciousness is formatted for the expression of reification. Through the principle of rationalization, and hence calculation and specialization, the work process achieves predictability and precision, but also in this process the worker is no longer the "master of the process; on the contrary, he is a mechanical part incorporated into a mechanical system" and so must "conform to its laws whether he likes it or not" (p. 89). Hence, "the emergence of modern capitalism tends to replace 'natural' relations which exhibit human relations more plainly by rationally reified relations" (p. 91).

Lukács's primary point is that human functions and human relations are transformed into commodity relations and so become dehumanized and dehumanizing. Hence, "as the capitalist system continuously produces and reproduces itself on higher and higher levels, the structure of reification progressively sinks more deeply, more fatefully and more definitively into the consciousness of man" (p. 98). The commodity relation "stamps its imprint upon the whole consciousness of man; his qualities and abilities are no longer an organic part of his personality, they are things which he can 'own' or 'dispose of' like the various objects of the external world. And there is no natural form in which human relations can be cast, no way in which man can bring his physical and psychic 'qualities' into play without their being subjected increasingly to this reifying process" (p. 102). Consequently, every aspect of human existence is something to be bought and sold like a commodity. Everything is now for sale. Whatever is wanted can now be purchased or exchanged, e.g., love, happiness, health, peace of mind, even other people. "Reification is, then, the necessary, immediate reality of every person living in capitalist society" (p. 197), i.e., the totality of human existence is a reified existence.

Feuerbach, Marx, and Lukács are intellectually connected, although each one provides a different perspective from which to understand reification and its problematic social implications. Each one of these thinkers indicates that reification impedes and corrupts genuine, authentic human relations. The genuineness and authenticity of human relations is impeded and corrupted by false relations with self, false relations with others, and an incomplete social existence.

Reification begins in self-alienation; this is acknowledged by Feuerbach, Marx, and Lukács. Therefore, reification is a consequence of alienation or at least a special case of alienation. It is a psychological manifestation in which perception is confused, in which the individual dissociates a part of self and projects that dissociated part of self into an independent existence that confronts the self as alien. What is *me* is now *not me*. Reification, on a psychological level, is a split personality. This understanding of reification is most evident in Feuerbach. Marx agrees with Feuerbach's understanding of alienation but extends it beyond the realm of religion. For Marx, reification is also a special case of alienation, but the alienation is a manifestation of capitalist production, specifically of the commodity process in which the laborer looses control over the commodity, the laboring process, and hence the self. The laborer, in Hegelian terms, becomes a being-for-another and hence a being without self-determination. It is the Hegelian "Lordship and Bondage" moment described in *The Phenomenology of Spirit*. Hence, all alienation is self-alienation with reification becoming a characteristic of capitalist production in which things are personified and social relations thingified. However, it is Lukács who elaborates a theory of reification and extends the Marxian interpretation into the realm of *all* social relations. All social relations take on the form of commodity relations, i.e., social interaction becomes a commodity, a thing to buy and sell, own and dispossess, use and discard. Reification, hence, becomes the commodification of human relations, the dehumanization of human relations. Hence, self-alienation is a disingenuine relationship with self. As a bifurcation of the personality a part of the self is spun-off, objectified, and estranged. However, the alienated pieces of the self are unrecognized as part of self and so transformed into independent forces. The falseness of this way of being is that the self does not recognize self and so is unrelated to self.

Consequently, this inability to relate to self leads to false relations with others. As Feuerbach observed, by positing parts of the self onto the Divine humans are unable to acknowledge in each other what they acknowledge in the Divine. Marx, on the other hand, sees a breakdown in social relations as a consequence of the productive process in which estranged labor's relation to work and the product of labor also holds with regard to social relations, i.e., relations to other humans. Alienation thus colors relations with others, as a self-alienated being all social relations are estranged relations because the dissociated self can only relate to others in a dissociated way. Hence, the relationship with others is as false as the relationship with self. Finally, for Lukács because social relations have become commodity relations then social relations have become thingified. Social relations have value in terms of usefulness, i.e., social relations take the form of possessions, and as possessions social relations are subject to the vagary and caprice of the individual. Another way to understand this is that social relations become objects susceptible to individual manipulation and so the commodification of social relations inverts the Kantian principle which says treat persons as an end and not as a means. Consequently, social relations are transformed into market relations, i.e., economic transactions.

Finally, the inability to relate to self and others leads to an incomplete social existence. The reification of self and others has a corrupting influence on society as a whole. Feuerbach, Marx, and Lukács all understood that alienation and reification are states of being or ways of being that inhibit not only human potential but also human possibilities. It is a way of being that Martin Heidegger described as loss of self, a self "submerged in a kind of anonymous routine manner of life in which its possibilities are taken over and dictated to it by circumstances or social pressures" (Macquarrie 1968, p. 14). Or, what Paulo Friere (1970) described as someone submerged in reality, someone who is trapped in a concrete situation unaware of the cause of the condition and unable to achieve understanding or become aware of what reality is, or at least interpret reality objectively. Consequently, the encounter with alienation and reification results in relationships of indifference and domination which takes away the distinctive existence of self. It is a way of life imposed upon the self, stripping it of possibilities of choice and compelling it to a uniformity and conformism dictated by conventions brought on by alienation and reification. Hence, between the self and others there is no genuine communication and no authentic being-with-one-another. The reality of the situation is concealed and obfuscated, manifesting itself as a tranquilizing that expunges responsibility and anxiety, as alienation that diverts the self from authentic selfhood and authentic community, or as scattering in which possibilities are dictated from outside the self. Hence, social existence deteriorates into a falseness that obscures reality.

Therefore, for these reasons, a deep level social transformation is necessary to interrupt and dismantle the problematic and oppressive effects of alienation and reification. Individuals are enmeshed in social illusion that alienate them from their own experience and shape their worldview while prohibiting skepticism or disbelief among those in the fantasy system, because the social fantasy is shared. This is a state of being in which one is divorced from one's own experience. This is analogous to what philosopher Martin Heidegger expressed as the "they-self." Here the individual has fallen under the domination of the collective mass which is deluded by the current system of institutions, values, and ethics; their standards and way of life are determined for them by the conventions of bourgeois, capitalist society; their possibilities of choice are taken away, and a uniformity and conformism is imposed upon them (Macquarrie 1968, 18). Heidegger refers to this state of being as "falleness," in which the individual is deprived "of freedom through the dominance of the 'they,' the depersonalized collective anonymous mass" (Macquarrie 1968, 27). But it is also part of the social pathology developing out of the system of capitalism. In such a state the individual is tranquilized by the relief of responsibility, alienated from self, directed by factors outside of self, and hence lives an inauthentic life (Macquarrie 1968, 27). Another way of looking at this state of being is what psychiatrist David Cooper (1971) described as "being out of one's mind," that is, a separation from self, and an inauthentic existence. The pay-off in living such an estranged life is the fact that it is normal; it is how everyone else lives. So, "on reflection, there's nothing like as good as being out of one's mind" (Cooper 1971, 11).

However, the individual only becomes aware that they are in a social fantasy system dominated by reification retrospectively. The demand for radical change must be consciously developed. If they begin to wake up from the social fantasy system, they can expect the system to react and so be classified or labeled as bad, sick, different, abnormal, ungrateful, and even psychotic; and in political terms they are classified as unpatriotic and hence disloyal, traitorous, subversive, seditious, insurrectionary, rebellious, and even revolutionary. If the individual attests to any experience outside the reified world of what society takes to be real and true they are subjected to correction and therapy or in political terms punishment and incarceration. Hence, it is only through the social movement that a transformation in consciousness and behavior can emerge in which the masses can begin to perceive the illegitimacy of the current institutional arrangements, become defiant, and collectively demand change.

References

Bottomore, T. (Ed.). (1983). *A dictionary of Marxist thought.* Cambridge, MA: Harvard University Press.

Cooper, D. (1970). *The death of the family.* New York: Vintage Books.

Feuerbach, L. (1989). *The essence of Christianity.* (G. Eliot Trans.). Amherst, NY: Prometheus Books. (Original work published 1854)

Freire, P. (1970). *Pedagogy of the oppressed.* (M. B. Ramos Trans.). New York: Seabury Press.

Lukács, G. (1971). *History and class consciousness.* (P. Livingstone Trans.). Cambridge, MA: The MIT Press.

Macquarrie, J. (1968). *Martin Heidegger.* Richmond, VA: John Knox Press.

Tucker, R. C. (Ed.). (1978). *The Marx-Engels reader.* (2nd ed.). New York: W. W. Norton.

ABOUT THE AUTHOR

Ronald A. Kuykendall is instructor of Political Science at Trident Technical College in South Carolina. He is the author of *Social Crisis and Social Demoralization: The Dynamics of Status in American Race Relations* (2005). He has also published articles in the *Journal of Black Studies*, the *Western Journal of Black Studies*, and was a contributor to the multivolume *Encyclopedia of the Great Black Migration* (2006) published by Greenwood Press. His research interests include radical African American social and political thought and the intersection of race and politics. He has also made presentations on *"African American Affiliation with Socialism, 1825-1925"* presented at the annual meeting of the South Carolina Political Science Association, University of South Carolina-Spartanburg, Spartanburg, SC; *"The African Blood Brotherhood, Independent Marxists During the Harlem Renaissance"* presented at the conference "The Future of the Harlem Renaissance" University of Tennessee, Knoxville, TN; *"Political Institutions, an International Perspective"* presented at the meeting of the South Carolina International Education Consortium, McCormick, SC; *"The Political Significance of the Plessy v. Ferguson Case"* lecture presented at the Symposium on the 50th Anniversary of Brown v. Board of Education, Greenville Technical College, Greenville, SC; *"Multicultural and Poverty Issues"* presented at the Training For Attorneys Appointed in Abuse and Neglect Cases in the 13th Judicial Circuit sponsored by Children's Law Center School of Law University of South Carolina and The South Carolina Bar Foundation.

CHAPTER SIX

THE BEGINNING OF THE END

JONATHAN PAUL

JONATHAN PAUL

This Country Must Change

Our world we live in is in peril. The crisis we face is real and is getting worse every day that goes by. Species extinction is at the highest rate in tens of thousands of years. The destruction of the land base through deforestation, resource extraction, pollution, and the burden of human overpopulation is putting the planet at the brink of disaster. The human species has encroached on every habitat on this planet with devastating consequences. We are literally killing the only world we live on and doing so without impunity.

Although this planet can be very resilient, the delicate and intricate web of life keeps the planet and all of her species in balance. The predator-prey relationship, though sometimes seemingly harsh, has been effectively disturbed by human activities and therefore the eco-systems are becoming out of balance and die offs are now a scary reality. It is humans, in fact, that behave like an introduced non-native species and are creating havoc on the ecological balance. Although humans have been on this planet for a long time, it is our prevailing attitude that we are above all other life forms that is causing many of the problems we face today. These beliefs and attitudes are keeping us on the road to our demise.

Before white European settlers came to North America this land was teeming with life. From the hardwood forests of the east to the plains of the midwest and to the towering forests of the west, this country was overwhelmed with wild animals from bison to ferrets. Snow capped mountains fed rivers with crystal clean water that eventually made its way to the Gulf of Mexico. Salmon filled the rivers of the west providing nourishment for animals and the land while they spawned. When the salmon laid their eggs, they died and created nourishment for the streams and forests that surrounded them. If one could be there, there could be no doubt that the enormity of life could never end. But with the introduction of European settlers fleeing religious persecution in Britain, everything began to change. From the shores of the east, white man began cutting the hardwood forests and slowly began moving west. With religious dominance in mind, the land base began to change dramatically. With the rush for gold and population boom, the move west became a destructive path that still is around today. With the local indigenous populations driven off of their lands and their food sources depleted, genocide was in full force. Bison were exterminated from a population of around 60 million to about four hundred in a matter of years in order to cut the food supply of the plains Indians and also to allow more land for cattle and sheep. It was not long before most native peoples were either on reservations or dead and the continued and systematic destruction of the environment was not only ignored, but encouraged.

With the boom of population came the boom in the populations of cattle and sheep. With the raising of these animals you need grazing land, and a lot of it. But in order to have this land, you needed to exterminate the competition. Soon, the conquering of the wild animals began. Predators like bears, wolves, coyotes, and mountain lions were being killed to the brink of extinction by the guns, traps, and poison baits of government exterminators. With this slaughter, many other animals also died as unintended targets of strychnine-laced traps. The wolf and grizzly were brought to near extinction while other animals, like the carrier pigeon that was numbered in the hundreds of millions, was brought to extinction by hunting. These species, along with other species that were hanging close to extinction, were just a prelude to what we are experiencing today.

Even the oceans were not immune to human encroachment. Once full of life, the seas around the world are in peril due to human impact. Almost all of the great whales were hunted to near extinction for their oil to light the cities, while many species of fish were being unsustainably harvested. As humans began to modernize, our methods of resource extraction became more efficient and deadly. Along with massive over-fishing, pollution began to poison the oceans. Although fossil fuels began to replace the need for whale oil, soon another problem began to emerge. With the amount of carbon being released into the atmosphere, the earth's natural scrubbers could not cope. Along with this came the warming atmosphere and a huge environmental problem was now in the making with no end in sight.

The world's forests scrub the carbon out of our atmosphere along with the world's oceans. With massive deforestation, almost eleven football fields per second, this natural carbon scrubber is decreased and the oceans cannot handle the massive amounts of extra carbon released by human civilization. This, in turn, leaves much of this carbon in the atmosphere, creating a greenhouse effect that captures too much heat, therefore warming our planet. Large melt-offs in the north and south poles along with glacial melting is causing havoc on all levels. Although debated and ignored for many years by industry-infested government and confusing information put out by the captains of industry, we have surely put ourselves in a position in which revolutionary change may not even be enough.

We have to realize, however, that carbon dioxide is not all bad. In fact, the release of carbon dioxide by natural means, by volcanoes for instance, is what keeps our planet a livable place. If we had no carbon in the atmosphere then this planet would be a lifeless ice ball. But, like anything, too much carbon released is causing many serious problems in our environment. Humans have knocked the earth out of balance and somewhere in our deepest parts of our collective consciousness we have lost our way. The whole world, our only home we share with millions of other species, is being killed because we refuse to acknowledge our ignorance, apathy, and greed.

The next question we need to explore is why and how we let ourselves get into this situation and how we are going to get out of it. The first thing we need to acknowledge is that we cannot "save" the planet for just ourselves, but for all species. In the mainstream of society, our only discussion of dealing with the issues at hand are only at an anthropocentric level, which is ironically the same thinking that got us here in the first place. Our collective thinking must include all species and all of the land base. Trying to save the planet for humans only will not work because making the eco-systems healthy can only be achieved by saving all aspects of the planet's ecology. Because of human arrogance and self-centered thinking, being able to go beyond the closed "box" is revolutionary in itself.

When awareness of environmental issues began to grow in the early 1970s, our situation was already critical. If real change was to happen it had to start then. Moderate change would not be enough even at this time. Even with the Clean Water Act and the Clean Air Act, it was too little, too late. Although some milestones can be attributed to these laws, the rate of exploitation trumped the environmental laws, which could not keep up with rising populations and industry growth. In fact, the industries were making way too much money in order to be willing to change.

With the election of George Bush in 2000, and with the September 11th attacks, the issues concerning the environment were not only put on the back burner, but were buried in the back yard. With the Bush family heavily in the oil business, there was no motivation to find alternatives to fossil fuels. In fact, the Bush regime was neo-conservative and in such a cozy relationship with corporations, that many of the previous laws protecting the environment and species were watered down or ignored in order to allow these industries to continue without proper oversight.

The years from 2000 to 2008 were critical for change, but it was not so considering we had the most anti-environmental administration in our nation's history. Bush's war on nature was calculated and efficient influencing the growing separation of the rich and the poor. Part of this was the war in Iraq. Although the Bush regime attempted to dupe the people by stating that Saddam Hussein was making WMDs and was involved with the attacks of September 11th, this was in fact a lie to justify invading a country with one of the largest oil reserves in the world. The trillions spent to keep the war effort going could have been spent on a Manhattan-style project to wean us off of fossil fuels, but instead the Bush regime opted to continue the status quo and allow his rich oil friends to make the biggest profits in American corporate history.

In the summer of 2008, oil prices skyrocketed to $140 plus a barrel and up to $5 a gallon at the pump. Sales of gas guzzling vehicles plummeted and talk of high fuel efficiency and alternative vehicles came to light not for environmental issues, but for economics. It was not surprising that soon oil prices decreased to the lowest levels in years. Suddenly, the talk of this change disappeared from the mainstream.

The irony about all of this is that over the years activists who work for the environment and issues concerning animals have been put on the fringe and discounted as alarmists and eco-terrorists. This has been a calculated move by the industries and the organizations that support them. Misinformation used to confuse the average person has led to a debate that has wasted precious time and all of the while polluting corporations have made record profits. ExxonMobil is a perfect example of this behavior. For the last twenty years, this oil giant has put out misinformation in order to keep the public confused. Industry-hired scientists debunked the reality of climate change while scientists like Robert Hanson of NASA was silenced by the Bush regime. While many cried foul, the industries and their friends in government allowed business as usual. With this we can ask the real questions and wonder who the real eco-terrorists are and who is really responsible for the destruction of the planet. Although the finger points at the captains of industry and the governments that support them, we cannot discount the responsibilities of the average citizen who chooses to not stand in disgust and to change the way that they consume products made by those industries. The reality is that the industries will not change their ways unless people demand it. Changing this is easier said than done because, I hate to admit it, many people do not seem to care enough. Whether this is because of social-economic status or the fact that they are gullible to what the corporations make us believe - that we need them as much as they need us - I am not sure. But there is one fact that exists that is a true reason for our present problems and that is overpopulation.

We cannot even begin to face the problems without looking into the fact that the human species is overpopulated beyond sustainability. With predictions of populations increasing at enormous rates in the next twenty years, we have to take a serious look at this issue. It seems that population is an issue we cannot accept or are too afraid to challenge because it is not politically correct or just inconceivable for us even to imagine that we would have to lose our ability to breed as we please. And, of course, some will question why we should change if it is too late.

It is true that there are some eco-systems that may be beyond help, but we have no choice but to do all we can anyway. Although we have put ourselves in a position that seems to be an overwhelming process, we are not beyond our abilities to find change within our hearts and minds. There are a number of options we can embrace in our society that will and can be utilized in order to allow ourselves to climb out of this seemingly bottomless pit we are in. Although the process is enormous, it can be done if the desire is there. The key issue is time. Humans are, in my opinion, overwhelmingly anthropocentric and have difficulty thinking out of the box, let alone seven generations into the future. It seems we will only face change when it directly affects our lives - when certain foods become scarce or nonexistent or when the air quality is so bad that the sun is not seen anymore. Because we have procrastinated for so long, change must be radical and even revolutionary at best.

When we think of the term *revolutionary*, we need to understand the definition can be viewed in a broad scope. In Webster's Dictionary, the term *revolution* is defined as "the overthrow and replacement of an established government or political system by the people" and "a sudden, complete, or radical change." Although many identify the term *revolution* as violent in scope, this does not mean it is so. This type of revolution can be justified as a last resort but does not necessarily mean this is needed here.

From an eco-centric perspective, and controversial at best, is the reality that the most efficient and effective process to heal the planet would be if humans literally ceased to exist. Even with the release of all the nuclear waste and other industrial toxins around the globe, without the continual impact of human existence the earth and all of its bio-systems would return to a healthy place within a thousand years or so. Habitat, animal, plant, and insect species would be allowed to recover and once again find their place in the delicate circle of life. This, however, is not a reality barring a virus or war that wipes all life off of this planet. Since we are here to stay we need to find a balance between our way of life and how we effect the way other life lives on this planet.

In order to facilitate any kind of change in the way we live in this planet, we need to understand our own culture and how it got this way. Our modern society is really a death culture beginning the moment Christopher Columbus "discovered" the Americas. Columbus landed in the Bahamas in 1492, where he was met by the Arawak Indians who lived there. The moment the Arawaks made contact with the Spanish explorer, they were taken prisoner and Columbus demanded they show him where the gold was. It seems Columbus's main goal was to find gold and bring it back to Spain no matter what the cost to human life.

Although now the United States celebrate Columbus Day every October 12, in reality we celebrate a man who committed genocide on native peoples. In order for Columbus to pay his debts, he enslaved every Arawak Indian fourteen years or older to find a certain amount of gold every three months. If they failed to do so their hands were cut off and they bled to death. Although the Arawaks rebelled, they faced Spaniards with muskets, swords, and armor. Those who were captured were executed. In only two years, one-half of the population of 250,000 Indians were dead. After Columbus came more genocidal explorers like Cortez (who wiped out the Aztecs of Mexico), Pizzaro (who destroyed the Incas of Peru), and the settlers of New England who committed genocide on the Powhatans and Pequot tribes.

This country and many others were built on the blood of innocents. When that genocide was completed, ecocide continued until this very day. Still the corporate elite, and the governments they rule and dominate, decimates the land base for profit. This ecocide is so massive and so ingrained in our society that changing the way we live is as unimaginable as contemplating the edge of the universe.

As soon as our society can acknowledge the extent of the damage we have created, we need to begin the process of healing our planet we live on. But even if we stop all the destructive practices humans commit on a daily basis, we still will feel the effects of our actions in the near future. The step we need to take will be the most significant and important step that humans will take since we first began walking on this earth. There will be much resistance from the captains of industry. These powerful corporations rule the world and create massive environmental destruction, genocide, and war to continue their greed and power. Unless all of the people stand to these corporations and demand change there will be no change.

The real question we need to ask ourselves is can we actually do this and change the way we live and allow the planet to heal and species to recover? There are many that believe we can and feel we must have a positive thinking in order to allow this change to come. Personally, I do not think our culture has the means and wants to create change. Our culture is designed to dumb us down and keep us complacent. As long as we have our "stuff" and we can have our own little bubble to exist, things will never really change in the way that needs to happen. I believe we need to be realistic about the way things are. Although we have the responsibility to change the way things are going, I really do not believe that anything we do will be enough. Our future looks grim and even with a revolutionary change the impacts will still hit us hard. In contrast with believing we can turn the tide, I believe it is time to prepare for the future. Just as we put on our seat belts when we drive our cars, we must also put on our seat belts to survive the coming impact of life.

As time comes and goes, more species will disappear and more of the land base will become unfit for life. Although scientists have predictions for the future we can never really know the true impact of planetary ecocide because we have never experienced this before. Ecosystems are connected and as they fall the impacts become greater and the snowball effect becomes a reality. Our small and moderate changes we may enact will be dwarfed by the massive changes we choose to ignore. We are now forced into survival mode. Buckle up, because the impact is coming and it will hit us hard and sooner than many think.

Although the reality I am putting out is grim, this does

not release us of our responsibility to do all we can to minimize the impact we are heading for. Anything we do that can make the recovery of any land base or species is a necessity we must endure. In order to do this we must accept that life will be different and we must embrace that. Banding together in small communities that are self-sustainable and using both modern green technologies and simpler living must be accepted in our mindset. With a massive reduction in our population and with cleaner living we can have an affect on the problems we face today. So instead of being overwhelmed by the huge scope of our problems, we need to acknowledge it and change all we can in our personal lives and in our communities.

Barring a major catastrophe, I have a hard time imagining a willingness to make revolutionary change in the way humans exist on the planet. Call me negative or a cynic, but I think I see things in a realistic way. In my short life on the earth, I have witnessed destructiveness on a massive scale. This destructiveness has come from an attitude that has dominated human kind for generations. Turning this prevalent attitude around seems more of a struggle than any other we face today.

While resistance to change causes delay in the way we live and view this world, there are those who want change and are fighting for change right now. Although the system we live in resists these people by marginalizing them, there is still hope in the spirit of those who fight for justice and especially for those who fight for the planet as a whole.

This is a true battle against Goliath. The captains of industry, government agencies, the neo-conservative wise-use anti-environmental activists, along with a majority of the population who chooses to ignore or become passive to the issues, and for those who simply do not care - our struggle is going to be a long and difficult one. But no matter what the outcome or the reality of what looms ahead, I am grateful and honored to be one who fights against the darkness. Even if I were told we would lose the fight to save this planet, I would not give up. To save this planet and all of her species upon her is the ultimate struggle that trumps any other issue. I am not dismissing the importance of other struggles around the globe, but merely stating that without an intact home, planet earth, there are no other struggles because is it clear that all struggles stem from one prevailing attitude that has dominated our existence since the beginning of time on earth.

To see the forests fall, species disappear, rivers choked

in pollution, animals slaughtered by the millions every day, I feel despair and loss of hope. To witness the superficial and selfish attitudes of our society and to observe the ignorance and the unwillingness of humankind to get out of our collective denial, is to realize that hope for change seems to be fading fast. But we should not let this reality dim our spirits and make us lose hope. This planet we live on is unique and a rare anomaly in the universe. Earth is situated in the perfect orbit around the perfect star and is able to create and sustain life. Earth is a living organism that deserves our respect and honor.

Instead of losing hope, we must take our despair and turn it into action to reverse the damage we have done. No matter the future forecast and how gloomy it may appear, we owe it and are responsible to do all we can to reverse and stop the damage we create. If we can turn the tide, then all may not be lost on this beautiful planet. A revolutionary change can happen if we are willing to do it and face the challenges both of change within ourselves and of our outside surroundings. Somewhere deep within our collective mindsets, we need to break the chains of oppression and move forward to a life of peace and live with the planet, not against it.

ABOUT THE AUTHOR

Jonathan Paul was born in 1966 in New York City. Since the early 1980s, he has been an activist for animals and the environment. Jonathan was one of the co-founders and was the organizer for the U.S. Hunt Saboteurs from 1987-1991. He was also the co-founder of Global Investigations, which participated in an 18-month investigation into the fur industry in the U.S. Additionally, Jonathan was a co-founder of Siskiyou Forest Defenders, Sea Defense Alliance, and Ocean Defense International. A vegan since he was 17 years old, Jonathan has dedicated his life to campaigning against the use of animals in laboratories, food and entertainment, combating corporate dominance, and working on various environmental issues. In 1992, he spent six months in jail for refusing to cooperate with a grand jury investigating animal and environmental activists. In early 2006, Jonathan was arrested by the federal government and charged with arson and conspiracy for the Animal Liberation Front's destruction of the Cavel West Horse Slaughterhouse in 1997, an action that effectively shut down the company for good. Currently, he is serving his 51-month sentence at the federal correctional facility in Phoenix, Arizona. He is scheduled to be released in January of 2011.

www.supportjonathan.org

CHAPTER SEVEN

LONG LIVE JOHN AFRICA!

RAMONA AFRICA
THE MOVE ORGANIZATION

RAMONA AFRICA

This Country Must Change

ONA MOVE! The MOVE Organization wants you to know that the information you read in this chapter comes from the Teaching of MOVE'S <u>Founder and</u> <u>Coordinator, JOHN AFRICA.</u> There are some direct quotes from <u>JOHN AFRICA</u> contained in this writing but <u>all</u> of the information in this chapter is from the Teaching of <u>JOHN AFRICA.</u>

We of MOVE have been asked to write about the need for revolution so we're starting with a quote from <u>JOHN AFRICA.</u> TO QUOTE <u>JOHN AFRICA</u> <u>THE COORDINATOR, QUOTE-</u> ...REVOLUTION <u>AIN'T</u> A PRINCIPLE THAT IS <u>APPLIED</u> WHEN THE OPPRESSOR IS OPPRESSING, REVOLUTION IS THE PRINCIPLE OF FREEDOM EVEN WHEN THE OPPRESSOR <u>DOES NOT</u> EXIST....-END QUOTE, <u>JOHN</u> <u>AFRICA.</u> You can only be a revolutionary if you understand and believe in the principle of freedom, not in categories but the totality of the principle of freedom. <u>JOHN AFRICA</u> teaches us that every living being is coordinated by MOMA Nature, the Mother of life, to be free; free of disease, free of poison and pollution, free of crime, free of oppression, free of brutality and torture, free of enslavement and exploitation. Man's system is built on all of these things-crime, disease, pollution, exploitation, enslavement, brutality and torture, etc. As long as this system exists, all of these problems will continue to exist because they ARE the system. This is why there is such an urgent need for revolution. Everybody complains about this system and the conditions coming from it but some people want to hold onto it at the same time. It's not enough to simply complain about this system, people have to seriously take action to put an end to this horror. <u>JOHN AFRICA'S</u> MOVE Organization is committed to this fight and have demonstrated our commitment to this revolution. For over thirty-five years MOVE people have been uncompromising in our fight against this rotten system, despite all that this system has attacked us with. MOVE people have been beat bloody, have been beat into numerous miscarriages, had a 3 week old baby trampled to death by cops, we've been wrongly convicted and received 100 year prison sentences. We've been attacked with water cannons, tear gas, guns, automatic weapons. We've been bombed, had our family (including our babies) set afire and burned to death but we're still fighting this rotten system. <u>LONG LIVE</u> <u>JOHN AFRICA!</u> We instill the principle of revolution in our children. In fact, the police commissioner involved in the bombing and murder of our family stated publicly that our children are viewed as more of a threat than the adults. Those who run this system are very intimidated by and afraid of the youth. Young people are coordinated by MOMA Nature to fight for what is right and they are also coordinated with the energy it takes to fight for what's right. Those running this rotten system know that they are no match for the natural coordination of the youth so they do everything possible to sabotage and drain the energy, the fight out of the youth. They know that they can't keep this system afloat unless they trick people into accepting it and believing that it's OK or make people too weak to defend themselves against the system . That's why they push all types of diversions on young people, like video games, drugs, liquor, cigarettes, designer clothes, PSPs, Nintendo, etc. All of these things anesthetize the youth and drain their energy so they can't defend themselves against what this system is doing. They don't even realize what's happening to them. Young people think that these things are cool, that they make them feel good, that they're just having fun so why would they feel the need to fight against something that they see as cool, as fun. It's no different than what drug pushers do. They seduce people with drugs that seemingly make people feel good. They get people addicted to drugs and once they're addicted they keep coming back because they feel like they can't live without the drugs. People don't even realize how the drugs are robbing them of their health, their strength and satisfaction. Drug addicts think they feel good when they're high on dope but they're out of it, unaware of what's really happening to them. They're completely dependent on and at the mercy of the drug pusher. That's exactly how this system's officials operate. They get people, starting with children, hooked on these diversions, diversions provided by the system, diversions that people think makes them feel good, makes them happy, but really locks them into this system that is robbing them of their happiness and everything they're supposed to have. They get young people hooked on these diversions, get them addicted to these things and therefore addicted to this system. This is how people become addicted to the system, get tricked into thinking the system is fun, is cool and that they've got to have it, can't live without it-just like drug addicts.

There is absolutely no question about the need for revolution, the need to stop this rotten system and all of its influence when you can see things clearly.

142

This Country Must Change

JOHN AFRICA teaches that you can only influence your influence and this system is people's influence. Ask yourself – have things gotten better since the inception of this system or have they gotten steadily worse? Is the air cleaner, the water purer? Are people healthier? Are children happier? Is there less crime? Are there less dope addicts and alcoholics or more? When you see, read, hear about a 5 year old child killing a baby just to see what it feels like to kill, that's the influence of this system. When you hear about teenagers putting puppies in an oven and cooking them to death while the puppies claw and yelp in horror, that's the influence of this system. When you hear about people that breed pit bulls to fight and tear each other apart and also feed these dogs innocent little puppies to instill the thirst for blood in these pit bulls, that's the influence of this system. When you find out about Love Canal, NY. and Toms River NJ. where corporations dump toxic chemicals in the earth and water causing babies to be born with all manners of birth defects or die of cancer, that's the influence of this system. When you read about a pregnant girl going to her prom, giving birth in the bathroom and throwing the baby in the trash like it was a piece of paper, that's the influence of this system. When you have politicians and officials tell you that it's OK to execute an innocent person, that's the influence of this system. When you have cops shooting people 20, 30, 50, 80 times, that's the influence of this system. When you have judges involved in a case of sexual abuse of a little girl by her father ruling that the abuse, the rape is OK, because what a man does in his bedroom is his business, that's the influence of this system. Every time students go off and shoot up their high school or college and kill their classmates, that's the influence of this system. When a person goes off and arbitrarily shoots people to death in a mall, that's the influence of this system. When sweet innocent little babies are born and are turned into Hitlers, Jeffrey Dahlmers, Son of Sams, that's the influence of this system. TO QUOTE JOHN AFRICA THE COORDINATOR QUOTE-...THIS IS A SYSTEM FOLKS ARE LIVING IN, IT WAS DEVISED FROM AN IDEA, AND THE RULES, THE SO CALLED LAWS, THE PRACTICES OF THIS SYSTEM, THIS IDEA, THIS CIVILIZATION HAS INFLUENCED EVERYBODY IN THE SYSTEM SINCE THE BEGINNING OF THE SYSTEM, SO IF YOU GOT CRIME NOW IT IS BECAUSE YOU HAD IT WHEN YOU STARTED, CRIMINALS DON'T COME FROM THE WOMB OF A WOMAN, THEY'RE INFLUENCED TO BE

143

CRIMINALS WHEN THEY ENTER THE CRIME-ORIENTED CAVITY OF CIVILIZATION...END QUOTE, <u>JOHN AFRICA.</u> It's very clear that the only way to make things right, to get back the health, happiness, satisfaction we're supposed to have is to rid ourselves of the system that is robbing us of these things. Ever since the inception of this system, this civilization, man has resisted it, nobody accepts oppression, being poisoned, being unhappy, without resistance, without a fight. Over time, some people have been beat down, become disillusioned and thrown up their hands, given up, because they couldn't see any way to win. Others, like JOHN AFRICA'S MOVE Organization, continue to resist and this system really comes down on people like us. This system has also tricked people into believing that resisting the treachery of this system is a crime, is criminal, and that people have no right to resist it. They invented the word, the concept, called "legal". They have trained people to believe that "legal" is the same as right and that illegal is the same as wrong but that's a lie. <u>JOHN AFRICA</u> has proven that legal is not the same as right. Apartheid, The Holocaust, Slavery were all legal and all wrong. Resisting these horrors were all "illegal" but they certainly were not wrong. It is our duty, our obligation to revolt against anything that wrongs us, our babies, our family in any way and nobody can prove this position wrong. What hope do our children, our grandchildren and our great-grandchildren have if we don't fight to put an end to this treachery. Even the officials that want to call our resistance wrong, illegal, can't stand by that position because every one of them celebrate the 4th of July where they claim revolutionaries went to war against the English government, went to war against cops called Red Coats. Nathan Hale, Patrick Henry, Paul Revere are all celebrated as heroes, freedom fighters, for resisting tierney, for fighting what is called a revolutionary war, an illegal war against the British government so how can these same officials also say that it's wrong. How can it possibly be wrong to fight those that are poisoning the very air, the very water, and the very earth that we need in order to live? It's instinctive to fight for your life and for what you need in order to live. It ain't criminal.

True revolution, as taught by <u>JOHN AFRICA</u>, begins with self, begins with how you think, which determines how you live. If we are ever to reverse the self destructive downward spiral that this society is on; if we are ever to be healthy, happy, free of crime, disease and degeneration; if we are ever to be free of oppression, brutality and torture; we have to change how we think and therefore how we live. The urgent need for true revolution is not a theoretical discussion, a topic to be debated or a conversation piece. It is an absolute necessity and an absolute certainty. The only question is whether we are in harmony with the healing correcting force of revolution to make things easier on ourselves or whether we foolishly try to resist that force and make things harder on ourselves by fighting a losing battle. MOVE people have been taught by JOHN AFRICA that what is right is strong, it's lasting and it has always been here. What is wrong is weak, temporary and cannot, does not last. That's why there have been so many empires that have come and gone. They don't last because they ain't right, no matter how powerful they may appear to be at any particular time. They all go down and get replaced with another empire that doesn't work and it's gonna be that way until we truly change the way we think, start respecting all of life and start living in harmony with MOMA nature, the mother of life, the coordinator of life. Revolution simply means change and we have to change from a self-destructive society that puts priority on money and things to a society that puts priority on life. There is no true revolution and cannot be a true revolution until we do this, no matter how many times governments are replaced with seemingly different brands of governments; or how many politicians are replaced with seemingly different politicians or how many societies are replaced with seemingly different societies. The proof of what is being said here is in all of the governments, politicians and societies that have come and gone since the creation of this failing system.

TO QUOTE JOHN AFRICA THE COORDINATOR, QUOTE- ...IT IS PAST TIME FOR ALL POOR PEOPLE TO RELEASE THEMSELVES FROM THE DECEPTIVE STRANGULATION OF SOCIETY, REALIZE THAT SOCIETY HAS FAILED YOU, FOR TO ATTEMPT TO IGNORE THIS SYSTEM OF DECEPTION NOW IS TO DENY YOU THE NEED TO PROTEST THIS FAILURE LATER, THE SYSTEM HAS FAILED YOU YESTERDAY, FAILED YOU TODAY AND HAVE CREATED THE CONDITIONS FOR FAILURE TOMORROW...-END QUOTE, JOHN AFRICA

Ramona Africa

ABOUT THE AUTHOR

Ramona Africa is the sole adult survivor of the May 13, 1985 massacre of 11 members of the MOVE organization. The FBI and the City of Philadelphia dropped a C4 bomb on MOVE's Osage Avenue home in West Philadelphia. Both 30-year old Ramona and 13-year old Birdie Africa (the only 2 survivors) report that as the MOVE family attempted to escape their burning home, they were met with massive rounds of automatic gunfire, forcing 11 members of the MOVE family to be burnt alive. Ramona dodged gunfire and escaped from the fire with permanent scarring from the burns.

Ramona was charged with conspiracy, riot, and multiple counts of simple and aggravated assault. Subsequently Ramona served 7 years in prison. If she had chosen to sever her ties with MOVE and renounce the teachings of John Africa, she could have been released far earlier. In the face of this she held true to her revolutionary beliefs and was uncompromising in the face of state terror. In his essay, "May 13 Remembered," featured in his book "All Things Censored," Mumia Abu-Jamal writes:

> "Had Ramona Africa emerged from the sea of flames wrapped in fear, had she not instead escaped with her aura of resistance intact, she would have been free long before the seven years she spent in a hellhole. Her prosecutor, describing MOVE as a cult of resistance, demanded the jury convict her of a range of charges that, if they did so, would have exposed her to fifty years in prison. Only her naturalist faith, the teachings of John Africa, allowed her to competently defend herself, where she beat the majority of the charges. Ramona is "free" today."

Since her release from prison, Ramona has tirelessly worked on behalf of the MOVE 9, Mumia Abu-Jamal, and all political prisoners and prisoners of war. She travels around the world, working for the revolution.

www.onamove.com

146

CHAPTER EIGHT

POWER TO THE IMAGINATION!

ROB LOS RICOS

ROB LOS RICOS

This Country Must Change

The Revolution continues not to happen, despite the presence of many revolutionary organizations in this country. Or is the presence of these groups actually inhibiting revolutionary activity here in the US? I don't want to examine this point too deeply now, but I do wish to address the first point above, and that is the failure of allegedly revolutionary organizations to gain any following amongst the masses they always discuss at their meetings and in their literature.

The main activity of most revolutionary groups is to educate people about the need to rise up and overthrow the capitalist system, which oppresses them. No doubt, they are sincere in this desire to reach out and organize the masses. Despite appearances to the contrary, most people are too cynical to blindly follow self-appointed leaders – unless they see there is something immediately rewarding to them - personally - in doing so. The difficult part for the Revolutionaries is not the actual educational aspects of this form of organizing, but is to be found in the challenge of educating people while not awakening in them a sense of empowerment.

Sure, every revolutionary group would like to see people arise and fight the Powers That Be, but only if the resulting revolution would result in the rise to power of their revolutionary organization. In this regard, they are not to be seen as enemies of the system, but as yet another faction in contention for State power. The revolutionaries don't want to smash the State; they want to be the State. This is why so few people – college students, mostly – fall for their schemes.

It's all but impossible for people to live in this era and not have an opinion about the legitimacy of authority. Almost everyone has run afoul of some code of conduct, law or regulation at some point in their lives, and almost every one of these instances very likely convinced the transgressors of the unfairness of the enforcing authority's power, or the idiocy of the rule/law/code transgressed. With few exceptions, authoritative power is seen as something rather arbitrary by most people at some point in their lives. This distrust of authority can become a knee-jerk reaction that is difficult to unlearn, as it tends to burn itself deeply into the psyche of the person who has transgressed. Why do you think we have to attend school for so long? Definitely, it is because we must be trained in obedience. This is why so many kids detest school. They do not desire to submit to an authority that is pre-existent, one, which they were given no voice in establishing.

At some point in a person's life, she must learn to handle the fact that she must recognize some entity's power over her, whether that power emanates from a religion, school, family, or workplace. This generally does not make the person happy. To most people, this is humiliating.

Looking for a job is likely the least favorite activity most people experience during their lifetimes. Since almost all of us are forced to work by the economic structure our society imposes upon us, we manage to struggle through the pain and humiliation as best we can, often with some combination of booze, drugs, pharmaceuticals, religion and sex.

And when we hear someone speak about the need for revolution in our country, even when sympathetic to the message, folks generally tend to hope that someone else will take up the challenge, seeing as how they don't have the time or energy, or think they don't have the strength and courage needed to fight against the authorities. This is the weakness the revolutionary groups seek out in their intended victims. If there is a general feeling of something being very wrong in our society, but people feel helpless in the face of the overwhelming task of overthrowing the social order, the revolutionary group has at least a slight chance to convert some of the population into followers.

But, here lies the trick – how does one awaken another person's sense of indignation at the ills of society, while maintaining that person's willingness to submit to the group's purpose? It would be so much easier if the revolutionaries could hypnotize their intended followers into accepting the group's leadership. This is, of course, precisely what the revolutionaries attempt to do. By ceaselessly bleating the same slogans, the group can entrap their intended victims into believing that their group is much different than the many other tiny revolutionary groups. Some gullible people will accept the group's message and begin to adopt that party's doctrine. If the hypnosis doesn't take effect, the revolutionaries can always try to use guilt, try to shame people into submission. This works particularly well on people who were raised as Catholics, by the way.

It's quite a difficult trick, trying to move people to action, while keeping them docile enough to be herded around by the leadership of the revolutionaries. No wonder revolutionaries find so little success in these endeavors. Most revolutionary literature is more boring than can be tolerated. And it is often written in some obscure idiom that is only decipherable to the initiated

– much like the Bible. Indeed, the revolutionaries often offer the same thing as the bible-thumpers: salvation! By joining their movement, people are told, together they can save the Nation, the Earth, the Blue Footed Booby - depending on the focus of the group.

Still, there's that knee-jerk reaction to authority that most Americans never seem to fully outgrow. Why awaken to one scam, just to be lulled to sleep again by a different one? Why choose Boss B over Boss A? This changing-of-the-guard has happened so often that its futility is glaringly obvious, even though this is not bluntly stated in textbooks.

The combination of boring obscurity and yet-another-authoritarian-wannabe the revolutionary groups represent is not a winner in many people's hearts and souls. In a nation obsessed by the mythology of self-reliance, it's difficult to sell doctrines, which require blind obedience. Not to the people most likely to arise with the furious rage needed to achieve any drastic changes in the systems that oppress us.

In the marketplace of ideas, then, although the System gets much of the blame for what is going wrong, the revolutionary's attempt to take over State power - rather than overthrow the System and disperse power into the population - does not gain a wide following. The revolutionaries are content to sit on the sidelines of history and make a fuss when some weakness in the System presents itself – like the current economic depression. Inevitably, they will attract a number of people with their own ideas about what should be done about the situation at hand, and the revolutionaries will patiently explain that only their leadership can provide the proper solutions. Maybe not in this lifetime, though.

During the Bush Junta's reign, Junta leaders demanded that leftists, environmentalists, and scientists never condemn the American Way of Life. That is to say, they were willing to go to war in order to secure oil and gas for Americans to use for whatever purpose they desired. As long as American citizens are willing to send their children off to war in distant lands to ensure the flow of petrochemicals to the Fatherland, we can rest assured in knowing that there will be plenty of gas for our commutes to work, trips to the mall, and riding lawnmower races.

Rather than criticizing consumers about the incredible amount of damage their lifestyles are inflicting upon the biosphere – as the revolutionaries often do – the Bush Junta insisted that it was inexcusable to suggest that the American Way of Life was in any way wrong. Which message do you think most people wanted to hear? That their over-consumption of the world's resources must end before we destroy our planet's ability to support life, or that everything's just fine the way it is? Yes, Americans, like most people, are guided more by immediate self-interest than they are by wisdom gained by introspection and observation.

This is what the revolutionary groups recognize as well. They do not call for a drastic change in the way we live our lives, they just want the ability to collect and spend the tax money we pay to the government in order to do so.

It would be wonderful to think that the emergence of radical environmentalism would have produced some sort of alternative vision for our collective future at this point in the (end)game, but it hasn't, and perhaps can't. Here we are, 30+ years after the first Earth Day, and the most extreme change most people can envision in their lives would be to drive hybrid cars to their wretched, demeaning jobs. (Just for the sake of enlightenment – there are regular, internal-combustion engine cars that are more fuel-efficient than hybrids. You IDIOTS!)

Youth are at least acknowledging the horrors they will have to face during their lifetimes, but even though they are questioning the consumerist lifestyle, what they generally come up with is more of the same – like riding bikes to their wretched, demeaning, collectively-owned-and-managed jobs, with some recycling thrown in along the way.

It's clear to me that what we are suffering from is a failure of imagination. We cannot envision a world, or a way of living, that is vastly different (personally rewarding, nurturing, co-operative, gentle on our planet) because it is beyond the reach of our imagination.

At least part of the blame for this is the prevalence of Pragmatism in most educated people's minds. Pragmatism is a way of thinking that is meant to defeat imaginative thinking and stifle creativity. We are told to be "practical" or "realistic." This is a way of thinking that is inherently submissive. It is how a slave justifies her continued obsequience to her master, or a person trapped in an abusive relationship rationalizes her consent to remain in the relationship. Pragmatism discards the immense possibilities for the future in favor of those more immediately obtainable. In this era of dwindling resources, Pragmatism is the logic of gradual, mass suicide, which rejects life and its infinite potential.

So few of us find any meaning, comfort, or reward in our present lives, yet we cling to them. It's all we know. Pragmatically thinking, there are powerful forces in place – economics, religion, police and military, to name a few – which enforce consumerism, to ensure we do not wander astray of the Ruling Powers' plans for our lives. This is a philosophy of fear. We are afraid of what will happen to us if we turn away from economics as our source of survival. We are afraid of how the police will treat us. We are afraid of the concentration camps and prisons our government is busy building to contend with the future unrest which will arise as the economy continues to take more from the majority of the population and hands it over to those already massively wealthy.

But, by abandoning the workers here in favor of cheaper labor overseas, the Ruling Powers have left us little choice but to look for answers elsewhere. Their economic models just do not work, and require government intervention every now and then in order to continue to exist. While preaching to the voters that it is tragically inappropriate - even evil - to suggest the government provide healthcare to its people (the way almost every nation on Earth already does), the public mouthpieces of the monied elite demand taxpayer money to protect their investment swindles.

When the current economic meltdown began to spiral out of control, the voting public expressed their disapproval for any sort of bailout for the embezzlers and con-men responsible for the mess. Most public officials acknowledged that their constituents were voicing their opposition to such subsidies by a margin of 10-1. Yet there was never even a hint of doubt that the swindlers would get the funds they demanded. The needs and opinions of the general public mean nothing to the people in power in this country. Money – huge, mountainous piles of money inaccessible to the vast majority of the population – is what this economy is all about.

And where is the outrage over this debacle – the greatest single instance of theft in recorded history? The public has moved on to other issues, mostly because they have to work so much harder in order to maintain their standard of living. Also, many of them were suckered into believing that a changing of the guard in the White House could potentially lead to a re-assessment of priorities by the government.

What most people desire is a fix to the economic ills the nation is experiencing? They want what they see on TV. They desire to purchase the good things in life – a home and everything that makes a home life comfortable and desirable. They want this without having to sacrifice their privileged positions as first world consumers in order to achieve it.

If we are not capable of envisioning a life different from the one handed down to us, or the one depicted in advertisements and sitcoms, it's because any sort of alternative vision of how to organize our lives has not been presented to us.

The one model we have now (Work or Starve!) was originally forced on people through overwhelming military force. Where people did not acquiesce to such a lifestyle, campaigns of genocide were – and still are to this day – conducted until the resisters are unable to continue with their ways of providing for themselves outside of Western economics.

Instead of radically transforming our lives so that we can meet our needs without over-taxing what our environment can provide for us, even the visionaries among us can only seem to envision more of the same – only "New and Improved", or "Sustainable!"

This society is horribly sick and twisted. Even now, as our elected (or self-appointed) leaders demand human sacrifice (the war in Iraq, the War on Drugs, etc.), many people refuse to question the values that shape our society. And how can we, when so many of us require pharmaceuticals, booze or other coping mechanisms in order to function in our day-to-day roles? Our consumer-driven way of life is destroying us as human beings as well as our planet's ability to support life, and still we reproduce our place within it, day after wretched day. What the fuck is wrong with us?

This may sound silly, but it's something that bothered me as a child and pisses me off to this day: Some of the iconic cartoons I grew up watching on Saturday morning served to re-enforce consumerism in the viewers by presenting it as both natural and never-changing. From the Flintstone's Stone-Age to the futuristic lifestyle of the Jetsons, the lives depicted were little different from the ones being lived by the viewers. The level of technology may have changed from one show to the next, but the consumerist lifestyle was never any different: Work, buy, try to get ahead, buy some more!

How can we break out of this cycle, when every element of society forces us to accept it as some sort of natural occurrence? It's not enough that some of us attempt to think outside of the proverbial box – we have to think beyond the means used to produce boxes.

The imperative we face now – those of us who can see beyond the mechanisms of the Ruling Powers – is to enact our visions of very different ways of relating to the places where we dwell. In order to do so, we must band together with strong-willed and like-minded people in order to produce working models of how we think life could be, were there not coercive forces severely limiting our options.

It's also important that more than one model of a different society be created. There should be as many as there are people committed to making their visions manifest in reality. There are, after all, many different ecosystems here on Earth, and each provides for different challenges for the people who desire to live within them, based on their unique attributes, as well as the amount of damage industrialism has inflicted upon them.

It is not difficult to live on this planet. It has nurtured an astonishing variety of such ecosystems capable of providing for every imaginable need a human population requires in order to thrive. Everything we need is available almost everywhere, if we only know where (and how) to look for it.

The greatest danger and difficulty will be found in the struggle to rid ourselves of the control the Ruling Powers possess in enforcing their lifestyle upon the rest of us. They will use every method of coercion and violence available to them to either force us back into the vast herd of their docile servants or kill us if we will not be enslaved. As it stands now, they seem to be poised to jettison the bulk of humanity, as tremendous numbers of us are no longer required to fulfill their needs. To use the U.S. as just the most glaring example: Our standard of living has (just in my lifetime) gone from being equal to or above that of any nation on Earth to being "better than Somalia." The U.S. ceased being a First World nation when it was crushed under the heel of the Reagan regime. And the bottom of this downward trend is nowhere to be seen. Food prices continue to rise, while people's ability to purchase food continues to erode – even among those still legally employed.

What we truly require in these times are courage and resolve.

We must turn away from slavish obsequience to this deadend society. Because we are all but blind to any other vision of a society, there is no blueprint or pathway prepared for us to follow in order to establish a radically different means of conducting our lives. But we must turn away from the one we are trapped in now. In doing so, we will suffer - and not a little. But not to do so is suicide. We can create options for ourselves and our offspring – human beings are clever and adaptable creatures - and we need to do it immediately!

The one issue that continually comes to my mind is the abolition of economics. At the very least, the use of money as a means of exchange and accumulation should be abandoned. There is absolutely no sane argument for continuing along that path. It has only brought about severe limitations in the way most people conduct their lives, while rewarding thieves, thugs, warlords and swindlers.

If that is not readily apparent to you, you should remind yourself every day that during this economic debacle, where over one-third of America's accumulated wealth has evaporated in less than one year, the oil corporations and their subsidiaries are recording unprecedented profits. Then, ask yourself a question: Is this something worth the sacrifice of our children?

ABOUT THE AUTHOR

Rob los Ricos is the beer-drinkingest, shopliftingest, controlled-substance possessingest, riotingest, assaulting-a-cop-with-a-rock-ingest, rantingest anarchist writer wandering the streets and mountains of Cascadia to have come out of the state of Texas since Albert Parsons. Believe that!

THE EARTH LIBERATION FRONT AND REVOLUTION

LESLIE JAMES PICKERING

LESLIE JAMES PICKERING

This Country Must Change

A crucial factor in my support of the Earth Liberation Front has been the effort's relationship with revolutionary struggle. I've worked to present the organization as a contemporary phase of an ongoing legacy of revolutionary struggle in America, but there are also indications to the contrary.

For well over a decade, the Earth Liberation Front has remained in a position that can be understood either as an environmental effort, or as a current incarnation of revolutionary struggle. The list of costly arsons attributed to the organization has earned its place atop the FBI's inventory of domestic threats to national security. So, is this guerrilla warfare, or radical direct action protest? Is the organization a developing revolutionary effort, or special interest extremism?

This distinction is critical not just in gaining a true understanding of the Earth Liberation Front's position and significance, but is a crucial issue as we prepare for the struggle ahead.

There is a long and complicated history of revolutionary struggle here in America. Individuals and organizations have fought for revolution in the United States on a more or less continuous basis throughout this country's history.

In relatively recent memory, revolutionary struggles have sprung up from the civil rights movement and the movement against the Vietnam War. These examples originated from efforts looking to end a specific war and to gain equal rights for a racial segment of the population, yet portions of these movements clearly reevaluated their scope and activities and began struggling for revolution in America.

As Students for a Democratic Society spread across college campuses in the 1960s, the organization's scope grew to include the interests of civil rights and ending the Vietnam War. By the end of the decade, offshoots of the organization, most famously the Weathermen, embraced guerrilla warfare in a struggle for revolution in America. The Weather Underground Organization left little to doubt over its intentions as it announced, "a declaration of a state of war," to join "people fighting Amerikan imperialism," "adapting the classic guerrilla strategy of the Viet Cong and the urban guerrilla strategy of the Tupamaros to our own," "strategic position behind enemy lines to join forces in the destruction of the empire."[1]

Malcolm X abandoned the black separatist strategy of the Nation of Islam and publicly promoted revolutionary struggle by means of guerrilla warfare to bring about the liberation of blacks in America. Malcolm spoke this message powerfully at large speaking engagements and in national media until he was assassinated on stage. His words and actions inspired a large number of individuals and organizations, including the Black Panther Party who armed itself to defend its communities against brutal, racist attacks from the Police, and became an international symbol of black liberation. After federal law enforcement launched a murderous campaign to repress the Party, a number of members, including Assata Shakur, joined the Black Liberation Army, engaging in guerrilla warfare as a means of revolutionary struggle. In their first communiqué, the Black Liberation Army wrote, "the domestic armed forces of racism and oppression will be confronted with the guns of the Black Liberation Army, who will mete out in the tradition of Malcolm and all true revolutionaries real justice. We are revolutionary justice."[2]

After growing frustrated with involvement in anti-war protests and student strikes at Columbia University, Sam Melville led a guerrilla bombing spree that devastated skyscrapers in Manhattan housing the offices of the U.S. Army, Selective Service, Chase Manhattan Bank, Marine Midland Bank, Standard Oil, General Motors, and others, all within a three-month period. In their communiqués, the group referred to their actions as, part of a "war in the U.S.", "striking blows for liberation", "fighting to rid the world of American domination and exploitation", and "fighting for revolution."[3]

The case of the Earth Liberation Front is similar to the cases of the Weather Underground Organization, Black Liberation Army and Sam Melville's group in a number of ways. Through strategies encompassing anything from educational campaigns to sensational acts of civil disobedience, the young environmental movement slowly gained popularity. As the efforts that pioneered the environmentalism gained public acceptance in the 1980s, new organizations, such as Earth First! began to blend strategies of civil disobedience and guerrilla warfare, sabotaging property utilized to destroy and exploit the Earth. By 1996, The Earth Liberation Front had emerged, combining Earth First!-styled sabotage with a brand of arson then associated with the underground Animal Liberation Front. Within a few years, the Earth Liberation Front had modeled its own brand of guerrilla sabotage, embodying the most costly spree in American history.

Yet while the actions of Earth Liberation Front are

arguably on par with, or even surpass, a number of past revolutionary efforts, the organization his fallen just shy of producing a revolutionary ideology, let alone a revolutionary declaration of war.

Beltane, 1997

Welcome to the struggle of all species to be free. We are the burning rage of this dying planet. The war of greed ravages the Earth and species die out every day. ELF works to speed up the collapse of industry, to scare the rich, and to undermine the foundations of the state. We embrace social and deep-ecology as a practical resistance movement. We have to show the enemy that we are serious about defending what is sacred. Together we have teeth and claws to match our dreams. Our greatest weapons are imagination and the ability to strike when least expected.

Since 1992 a series of Earth-nights and Halloween smashes has mushroomed around the world. 1,000's of bulldozers, power lines, computer systems, buildings and valuable equipment have been composted. Many ELF actions have been censored to prevent our bravery from inciting others to take action.

We take inspiration from Luddites, Levellers, Diggers, the Autonome squatter movement, the ALF, the Zapatistas, and the little people – those mischievous elves of lore. Authorities can't see us because they don't believe in elves. We are practically invisible. We have no command structure, no spokespersons, no office, just small groups working separately seeking vulnerable targets and practicing our craft.

Many elves are moving to the Pacific Northwest and other sacred areas. Some elves will leave surprises as they go. Find your family! And lets dance as we make ruins of the corporate money system.

This initial communiqué of the Earth Liberation Front

addresses environmental concerns with a hint of revolutionary ideology in the assertion that the group works to "undermine the foundations of the state" and "make ruins of the corporate money system." There is nothing in the Beltane communiqué about the responsibility of government to protect the people from the threats that are posed by the destruction and exploitation of our environment. There is no direct mention of any understanding that the system must be overthrown to bring about the liberation of the Earth. While these notions are arguably implied, the lack of a clearly defined allegiance with revolutionary struggle lends credibility to concerns that the organization believes that its sabotage adequately answers the exploitation committed against the Earth, or that the organization simply doesn't have any further analysis.

In theory, the Earth Liberation Front is a loose network of cells, each consisting of a small number of people, which have no contact or awareness of each other's membership and no overarching hierarchy. The cells act on an undefined ideology, under three very basic guidelines.[4] Each cell is free to take action where it sees fit, so long as the action fits within these guidelines.

This structure makes it difficult, if not impossible, for law enforcement to eliminate the organization, because the capture of one cell or member wouldn't, theoretically, lead to the capture of any other cells of the organization. Without a governing body leading the organization, law enforcement are unable to destroy it by eliminating its leadership and a new cell can form any place, any time.

On the other hand, this structure can create a leadership void. The lack of a unifying and decision-making body can lead to stagnation and obsolescence. With no defined method for change within the organization, evolutions happen organically, if they happen at all. In this scenario, outside factors, such as arrests and state repression, are at least as likely to have an effect on the organization as anything organically emerging from within.

In addition, antiauthoritarianism is essentially a principle of the Earth Liberation Front, embodied in its non-hierarchal structure. If initiative and skill were to elevate any individual or group to a level of authority within the organization, this principle could work to discredit and invalidate that authority. Again, this serves to strengthen the organization in ways but has not brought the Earth Liberation Front to the point of proclaiming or its allegiance with revolutionary struggle.

Since one of the organization's guidelines called for actions causing as much economic damage as possible to environmental offenders, the Earth Liberation Front Press Office[5] concluded that an operational strategy of the Earth Liberation Front is economic sabotage.

The theory behind economic sabotage, in the case of the Earth Liberation Front, would be that government and other capitalist interests were destroying and exploiting the Earth for the sole interest of making money. Therefore, the Earth Liberation Front would work to remove the profitability of environmental exploitation by costing environmental offenders considerable damages on an ongoing basis, thereby driving environmentally destructive entities to reconsider their actions or putting them out of business entirely.

In many ways this strategy makes sense in combination with a range of other strategies working in unison to protect the Earth. The Press Office often argued that economic sabotage made more sense than sticking strictly to the general strategies of the mainstream environmental movement, which have continually failed to solve the overall environmental problem. However, at the scale of environmental exploitation and destruction that we have seen in recent decades, this kind of economic sabotage would need to be practiced at an incredible frequency to protect the Earth on its own.

While this attempt to clarify and gain public support for the operational strategies of the Earth Liberation Front was a positive step for the Press Office, it was far from adequate. Economic sabotage identifies capitalism as the driving force behind environmental devastation but it only answers the evils of capitalism by becoming a nuisance in the scenario. While capitalism has been criticized in communiqués, no strategy was openly embraced by the Earth Liberation Front to combat this motivating force behind the destruction of the Earth.

The Press Office also understood the Earth Liberation Front as operating a strategy of armed propaganda. Similar to many past revolutionary efforts, the Earth Liberation Front was taking action to inspire others to take action. The organization did not believe that its actions would liberate the Earth on their own, but would inspire and give hope to countless others who would then lead the struggle forward.

In the cases of the Weather Underground Organization,

the Black Liberation Army and Sam Melville's group, which all openly espoused the need for a revolution in America, armed propaganda was a logical step along the road to revolution. In the case of the Earth Liberation Front, being the most radical organization in the environmental movement with no clear sense of further action towards liberation, armed propaganda may have only called for people to engage in more armed propaganda.

Without a strategy embracing the need for a revolutionary struggle to overthrow the existing power structure of society, organizations like the Earth Liberation Front can suffer from being categorized as special interest extremists.

The charge of 'special interest extremism' works to pigeonhole the effort into a category of 'extremism,' which is considered unjustified and frightening to a significant percentage of the population, while defining its cause as a 'special interest' and unimportant to the average person. Branded as a special interest extremist organization, the Earth Liberation Front it is not viewed as an effort to do what is needed to resolve issues important to each one of us, such as protecting our ability to survive on this planet, but an effort that goes to terrifying lengths towards a cause that is of no importance to the general population.

The objective of the Earth Liberation Front is vital to all of us. The Earth is our biosphere, our life support system. As the Earth is destroyed, so are we. The ominous importance of environmental protection to each and every living being on Earth is potentially the most compelling argument for a worldwide revolution that could be voiced. It needs to be heard.

The closest the Earth Liberation Front has come to proclaiming allegiance with revolutionary struggle was after the $700,000 arson of the United States Forest Service Northeast Research Station in Irvine, Pennsylvania on August 11, 2002.

The communiqué read in part, "Segments of this global revolutionary movement are no longer limiting their revolutionary potential by adhering to flawed, inconsistent 'non-violent' ideology… Where it is necessary, we will no longer hesitate to pick up the gun to implement justice… The diverse efforts of this revolutionary force cannot be contained, and will only continue to intensify as we are brought face to face with the oppressor in inevitable, violent confrontation." [6]

The targeting of a government agency, especially the United States Forest Service, was not uncommon for the Earth Liberation Front, or the broader radical environmental struggle.

Arsons at the United States Department of the Interior Bureau of Land Management ($120,978.61 in damages on 11/30/1997), the United States Department of Agriculture Animal Plant Health Inspection Service ($1,200,000 in damages on 6/21/1998), the United States Department of Agriculture Animal Damage Control ($500,000 in damages on 6/21/1998), United States Department of the Interior Bureau of Land Management ($207,497.60 in damages on 10/15/2001), as well as several actions taking place on various State Universities, have all been claimed by the Earth Liberation Front. Earth First! had set a precedent for waging environmental campaigns against these and other governmental agencies prior to the Earth Liberation Front.

The first major act of sabotage attributed to the Earth Liberation Front took place at a United States government facility. The arson at the United States Forest Service's Oakridge Ranger Station in Oregon on October 30, 1996 caused an estimated total loss of $5,074,189. Two days earlier, trucks belonging to the United States Forest Service were torched at the Ranger Station in Detroit, Oregon. An incendiary device placed on the building's roof that failed to ignite was found along with graffiti including the words, "Earth Liberation Front." Damages there were estimated at approximately $21,500.[7]

The communiqué from the arson of the United States Department of the Interior Bureau of Land Management on November 29, 1997, is a good example of what could be considered more standard environmental language from the organization, "This hypocrisy and genocide against the horse nation will not go unchallenged! The practice of rounding up and auctioning wild horses must be stopped. The practice of grazing cattle on public lands must be stopped. The time to take action is now. From an investigation like the Associated Press', to writing the BLM, to an action like ours, you can help stop the slaughter and save our Mother Earth."[8]

In the Bureau of Land Management communiqué, the clearly stated objective of the arson is to "challenge" and "stop" the practices of "rounding up and auctioning off wild horses" to slaughter and "grazing cattle on public lands." The only broader objective stated in the communiqué is to "save our Mother Earth." The communiqué suggests that arson, as well as investigative reporting and letter writing, are suitable tactics to achieve these goals. Outside of the use of arson as a guerrilla tactic, there is little here to suggest a revolutionary strategy behind the action.

167

The Forest Service Research Station communiqué explains that the facility was targeted because of its, "blatant disregard for the sanctity of life," "indifference to strong public opposition," "irrevocable acts of extreme violence... against the Earth," and that the agency was responsible for, "threats posed to life in the Allegheny Forest by proposed timber sales, oil drilling and greed driven manipulation of nature."[9] The communiqué also, however, reserved paragraphs for much broader revolutionary rhetoric, not only championing arson attacks, but arguing that it is justified to, "pick up the gun" and, "fight for our lives" in an "inevitable, violent confrontation."

What makes this communiqué stand out is its posture. While references to Malcolm X and threats of increased retaliation are present in other Earth Liberation Front communiqués, none went quite as far as the Forest Service Research Station communiqué in mentioning revolution, denouncing nonviolence and suggesting future evolutions in strategy.

Yet, while the communiqué pronounced the Earth Liberation Front as a "revolutionary force" allied with a "global revolutionary movement," it is only one among dozens of communiqués from the organization and remains shy of the kind of allegiance to revolutionary struggle that can be seen from the Weather Underground Organization, the Black Liberation Army, Sam Melville's group and numerous other examples.

In the first several years, we saw the strengths of the Earth Liberation Front bearing fruit. Actions were steady, if not increasing in frequency, while impact was improving in both economic damages and publicity. The Earth Liberation Front was striking devastating blows to impressive targets and its popularity was on the rise.

Since, we have seen the weaknesses of the organization play out. The frequency of Earth Liberation Front actions has drastically declined and little strategic evolution has been apparent. Not only have some members been captured and convicted, but also a number have turned state's witness, snitching on each other in selfish and pathetic pleas for mercy. The effect that all of this has had on the public support for the Earth Liberation Front is considerable.

The decline of the Earth Liberation Front over the last several years is disturbing. A level of state repression was focused on the Press Office and supportive individuals and communities for years before the decline of Earth Liberation Front actions.

This Country Must Change

Arrests of members didn't occur until years after the decline began. So, direct connections between repression and decline are questionable. What became of the inspiration and hope that the organization once bestowed on so many of us? Why did Earth Liberation Front activity suddenly decline shortly after the turn of the century?

According to the Government's Sentencing Memorandum from the FBI's Operation Backfire cases, the Backfire defendants were responsible for a good percentage of Earth Liberation Front activity between 1996 and 2001. Their cell(s), the Memorandum claims, fell apart largely due to internal issues. Inactivity of these individuals following the collapse of their cell(s) could have been a significant factor in the decline of Earth Liberation Front activity that occurred at that time. Other factors in the decline could be the lack of a fully functioning Press Office, which first shut down on September 5th, 2001, and the sudden anti-terrorism hysteria in America following September 11th, 2001.

At its peak, the Earth Liberation Front was averaging well over a million dollars in damages per arson and was striking at a near monthly frequency. News of the organization rapidly spread from local media markets in the Pacific Northwest, into national media based in Los Angeles then New York, and had begun to break as international news as we entered the new century.

Could the decline of the Earth Liberation Front have been influenced by limitations of the organization's scope and capabilities made apparent by mid-2001? After a half decade of actions, a recipe for considerable economic damages and substantial media coverage was apparent, but the effort failed to provide further possibilities or an ideology with the capability to truly resolve the environmental problem.

The fundamental issue is that a revolution in America, and throughout a good portion of the rest of the world, is necessary to bring about the changes that the Earth Liberation Front struggles for. It is the governmental system in this country, and similarly capitalist-oriented systems across the globe, which foster and enable the levels of exploitation and destruction against the Earth that the Earth Liberation Front condemn. Reformist environmental efforts will continue to have insufficient overall impact so long as we allow a system that treats the Earth as a commodity to reign. Economic sabotage and armed propaganda are powerful, but in order to be sound strategies, they need to be practiced under an ideology committed to revolutionary struggle.

Furthermore, as important as the protection of the Earth is, it is far from the only cause worthy of our attention and active involvement. The Earth Liberation Front recognized this through a number of their communiqués. Evolving into a revolutionary struggle would enable us to better act in solidarity with other efforts for liberation. When placed in the arena of revolutionary struggle, the Earth Liberation Front is part of a righteous legacy, which includes the Weather Underground Organization, the Black Liberation Army, the Black Panther Party, Malcolm X, Assata Shakur, Sam Melville and many, many others, which is exactly where the Earth Liberation Front belongs.

The fact remains that the system we live under exists to exploit us, as well as our Earth. If we allow it to continue through our own inaction, or by failing to engage in revolutionary struggle, the outcome is our own. Revolution is liberation.

(Endnotes)
[1] Harold Jacobs, <u>Weatherman</u> (Ramparts Press, Inc., 1970) 509-511.
[2] Robert Daley, <u>Target Blue: An Insiders View of the N.Y.P.D.</u> (New York: Delacorte Press, 1973) p. 77.
[3] Leslie James Pickering, <u>Mad Bomber Melville</u> (Portland: Arissa Media Group, 1997).
[4] The Earth Liberation Front guidelines are as follows:
1) To cause as much economic damage as possible to a given entity that is profiting off the destruction of the natural environment and life for selfish greed and profit.
2) To educate the public on the atrocities committed against the environment and life.
3) To take all necessary precautions against harming life
[5] The North American Earth Liberation Front Press Office was co-founded by the author under the following mission:
The North American Earth Liberation Front Press Office (NAELFPO) is a legal, above ground news service dedicated to exposing the political and social motives behind the covert direct actions of the ELF. The NAELFPO receives anonymous communiqués from the ELF and distributes the message to the media and the public throughout North America. The NAELFPO provides a public face ideologically in support of the ELF and similar acts of economic sabotage against those who profit from the destruction of the natural environment. The NAELFPO is contacted by the media and public internationally to provide information on the political and social motives of the ELF actions, and the tactical necessity of covert direct action. Due to the work of the NAELFPO, individuals who are looking to learn more about these issues have a place to turn, and the public who may be

ignorant to the actions and motives of the ELF are exposed to more frequent and in-depth coverage in the media.

[6] Leslie James Pickering, The Earth Liberation Front: 1997-2002 (Portland: Arissa Media Group, 2007) p. 38-39.

[7] Government's Sentencing Memorandum, In the United States District Court for the District of Oregon, Case Numbers CR 06-60069-AA, CR 06-60070-AA, CR 06-60071-AA, CR 06-60078-AA, CR 06-60079-AA, CR 06-60080-AA, CR 06-60120-AA, CR 06-60122-AA, CR 06-60123-AA, CR 06-60124-AA, CR 06-60125-AA, CR 06-60126-AA (United States Department of Justice) p. 7-10.

[8] The Earth Liberation Front: 1997-2002 p. 10-11.

[9] The Earth Liberation Front: 1997-2002 p. 38-39

Editor's Note
The North American Earth Liberation Front Press Office can be reached online at www.elfpressoffice.org.

ABOUT THE AUTHOR

Leslie James Pickering was a Founder and Spokesperson for the North American Earth Liberation Front Press Office, serving with the organization from early 2000 until the summer of 2002. During this period the Press Office sustained two raids by the Federal Bureau of Investigation, the Bureau of Alcohol Tobacco and Firearms and local law enforcement agencies, responded to over a half dozen grand jury subpoenas, conducted public presentations, produced booklets, newspapers, magazines, and a video on the Earth Liberation Front and handled the public release of communiqués for dozens of the most vital Earth Liberation Front actions.

Through the Press Office, Leslie was the editor of *Resistance, the Journal of the North American Earth Liberation Front Press Office*, and many other independently produced materials regarding the Earth Liberation Front. Leslie has handled countless local, national and international media inquires, resulting in articles in *The New York Times, The Washington Times, The Los Angeles Times, USA Today, Christian Science Monitor, Rolling Stone, The Village Voice* and many more, conducted interviews with ABC, NBC, CNN, FOX, CBC, BBC, National Geographic TV and many others, and has given lectures at American University, Lewis & Clark College, Saint Michael's University, Furman University, Bard College, New York University, Fresno State College, Macalester College, University of West Los Angeles, Princeton University, Mercyhurst College, Syracuse University, Buffalo State College and others.

Leslie's most recent book, *Mad Bomber Melville*, the biography of Vietnam War era revolutionary Sam Melville, was published in 2007 and his first book, *Earth Liberation Front 1997-2002* was published in 2003 by Arissa Media Group. He has written articles in the *Earth First! Journal* and *Igniting a Revolution: Voices in Defense of the Earth* published on AK Press and others. He has a California High School Equivalency Diploma, a BA in Community Organizing and Journalism and a MA in History of American Social Justice Struggles and Journalism from Goddard College. Leslie lives in his hometown of Buffalo, NY.

THIS COUNTRY MUST CHANGE

JAAN LAAMAN

JAAN LAAMAN

This Country Must Change

"This country must change." Most people in the United States would agree with this statement today. The 2008 presidential race certainly latched on to this slogan of change, even if the official candidates' idea of change didn't come close to what most of the public wants and needs.

As a life long activist who came of age in the late 1960s, I think I may have a useful perspective on revolutionary change as a concept and some thoughts on what we should be trying to change now.

There are moments in history when change becomes a dominant force in the social and political life of a country. In my teens and early adulthood, as I became active in opposing the Vietnam War and pushing for social justice, the idea of then current and continuing change was assumed and expected by most people. There was a lot of debate, even disagreement about what to change and how to achieve it. There was very little disagreement about the need for change and there was a feeling all across the country that big changes were coming. Hope and expectation are positive factors that help feed a movement, and this is true regardless of how things ultimately develop.

If we look at the U.S., and the world for that matter today, the need for change is obvious. The world is also more connected than ever. The role America plays and the problems we create and confront are also global. Meanwhile, there seems to be a new understanding, maybe even a movement emerging, which includes different issues and problems, but agrees on the need for real changes. Barack Obama's presidential campaign also seems to be evidence of this desire for change. Whether Obama's ideas and plans for changes meets the public's desire or the planet's needs for new approaches and methods, is at least very questionable if not doubtful. What is not in doubt is that Obama and his campaign tapped into a growing social discontent and a growing hope for a new direction.

CHANGE

Before we look at areas where big changes are needed, let's examine what we mean by changes and reforms, let's examine the process of change, including revolutionary change.

First of all, change is universal and omnipresent. Everything in our lives and in our world is always undergoing change. The only constant, is constant change. We can also say that change is dualistic. There are internal changes within us and changes in the external world around us. We'll come back to internal changes, but first let us take a brief but sharp look at the process of change.

Looking at change scientifically and dialectically, we should recognize that everything, all reality, matter, life and thought is connected and in constant motion or change. This motion has a shape. Things arise and develop, then disintegrate and die away. This is particularly obvious in living things, like a person and in combinations like a society.

Change is both quantitative (change in size, number, quantity) and qualitative (change in substance, form, quality). The quantitative step by step changes at some point lead to an abrupt and rapid qualitative fundamental change of substance or quality.

One final point to keep in mind is that the primary basis of any change is internal. Change develops and springs from inside the thing, person or situation in question. External factors, the surrounding conditions, are also important, but the actual change comes from the inside. The internal factors or contradictions within a thing, person or situation is the basis of the change in that thing, person or situation. The external factors are the conditions under which the change occurs. External factors can help or hinder the change, but the change happens based on the factors inside of the person, thing or situation we are looking at.

Understanding that change is a basic reality of all existence, the question is what kind of changes will happen and do we want to happen, and who benefits from them? Turning to reform and fundamental change, we see that reforms can advance or hold back more substantial change.

REFORMS

From a revolutionary perspective, a perspective that sees the need for significant structural changes in the present political and economic system in the country, reforms can be steps on the road toward real change or obstacles preventing it. In a negative sense, reforms reinforce the system. A reform that brings some relief to a sector of the public, can help to solidify the idea that the system works, that change is possible under the rules and order that exists. This works against the effort toward deeper, more fundamental and revolutionary change. Reforms can work to block revolution. Reforms also often have the potential to dishearten the public. Even if the reform creates some improvement for some people, it was done by "the government," "the politician," "the system," or by some power somewhere else. In this sense, reforms do not empower people or give them the feeling and hope that they can challenge and change the system.

Conversely, reforms can be positive steps for more fundamental change. Sometimes reforms can create popular space, more freedom for organizing, and public activity. Sometimes reforms can push back police power, police abuses and excessive government intrusion into people's lives. Reforms, especially if they are the result of a long and large-scale popular struggle where many have marched, organized and suffered government repression, can create a real spirit of possibility. Not only will people take heart and credit for achieving the specific reform, but the idea that more can be done is created. Winning changes after a popular struggle builds enthusiasm in people and sets the stage for more people to be willing to struggle and take risks. Victories build spirit.

There is an important element to reform work, namely that revolutionary activists involved in and helping to lead popular reform oriented efforts, must always be honest with the people right from the beginning. Revolutionaries must make clear that all the marching and work and even being successful in making the government or corporation accept the people's demands, is not the end goal and should not be the end of the struggle. In other words, winning the reform is a good thing, but should be understood as just one step in the larger effort to create more fundamental changes.

FUNDAMENTAL CHANGES

Fundamental change means creating a more just and equitable system that will really serve the people's interests. It means a new arrangement where the people will be much more in control of their lives, their government and economic system.

The United States puts forth volumes of self important and self-aggrandizing talk about democracy, freedom and voting. In fact, an honest assessment of American elections, primaries, the two major parties and the media's coverage of all these things today shows that they are set up to discredit, prohibit, and block real fundamental change in this country. It is a system that uses voting to make the outcome of voting largely predictable and acceptable to the economic and political elites.

We can only speculate, and we should, on how major fundamental, that is revolutionary, changes and advances will be achieved. If we look at history, we can draw some lessons. Big popular movements organizing and pushing for change are needed. The movement, its leaders, activists and grassroots must be aware, or come to realize, that the struggle has to go beyond the "rules" and the "established way." Opposition and resistance movements cannot allow the ruling state system to set the limits on what is acceptable opposition. Every freedom struggle draws its own lines based on its own conditions, time and place.

A final historical lesson is that a movement for real change has to achieve a level of force. Sometimes even war is needed. The United States began its existence through our Declaration of Independence and a war against British colonialism. Founded as a slave owning republic with a limited electorate, the Civil War advanced the U.S. into a more just and open society. The Suffragist movement in the early 1900s, pushed and protested and finally advanced and achieved voting rights for women, although primarily, at the time, only white women. In the early 1900s, and again especially in the 1930s, American workers organized, had strikes, fought innumerable battles, some with guns in hand, and finally gained some rights to join unions and improve their wages and conditions of work.

The 1950s and 1960s saw the growth and struggle of the Civil Rights movement. Black people fought for their legal rights, the right to vote and against Jim Crow discrimination. They fought against night rider Klan and police terror. All these examples, except for the actual founding of the U.S.A., were reformist advancements. Not even the Civil War, nor any of these other struggles, was an actual revolution where the old capitalist ruling class was kicked out of power and a new more democratic and just working class centered system was initiated. Throughout American history, and similarly with other countries' histories, struggle, force, and even uprising and war have been necessary to bring about significant major change.

There is a revolutionary principle governing the process of change. In any country's, kingdom's or empire's existence, there develops a period of crisis, "revolutionary crisis." This is most simply defined as the situation when the rulers can no longer rule or keep control in their usual accepted manner. On the other side, large and growing numbers of the people being ruled, no longer can or are willing to accept being ruled and controlled as they have been. War, major economic breakdown, large-scale catastrophe or climate change, are usually present and big factors when a revolutionary period of crisis develops in a country.

There is no principle or guarantee that a system will fall or a revolution will succeed when a revolutionary crisis develops. The fed-up and hungry-for-change population, their revolutionary organizations, activists and leaders have to seize the moment of potential advancement and be smart, brave and determined enough to push the struggle all the way to ending the old corporate, capitalist rule to begin a new system and a new day. Of course, the more experienced, organized, prepared and established the popular revolutionary organizations are among the public, the more likely we are to advance and succeed.

There is no blue print or secret software that lays out the steps to winning a freedom struggle or revolution. Successful 20th century revolutions in other countries, as well as earlier major popular struggles in our country, do have important lessons for us today. More importantly though, every struggle must be based on and understood from its own conditions, time and place.

I believe there are three key things necessary for all modern revolutionary struggles. First, we need revolutionary theory. We need to scientifically analyze and understand the overall society and specific problems that must be overcome. Dialectical and Historical Materialism is the scientific method to view any situation or problem. It is a tool to analyze social reality. We need to break things down and see them in their component parts in order to, hopefully, come up with plans that can successfully tackle the problem. Scientific revolutionary theory shouldn't be seen or used as a dogma, but it should be an aid to action.

We also need serious, principled, and dedicated revolutionary organization. An organization will enhance, extend and multiply the effort of even the best individual activist. In today's reality of police intrusion and power, building and sustaining a revolutionary party or front is no easy task, but it is possible and needed. A number of Socialist, Marxist, Revolutionary Nationalist and Anarchist parties and groups do exist, and some have been around for decades. Personally, I think they all do some good work, and I am glad they are out there. So far, I do not see the one organization or coalition that is providing clear leadership and voice for our overall struggle. Perhaps it will come from one or a combination of existing organizations.

Perhaps it is up to you and your close activist friends to begin and create it.

Finally, I think revolutionary unity is always needed. Ideological struggle and differences about strategy and tactics are real. Sometimes they lead to more clarity and better actions. Sometimes organizations get very negative criticizing other revolutionary groups. Personally, I think we should always put our main emphasis, time and effort into criticizing the government and system, not other activists.

The United States is a very large, developed and established country. But we, the people of America, have an absolute and natural right and an ever-growing real need for fundamental change. Revolutionary change is not just for somewhere else, for South Africa or Nepal or Venezuela. We have the right and responsibility, especially to our children and future and the future of our planet, to imagine, to work for, and to create a new American revolution, a new system run by and for working people.

WHY MAJOR CHANGE IS HARD

Why has progressive and positive, let alone revolutionary change, been so hard to achieve? The United States, like all countries, has an economic, social and political elite, a ruling class. We all know that membership in this ruling class is based on extreme wealth. Direct ownership, as well as the control of huge wealth is the basis of power for the ruling capitalist class in the U.S. Most of this wealth and resulting power is inherited and maintained in a very small number of families. New individuals and families do enter into this top layer of privilege and power, but their numbers are tiny.

A small number of actual ruling class members directly get involved in running the government. We've seen Rockefeller and Dupont family Senators and so on. Most of the actual politicians, generals, Cabinet members, even Presidents, are loyal, tested, and well paid managers who actually run the government and system for the ruling class. The entire superstructure of the U.S., the government structures, the major private institutions, business institutions, foundations, education system, the major corporate information and entertainment media, are all designed and structured to perpetuate business as usual, to perpetuate a capitalist system, topped by a ruling class.

This Country Must Change

Within the confines of the American system, change does occur. They have made the practice of elections and voting almost a fetishistic ritual. At the same time the system still has mechanisms that disenfranchise millions of people. For example, today there are up to 8 or 9 million men and women, prisoners, people on parole and ex-prisoners who cannot vote. Elections bring new faces, sometimes even revised or new policies and methods of regulating, mediating and maintaining the status quo. Ultimately, changes as well as ongoing methods and laws are there to keep the power and purpose of the system in the hands of the economic and political power elite, the ruling capitalism class.

As much change as is necessary is allowed and accepted. In the 1930s, when a large working-class movement was questioning conditions and even challenging the right of capitalist rule, "New Deal" policies established social security, the right to unionize, unemployment benefits, etc. In the mid-1960s, after a decade of growing struggle and strength by the Civil Rights movement, voting and other civil rights legislation was passed. At the same time, federal and local cops and government were spying on, repressing and outright attacking the most militant, effective, and revolutionary groups. Similarly, during the 1930s and again after World War II, the government and F.B.I. launched major repression against communists, socialists, radical labor leaders, and unions. In both of these examples, the government repression included people being arrested, imprisoned, driven into exile, and murdered. These are just two brief examples of a long history of government repression against those working for fundamental change in the U.S. When the pressure and real need for progress and major change is strong, the system launches harsh and deadly repression against the most militant and determined groups and leaders. It also tries to intimidate or co-opt some leaders and groups. Finally, the government and ruling elite will accept as much change as necessary, while keeping the system going and in their continued control.

AREAS OF NEEDED CHANGE

Turning to issues where changes of all magnitudes are sorely needed, I'm afraid this list could be really long so I'll only look at what I feel are the crucial areas.

Any student of American history could definitely

identify situations crying out for change in every period, from the beginning of the U.S. republic up to the present. The suffering of people historically was certainly as painful and wrong as the suffering of people today. Still, some issues facing us today probably are more dangerous and critical than anything before.

WAR

Historically, the U.S. was based and founded on war, land confiscation and genocide. The land was taken from and genocide committed against Indigenous Native people living here. The wars were against the Native people, other settlers, colonies, countries and the British Empire.

All American government wars in modern times, beginning with the Korean War and into today's War in Iraq, have been wars of aggression to serve imperialism's interest - the business geo-political interests of U.S. imperialism. For well over 100 years, the United States has been an imperialist power. For the last 60 years or so, the U.S. has been a, or the, superpower, and today we are essentially the world's main empire. Like all past empires, the U.S. government and corporate media use different words and justifications to explain their attacks, invasions, embargos, sanctions, wars, and overall imperial policies. There is always some evil ruler, bad president, subversive or revolutionary ideology or dangerous dictator to overthrow. Sometimes it is to impose "democracy" or "freedom" or a "free market." Sometimes it is an outright fabricated attack against some U.S. military ship or outpost that is used to "justify" the American war.

The foreign and military policy of the U.S. government is primarily to protect and serve U.S. corporations in their exploitation of resources, labor, markets and investments around the world. Whether these corporate policies are beneficial to the vast majority of people in the U.S. is not a real consideration. Often in recent years, U.S. corporations flee America and close factories here. They move to some far away country that is often firmly under U.S. military and political domination, to take advantage of much cheaper labor and less strict environmental regulations there.

In order to make U.S. imperialism acceptable to us, the American public, the government in conjunction with the corporate news and entertainment media, work overtime to not only provide their version of the facts and information, but also to set out the limits of acceptable debate. Both the liberal and conservative commentator, the Democrat and Republican politician, accept, agree on and support the underlying corporate centric imperialist world view. Their commentaries and debates are about how best to implement and carry out imperialist policies and maintain the U.S. as the center of a corporate based empire. Very, very rarely will you see this paradigm questioned or opposed on any corporate or government news or media outlet.

While the United States acts and reacts like an empire, officially everything the President and government does, is done in our, the American people's name. Although we the public have very little, if any, actual say in the actions of the President and government, we do bear the responsibility for these actions.

Immediately after the Trade Towers and Pentagon attacks on 9/11, for a very short time some insightful and meaningful questions were actually heard in the corporate media. Besides the shock and sorrow, a few voices essentially asked, what have we the American public allowed this government to do that would cause people from other lands to travel thousands of miles to come here, so they could kill themselves in order to strike at America and Americans? Within a day or two, such questions were completely eliminated from all corporate and government news media outlets. Those were exactly the type of questions that mainstream America needed to and still needs to hear and ask today. Perhaps now it is a little easier to raise such questions with more of the U.S. public.

The issue is not whether the 9/11 attacks were somehow justified. The Trade Towers attack was terrorism. The Pentagon, as the headquarters of the U.S. government military, is a military target and subject to attack from known enemies. Neither is the issue about Al-Qaeda or radical Islamist ideology. Personally, I wouldn't want to live in any kind of theocracy, Muslim, Christian or any other religious rule. The question really is, what is the U.S. government doing around the world? Most Americans are not very informed and usually misinformed. But the public bears the consequences. We pay the costs - 440 million dollars per day in Iraq in mid-2008. It is young American soldiers who do the killing and dying. The U.S. has military bases, airfields, and other facilities in over 120 countries in the world! Who knows what the C.I.A., Defense Intelligence Agency, plus various private mercenary-security outfits like Blackwater are doing in who knows how many more countries? All of this falls back on us as a people and country. There is a lot of talk about making the U.S.

safer, but real safety for us as people in the United States begins with our first finding out, and then gaining control over what the U.S. government is doing in our name.

American soldiers will keep on being killed in invasions and occupations of other people's lands. There may be more terrorist-type attacks against the U.S., but none of this is likely to impact government policy. It is only we, the people in America, who can stop or change what the government does. It is our absolute right and duty to do so.

USA POLICE STATE

This country was founded on some fundamental inequality and injustice. The United States was not designed to be run by or for the masses. It has always been run largely by and mostly for the economic and social elite. With struggle, sacrifice and time, real progress has occurred.

Since 9/11/2001, the government has successfully advanced and implemented more police control and power than ever before in the country's history. Expanded police power based on laws like the Patriot Act, on executive orders, new regulations and the militarization, consolidations, and expansions of police forces, has resulted in a police state like power and reality across the country. Combat ready cops and soldiers with automatic weapons routinely patrol airports, rail and bus stations and government buildings. Secret prisons, in and outside the country, hold unknown numbers of prisoners. Basic long standing legal rights and principles have been wiped out. The right to torture prisoners of war and other captives is calmly and politely debated on TV news shows. Meanwhile, who knows how many people and how severely they are actually being tortured?

The wars being conducted overseas are complimented by the ever growing police state power domestically. These are the two raw faces of U.S. imperial power today.

Besides the special military prison in Guantanamo and the other secret prisons, the U.S. locks up almost two and a half million men, women, and children in its "normal" state and federal prisons. More people are locked up in this country, per capita and in actual raw numbers, than in any other country in the world. Recent statistics found that one out of every 99 adults is behind bars. If you break it down by race, it is staggering. One out of every 9 Black men between 20 and 34 is locked up. Race and class are the defining criteria for who is packed into America's overflowing prisons.

The costs are enormous. Many states spend much more on prisons than education. The human cost, not only to the prisoner, but also on their children, families and communities is staggering as well. This too is a part of the police state reality that is spreading through America.

Fundamental changes in U.S. society, ultimately require fundamental changes in the U.S. State. Yes, this is a radical statement, but it is also a concept that goes way back to the founding of the Republic. The Declaration of Independence, after boldly stating that all Men (women too of course) "are created equal" and have "Unalienable rights to Life, Liberty, and the Pursuit of Happiness," and that when a government becomes destructive of protecting these rights, "it is the Right of the People to alter or abolish it and to institute a new Government, laying its Foundation on such Principles, and organizing its Powers in such Form, as to them shall seem most likely to effect their Safety and Happiness."

END COLONIALISM

The United States, despite its own history of war against British colonial rule, is one of the few countries in the world today that still directly holds colonies. For one large powerful country to keep smaller countries in colonial bondage in the 21st Century, is shameful and against the flow of history.

The most obvious, glaring and classic colonial situation is with the nation of Puerto Rico. The U.S. seized this island, along with Cuba and the Philippines, during the Spanish-American War in 1899. Cuba and the Philippines many decades ago achieved their independence as sovereign nations.

The United States government has maintained Puerto Rico as its colony under a number of guises. Military occupation, martial law, limited local rule and a military Governor, and the last few decades as "dependent commonwealth status." The reality is the U.S. government has never allowed the Puerto Rican people to hold a vote for independence, that would be recognized as legitimate under international decolonization standards and law. Since the mid-20th Century, the U.S. government has been organizing and allowing colonial type elections that permit Puerto Rican people to elect local officials only.

Every successive generation of Puerto Ricans since the U.S. invasion in 1899, has sent forth freedom fighters that have worked and fought for Independence for their nation. Each generational wave of these patriotic men and women has suffered the repression of the U.S. government. Today, a number of Puerto Rican independence activists sit in federal prison cells across this country for their efforts to free their island nation.

The history of American relations with the Indigenous Native Peoples and their Nations, is a long sad and ugly trail of genocide, land theft, broken promises and treaties. The present reality is still largely harsh and unjust. The poorest counties in the U.S.A. are consistently on certain Indian reservations. Native American people have the lowest life expectancy rates of any group in the U.S. Substance abuse and suicide rates, including for youth, are extremely high among Indian people.

The genocide committed against the Indigenous people in North America, came close to wiping them out. Most of the land thefts and occupations are now just a historical fact. The overall situation of the several million Native Americans alive today and the question of lands they hold and lands they still have active claims to, is really another colonial issue. The United States never has and still must, honorably this time, deal with the colonial question of the Indigenous Peoples who were here long before there was a U.S.A.

Although their histories were somewhat different, the question of the Inuit people and their land in Alaska, as well as the Indigenous Hawaiian people and their lands, have also never been legitimately resolved. This too is a colonialism issue.

Probably the most substantial but complicated matter of colonialism, is the reality of the Black or New African Nation of African slave descendants that exists within the U.S.A. state. The history of African slaves brought to America, their ultimate release from slavery, and the subsequent legal and unofficial discrimination Black people were subjected to, is not the standard model of one nation being held under colonial domination by another nation. It has been recognized and described as a new or unique colonial type status.

The Black or New African Nation within the U.S.A. state does meet the international standards of a colonized people: a common history, culture, language; a common land base; a common economic relationship. For the majority of Black people today, the largest part of their heritage comes from the Africans involuntarily brought as slaves to America. When slavery was ended during the Civil War, no vote was ever offered or held to see if Black people wanted to return to Africa, become part of the U.S.A. state, or establish their own Black centered nation in the largely Black majority areas in the South. No vote was given in 1865, and Black people have yet to be given their right to decide the question of their national self-determination.

From the end of slavery, through the 19th and 20th centuries and continuing today, the idea of Black Nationalism has been an active part of Black America. Organizations and leaders advocating Black Nationalism have always been prominent. From Marcus Garvey and the United Negro Improvement Association, to Noble Drew Ali and the Moorish Science Temples, and especially to Honorable Elijah Muhammad and the Nation of Islam, all had and some still have large followings. The 1960s and 1970s saw a major surge of Black Nationalism, with leaders and organizations like Malcolm X, Huey P. Newton and the Black Panther Party, Assata Shakur and the Black Liberation Army, and perhaps the most developed modern advocate for Black Nationalism, the Republic of New Africa, with leaders like Dr. Mutulu Shakur.

These issues of colonialism and self-determination must be resolved. I believe that some of them, perhaps Puerto Rican independence in particular, can be mutually and justly resolved in the near future, even without a major change within the U.S.A. state. I do think that the ultimate resolution to most of these ongoing colonial issues will only be resolved as part of a fundamental revolutionary remaking of the government and system in the United States.

PROTECING OUR PLANET - ENVIRONMENT

This is an area where many Americans are informed and aware about some of the serious problems confronting us all. Being kind of knowledgeable about one's "carbon footprint" and switching to new style light bulbs and so on, like many people are doing, are small steps and changes. Real action on a national scale is lacking, even in some kind of reformist sense. As the world's biggest user (abuser and waster would also be honest terms) of energy and resources, as well as probably still the major polluter, this country has massive responsibilities to bear. The Bush government consistently fought international and national efforts to reduce global warming, pollution, and environmental degradation. Major corporations, oil companies included, spend more money on media campaigns trying to say they aren't as bad as critics and the public know them to be, than they actually spend on curbing, let alone stopping, their destructive practices. Real action on government or corporate levels to halt the ongoing destruction is lacking.

Huge economic interests, especially in energy production and transportation, are blocking and resisting important necessary changes. Much of the government, beholden to these same economic powers, goes along with, covers up or dismisses the corporate pollution and resists changes that all major scientific bodies, U.N. panels, other countries and so many people have called for.

We will see what the Obama Administration will do, and hope it will be radically more pro-active than Bush and his oil company backers. Destruction of the Earth is mounting and waiting is not an option. The government must be pressed hard and loud to take major substantive steps. Just as important, public campaigns to expose and pressure the most filthy corporations are crucial.

We should also become more aware of and keep our courageous elves and alfs (Earth Liberation Front and Animal Liberation Front activists) in our hearts and minds. Some of these folks are doing long prison sentences for trying to protect our planet.

We as individuals can and should make wise, less polluting and destructive choices in our daily lives. Just as importantly, we have to make polluting corporations and the government take major steps to stop destroying our planet. We have to make them join international efforts that begin to help our planet sustain itself and become more balanced. Time is not on our side, but more and more people are becoming aware and active. I believe at least some of the most pressing changes are achievable. The U.S. government and many of the major corporations can be forced to enact reforms that are necessary to protect us and our planet.

ECONOMIC ISSUES

We have economic problems because we have a worn out economic system. In 2009, the U.S. is in a recession. The home buying market has collapsed. The home mortgage crisis is causing hundreds of thousands of families, and soon it will be millions, to lose their homes. The mortgage meltdown has led to a banking crisis that will deepen, despite the federal government's bank bail out plan. Unemployment is rising steadily and sharply and of course this will only exacerbate the other problems and cause more misery for millions. The U.S. dollar is weakening and, as a result, prices are going up for all kinds of basic necessities.

Less and less is actually produced in this country, compared to even 20 or 30 years ago. Since 1979, the share of the labor force employed in the goods producing sector has fallen steadily from almost 28 percent to 16 percent (in 2005). Between 2000 and 2005, over three million manufacturing jobs were eliminated. The production of goods, food, clothing, machinery, appliances, steel, industrial products, and so on, used to dominate our economy. Today, corporations have moved most of these factories and jobs to places like Mexico, China, India, etc. Meanwhile, the banks and financial giants concentrate on currency trading and all kinds of financial speculation. They buy and sell mortgages, not homes. They produce hedge funds, not products.

There are many specific causes for this tottering economy. Some obvious ones are: the Iraq War (in mid-2008, costing over 13 billion dollars per month); a spreading banking crisis, igniting by massive mortgage failures; obscenely high salaries and bonuses for corporate CEOs; incompetent regulation by the Securities and Exchange Commission; corruption and theft in high places. Some of these issues can be reformed and moderated. The U.S. public will have to ride out this recession. Maybe it can be somewhat curtailed, so it won't plunge the country into a full-blown depression. There is no certainty for this though, and harder times are clearly ahead for most people in America.

The Bush government consistently advanced policies that supported corporate profits with little federal regulation of corporate practices. In 2000, when Bush took over, there was a 236 billion dollar federal budget surplus. By 2007, his government had run the federal budget into a 162 billion dollar deficit. The deficit will likely continue to be much worse, especially due to increased war costs and bail outs for Wall Street banks. No nonsense reforms by the Obama Administration could moderate and lessen some of this.

It is important to understand though, that the economic ills suffered by America's working masses are not fundamentally just the product of Republican government policies. There has been inflation, stagflation, recession and depression under Democrat governments also. The boom-and-bust cycle, driven by the anarchy of the market, is intrinsic to the capitalist system of production. Businesses must expand to beat out their competition. Endless growth inevitably produces more goods than can be sold.

189

Picture tons of potatoes or pinto beans rotting, not because they are unneeded, but because they can't be sold profitably. Every year, the federal government actually pays dairy cattle corporations tens of millions of dollars to dump millions of gallons of good fresh milk, so the price of milk at the retail store is maintained at a certain level. This natural tendency, basic economic law actually, of overproduction in the capitalist system, results in factory closures, layoffs, disappearing credit, dizzy stock markets, lost pensions and tremendous waste.

Measures that at some point bring recovery to the corporations, only build a worse crash the next time in this capitalist cycle. Smaller businesses get squeezed out or swallowed up by larger ones. Some workers lose jobs and other workers are forced to accept wage and benefit cuts just to keep jobs. The rich get richer which the poor and those in the middle sink further down.

This country is more than wealthy enough to provide good paying jobs, a decent standard of living and quality medical care, housing and education, respectful retirement and quality of life for young and old, for everyone who lives here. For that to be realized though, it will take more than reforms, a Democrat president or some new faces in Congress. It requires that the rapacious rule of the capitalist class be ended. Capitalism isn't cast in concrete. It had a beginning and it will have an end. It is man-made and it must be unmade. We, the American people, need to push into the future. We need to create a modern, equitable system where cooperation is rewarded in a planned economy in which production is based on the human needs of all, rather than profits for the few. A modern, well-planned, cooperative socialist democratic system will only be achieved by fundamental and revolutionary changes, but changes we can certainly make.

HEALTHCARE

Fifty million Americans don't have any healthcare insurance or coverage. Tens of millions more don't have adequate coverage. Yet, in this country where up to a third of all people have no or not enough coverage, the cost of healthcare is higher than anywhere else in the world.

The United States has an inefficient, extremely costly, unwieldy and wasteful healthcare system. In this very wealthy country, this is a disgrace, a dangerous and deadly disgrace. The problem is not the number or quality of doctors, nurses and other healthcare workers, or the number of hospital beds or medical equipment and modern technology. The problem simply is the profit based anarchic delivery system of medical care and insurance.

Every major industrialized country has a better socialized health system than the U.S. Some poor developing countries (Cuba stands out here) have very good and, in some respects, better systems than we do. Major capitalist countries like England, Canada, France, and Australia have well running socialized healthcare systems, that are well supported by their populations. There is no reason why the United States could and should not have a similar socialized healthcare system even under the present government and order of things. This type of reform, while major, is achievable with enough organizing and educating, and a loud enough demand from the people.

The principle opponents are the many private/for profit insurance companies. In a single payer socialized system there is no need or place for numerous for-profit insurance companies. All the wastefulness, duplication, costs and profit each company is making now, would be eliminated. It would cost less and work better.

For profit hospitals and hospital corporations are also against socialized medical care. The question for America to ask, is whether healthcare should be a private business where a few individuals should be making a big profit? Shouldn't healthcare be a societal service and right, like the fire department and firemen coming to any place there is a fire?

The pharmaceutical industry is opposed to a centralized healthcare system too. They are very powerful and spend huge sums to keep the price of medicine high and their profits even higher. The cost of medicine in a single socialized health system will be much cheaper. Drug companies will have to lower their prices when dealing with one nationwide operation of doctors and hospitals.

The American Medical Association has not been in favor of a socialized healthcare system either. Many doctors do support a national healthcare system and probably many more could be won over to a new system that would actually care for all the people in the country.

Another group of opponents are the conservative politicians in Washington, especially the ones who get big bucks from the insurance, pharmaceutical, and for-profit hospital corporations. But they can be overcome by a large enough popular voice and demand. The public is pushing for this already. Halfway efforts should not be accepted. The U.S. should establish a system at least as broad as Canada or European nations.

EDUCATION

Nationwide, public education has been a very important and pretty successful institution in U.S. history. It was a real tool in creating opportunity for most people to improve their lives. It helped create and develop an American culture and identity. Of course American culture has had its prejudices and inequalities and the public education system has too. Primarily though, it has been a good thing for individuals and society.

Today, from kindergarten to university level, the public education system is not working well and failing some people, thus failing society itself. There is a lot of disparity in K through 12 education. A lot of this is because of the amount of money that various local districts spend on their schools, students, teachers, pay and equipment. Where more funds are spent, the outcome is better, more children learn more, graduate in higher numbers and go on to college level schools. The difference between small town and especially suburban high school graduation rates and those in all large and even medium sized cities is extreme. Drop out rates among city high school students are huge. They run from about 55 percent graduation to 24 percent graduation! Dropout rates in wealthier suburbs and small towns are much lower. In the last few years, 1.2 million or more high school students have dropped out every year. Even state and federal education officials are calling this a drop out epidemic and crisis.

A big part of the changes needed are about money, getting much more money for all big city schools, especially high schools. Education is primarily failing for poor people from poor city neighborhoods. It is also disproportionally failing for people of color.

More than just money is needed. Parents, families, communities where students live can do more for these young people. Reading to small children, encouraging success and expecting success in school for our children all have an impact.

Education reform is certainly possible under the present system. New ideas and approaches are important, but we have to be firm in defending and demanding that universal public education is maintained and improved. There are many efforts to privatize particular schools and even entire districts. So called Charter schools must also be watched, because often these are just more attempts to privatize and destroy and existing public school district. Public education needs serious attention and improvement. It has long been one of the important and positive things in this country that we should defend and advance.

SOCIAL-CULTURAL AND A SPIRIT OF CHANGE

The dominant culture in the U.S.A. is based in inequality. Historically, America has had class, race and gender divisions and discrimination. The ruling elite, mostly using government authority (laws, court rulings, police power), has maintained and often advanced these divisions, in order to prevent unity among lower classes and oppressed people. Racism in the United States is historic and goes back to the early days of settler society, which seized Indian lands and held African slaves. It centered and justified itself, and continues to exist on the ugly and false ideology and practice of white supremacy. There are other forms and relationships of prejudice in this country. There are individuals or groups or people who dislike or even hate other individuals from different ethnic, national or religious groups. This is negative and has the potential to cause harm.

The primary white supremacy based racism against Black and other people of color, has been the official and unofficial practice of government, schools, banks, housing, real estate and other businesses. Injustice and discrimination, particularly against Black people, has been and still continues in too many ways to be, the way America works. The ruling and economic elite have always used racism against people of color to create divisions in the working class. I firmly believe that racism has been the single biggest weapon used against all progressive, labor, social, anti-war, and overall revolutionary struggles throughout U.S. history.

Racial discrimination is much less legal and somewhat less pervasive today. The 2008 primaries and elections were interesting and unique because Barack Obama as well as Hillary Clinton were for the first time serious contenders for becoming president. With Obama winning the Presidential race, this shows there has been a shift in old style bigotry. More people, especially many young people, are not as invested or caught in the lock of white supremacy, racism, and sexism. This is good and also an opportune moment for progressive and revolutionary groups to actively promote working class and revolutionary unity.

A spirit of change, of rejuvenation is needed and feels like it may be approaching. I'm not talking about religion, though religious people and groups should be a part of it too. I'm talking about creating a shared, across race, nationality, gender, generations, and religions, spirit of hope. A positiveness based on people working together for common needs and goals.

Most people in this country already share some important daily life impacting goals. An end to the utterly wrong, deadly and costly war in Iraq. A deepening worry about the economy and healthcare. A real concern about our environment and planet. The concerns and needs are clear. The reality that many people desire to seek change is also clear.

There is a two-fold impetus and psychology for change. There has to be real desire and need for change based on real hardships. But there also must be a belief and hope that change is now or soon will be possible. A belief that by joining with others and stepping forward, there is a chance that a new and better situation can be created. Now is the time to encourage and spread the belief that real and revolutionary change is possible.

REVOLUTIONARY CHANGE

Let's look at revolutionary change, first in a macro perspective. Particularly as activists, organizers and radicals, we shouldn't be limited by labels, misinformation or doubt. We should not let others, certainly not the corporate media, continue to set the paradigm for what is a legitimate society, economic model or leadership. We should not be limited by 18th and 19th century concepts of capitalist profit models.

Monopolistic private profit methods for organizing huge areas of life for our entire society, from healthcare to banking, housing and home buying, energy sources and sales, transportation, insurance and much more, no longer adequately meet our needs. We should look beyond such restrictions. We need to raise, and raise anew, new paradigms for change. In a modern industrial information driven society of hundreds of millions, in an ever interlocking world of billions, common control and socialized solutions are the future. Empires, invasions, wars, police state laws to serve and protect dog eat dog economics is not viable or sustainable for our country or the world.

The future is revolutionary. We already see more unity among people and cooperation among countries. This country and this world have to thrive to grow in a harmonious and balanced way. We need common efforts to solve common problems. We need environmentally sustainable socialist economic solutions, based on cooperation and mutual rewards.

Revolutionary change in a micro sense, is change of the individual, change within oneself. Change does begin inside. We experience and learn things, and then our consciousness expands, and we become more knowledgeable and aware. Personal inner growth is so clearly a dialectical process. We experience and learn things and change inside. With our new consciousness, we then impact the world around us, and in turn change further inside.

Personal revolutionary growth is occurring in many people. It is a struggle though, because we live, learn and adapt in a basically dog eat dog value system. Getting over getting rich is seen as positive, period. For example, a person like the notorious New York City slumlord, Donald Trump, is presented as a "great man." This man who added to the fortune his father gave him, by overcharging poor families who rented his cold water, roach infested apartments in Queens in the 1970s, today has his own TV show.

The corporate movie industry also advances the capitalist agenda. For example, in the 2007 movie, "American Gangster," which was especially aimed at city youth, a flamboyant New York City drug dealer and later police informant is featured and promoted. Meanwhile, U.S. prisons are overcrowded with drug dealers.

We need inner change in all layers of U.S. society. We need to question the "legitimate" and "official" information we get from the corporate news media, as well as the "official" perspective on this news. What is good for American business and the U.S. government is not necessarily or even probably good for us, the American people. More information is available today, especially with the internet, but it takes some effort to seek out alternative sources.

The United States is our country. All of it belongs to all of us, not to George Bush, Donald Trump, ExxonMobil Corp., or any of the political or ruling elite. Being connected and concerned about our city, country and world, enhances our humanity. Belief and hope that we the regular people can create new and better ways to live, trade, and share with each other while we sustain the planet, is spiritually and emotionally positive and strengthening.

It is a reality of life and revolution that liberation and

Jaan Laaman

change will come largely from the courage, spirit, and work of young people. The hope of youth is powerful for us all. Yet, while young people are often audacious and willing to challenge injustice, there are also obstacles in their way. Right now in many parts of the country, activists, mentors, cultural figures and revolutionaries have a task to reach out to youth of color in poor urban areas, to let them know and see that the idea of being revolutionary and intellectual is a cool thing once again. Many conscious youth point out today there are many distractions aimed at young people, to keep them away from organizing and revolution. Things like mindless consumerism, apolitical music pumped out by the corporate music industry, endless professional sports entertainment, movies and video games that glorify a capitalist dog eat dog mentality, etc. These are challenges, but young people need to change more than anyone and many are already leading the way.

In American today, we are faced with endless war and worsening economics. Defending and suffering for U.S. imperialism is not in the interest of most people in the country, let alone in the rest of the world. Our lives, our children and families, our country and world are at stake. It is time for us to change and to make revolutionary changes in the United States.

People are growing more fed up with the way things are and becoming more receptive to even radical change. We are never too young or too old to be activists, to be revolutionaries. Revolutionary change won't just happen. It will take work, sacrifice, the building and strengthening of revolutionary organizations. It is a process, more than a goal and it is a good way to live.

Change is a healthy growing process for us as individuals. At this moment in time, revolutionary societal change is a necessary process for our world and all of us in it. As a good friend often says, "The Future Holds Promise."

196

ABOUT THE AUTHOR

Jaan is a life long activist, organizer, teacher, healer, People's soldier. He has long been an advocate for our planet, and has always been a true friend to the poor and oppressed people and the working class around the world.

For the past 25 years, Jaan has been locked up as a political prisoner. He is one of over 100 men and women in captivity in the U.S. for their political beliefs, their voices of dissent and their acts in support of their beliefs.

Jaan was one of the original Ohio-7 defendants, who were convicted for being members and militants of the United Freedom Front (UFF). The UFF was a clandestine anti-imperialist organization, which was very active in the 1980s in the anti-apartheid struggle, in support of the Palestine people, the Irish people and the IRA, which fought against Reagan's wars in Central America, and police and government abuses in the U.S. Jaan was given a 98 year sentence.

From behind prison walls, Jaan has continued to reach out and remains politically active. He is the editor of www.4strugglemagazine.org. 4strugglemag is a vibrant voice of political prisoners in America. This magazine, put out since 2004, is published three times a year. It is primarily an e-mag, but hardcopies are available - free to prisoners - $4 for folks outside.

4strugglemag
P.O. Box 97048
RPO Roncesvalles Ave.
Toronto, Ontario
M6R 3B3 Canada

Early in 2008, Jaan began doing radio commentaries, primarily for www.kcblr.org radio. Other stations now carry his voice as well. The commentaries are also available as podcasts from www.freejaan.com.

Jaan is an officially listed political prisoner by the Jericho Freedom Movement and the Anarchist Black Cross Federation. He is also a listed class war prisoner by the Partisan Defense Committee. He has and continues to work on various campaigns and activities with each of these political prisoner advocacy organizations.

In 2007, Jaan began a vigorous and detailed review of his

unjust state and federal convictions and sentences (45 years for Massachusetts and to follow, 53 years for the federal government). Not trained as a lawyer, he established a defense freedom fund to finance the new appeal. Initial basic funding was secured and work is progressing on a legal challenge that has the possibility of getting Jaan out of prison - back to his family, his now young adult son, his comrades and friends, old and new. Continuing funds for this effort are still needed and truly appreciated. Checks can be made out to "Jaan Laaman Legal Freedom Fund," and sent to:

Jaan Laaman Legal Freedom Fund
P.O. Box 681
East Boston, MA 02128

For more information, contact and updates, go to www.freejaan.com (Jaan, like all prisoners in this country, has no actual or direct access to the internet, email, etc.). You can write to Jaan directly at:

Jaan Laaman (10372-016)
USP Tucson
P.O. Box 24550
Tucson, AZ 85734

While Jaan may be currently reached at this address, please refer to www.4strugglemag.org and www.freejaan.com for up-to-date address information.

CHAPTER ELEVEN

A New Path

Jake Conroy

JAKE CONROY

The first time I really saw direct action in practice was in October of 1996, a year or two into my activist "career." The local news had reported that the Animal Liberation Front had smashed out the windows and painted slogans on a Honey Bee Hams restaurant in Bellevue, Washington. The local animal rights group I had recently become active in decided to show their support of the economic sabotage by doing a follow up demonstration over the weekend.

Although I was fairly new to actual activism, I had been raised to know doing what's easy and what's right isn't always the same choice. My single mother, once disowned by her military father for her protest activity against the Vietnam War, raised her children on the ideas of Martin Luther King, Jr., Shel Silverstein's book, *The Giving Tree*, and Marlo Thomas's album, *Free to be you and me*. I was instilled with the notions that one should strive to be a good person, help those who can't help themselves and stand up for what you believe to be right. The tools available for such pursuits were never really discussed until much later, but politeness, like any parent will tell you, was essential. Up until I arrived at Honey Bee Hams, the idea of more radical forms of activism never crossed my mind.

The action would spark an internal dialogue about where I would fit into the animal rights community and what kind of roles I would participate in. I feel strongly that we need to be honest with ourselves from the get-go about what our capabilities, strengths, and weaknesses are and how we want to hone our skills to be the most effective activists we can be. I had decided that although I was, and still am, an unabashed supporter of direct action, that was as far as I could take my role in that arena. Where I felt I could be more useful was in taking above ground pressure campaigns to new and different levels; trying to push that envelope or just ripping it to shreds altogether.

Over the next ten years, I would be involved in many different causes and forms of activism. I mostly focused on the animal rights movement where I felt the most passion and saw the most creativity and results. I studied and watched how fur products were removed from all west coast Macy's stores. How protests turned into daylight liberations at Consort Beagle Breeder. How the Animal Liberation Front rescued over 1,000 animals in one night after breaking into a lab. I was mesmerized by the dedication and ingenuity these individuals possessed. Over the years, I worked with amazing activists from all over the world to participate in and accomplish some amazing goals. We fed off one another, exchanging ideas and strategies to strengthen our actions. Each campaign would grow in size and creativity. By learning from each other and our past accomplishments, we managed to shut down fur departments and stores, effect local legislation and bring news ways of thinking into a large community. We ran a successful, multiple year hunt sabotage that overcame almost every obstacle the local and federal governments threw at us with creativity and dedication. We formed what would become one of the most exciting grassroots campaigns in decades, that started out by taking on one of the world's largest laboratories of its kind, and eventually every multinational company and government that allied itself to them. The campaign grew in success and stature, coming just shy of closing the lab forever.

Then we went to prison.

I wanted to be sure of the proper definition of *revolution* before I spent too much time writing about it, so I took a walk down to my local prison library. *The 1966 Random House Unabridged Dictionary*, the massive book with tissue-like paper falling out of the spine, gave me the following: "Revolution: A radical and pervasive change in society and social structure, esp. one made suddenly and often accompanied by violence." That's what I thought. But it seems to have been co-opted into everything but that. I'm told in the magazines that the new "American Revolution" is the latest Chevy truck. That the next video game console is "revolutionary play." It's used by people as an excuse to drop out of any form of activism. After all, complete industrial collapse is just around the corner, and if we don't know the right mushrooms to pick during the revolution, we might starve. So to hell with campaigning. Revolution fills tomes of radical literature and books encouraging "direct action now!" and "armed rebellion," despite the authors only lifting a finger to type out their next diatribe. The talk of revolution has been used to boost the egos and societal standings of many activists, only to have it slapped back in their faces by new Draconian laws passed by Congress using these radical rantings as ammunition. The actual act of revolution is almost dead in America, either by fear, social standings, laziness or just a simple case of being asleep at the wheel for too long.

Revolution amongst activist communities is heavily

romanticized with no regard for the actual struggle. It's easy to wear the pins, shirts, bandanas that celebrate Ché, Marcos, or the Animal Liberation Front. But do we take the time to put ourselves on the other side of the mask? Do we fully understand what it takes to pick up a bullet, bomb or brick? I will be the first to admit that I've been guilty of such romanticism. I also feel as above ground activists, it's our responsibility to publicly support the ideology of radical, underground activism. But it's also our responsibility to try our best to understand the motivation, action and consequences behind revolution to better our ability to vocalize such ideologies instead of just to blindly embrace anyone in a balaclava.

In the end of 1999, on the day before activists completely shut down the WTO and Seattle, the downtown area was overrun with protests, marches, and direct action. The city was buzzing with anticipation. People were getting anxious, road blocks went up, banners dropped and windows were smashed. Rumors were abuzz that a delegation of Zapatistas would turn up. So when some activists in black bloc strolled through the crowd, they were greeted with cheers and pats on the back. March organizers were thrilled to have them. No one seemed to notice that behind the masks it appeared they weren't of a Latin American descent. They were blinded by the glamour of such revolutionaries that they didn't realize something was amiss, until the black bloc started smashing out the windows of Niketown. The march organizers responded with physical violence, trying to tackle the activists and form a human shield around Niketown until the police could arrive. They had romanticized the mask and the gun so much that they had forgotten that it belongs to an actual struggle. It got so bad that they were now protecting from property damage, multinational corporations who are raping, pillaging and enslaving people, but blindly embracing the idea of those who would put a bullet in the back of the head of those responsible for such atrocities.

My prison sentence is a short one, 48 months, but I have had the opportunity to meet some remarkable people. I spent most of the incarceration in a medium security prison in Southern California that had a reputation for housing "trouble makers." It was there that I met a Black Panther from Los Angeles. A man who fought in a guerrilla army in the jungles of Central America for his people. A Bay Area black nationalist/black power activist. An inmate who had over 170 disciplinary write-ups, many stemming from organizing "The Crack Riots" of the 1990s, where inmates took over prisons nationwide to try to change the racist crack laws. All of these people, all still in prison, some for over 25 years, are products of revolution. It's the unfortunate result of struggle that for every high profile case and inmate, there are hundreds more people spending decades in prison, forgotten. Each one of them has numerous stories of comrades who have died for the same cause. There are people all over the country sitting in prison, waiting and hoping that maybe after several decades, that their time to walk through the gates is near. Although when asked, they wouldn't take any of it back. It's these consequences that are often overlooked when many of us shout revolution from the pulpit, steering others into action.

So at this point, we as activists have to have an honest conversation amongst our ranks and question our tactics, ideas and motives. We have to realize that as much as we love our pins, t-shirts, bandanas, and rhetoric, there is real struggle behind it all. There's more than our internet rants, the patches on our sweatshirts and the felt cat ears stitched onto our hoodies. It's hard work, dedication, struggle and lots of sacrifice. But in this day of almost unprecedented oppression in the world, can we make the idea of revolutionary change a reality? The days of walking into government buildings armed to the teeth, blowing up police stations or kidnapping heiresses are all but over. Sure, it still happens on a political scope, but the backlash is way more damaging than the actual action, mostly due to the apathy of the general public. Malcolm X once said that there is "no such thing as a bloodless revolution," which, by its definition, is true. But are we able to sway the public to that way of revolutionary thinking, or do we as a collective activist community have the numbers, resources and skills to take on the most powerful nation in the world, regardless of what 99% of the public thinks of us? Unfortunately, the answer is no. Is there an alternative way to bring revolutionary change while tweaking its very definition? I think the answer is one that Bobby Seale, co-founder of the Black Panther Party for Self Defense had since the 1960s: "We need to capture the imagination of the people."

The Black Panther Party was one of the most important revolutionary groups of our time. Their ideology and ability to put it into practice was an uncompromising show of radical activism that is really unparalleled. Like anything, it had its bumps in the road, the criticisms and mistakes. But what it accomplished by uniting revolutionary activity with the run-of-the-mill grassroots activism is a lesson any future revolutionary should take to heart.

By studying their achievements and their mistakes and meshing them with present day realities, we can better understand a path to revolutionary change in the 21st Century.

The Panthers, heavily armed, would patrol their neighborhoods looking for abusive police. Often these scenarios would escalate into attacks, beatings and shootouts. This led to arrests, prison time and funerals. Would-be Panthers would be taken from the neighborhoods, sometimes from street gangs, and schooled in weapons, law, and radical thinking. In its simplest form, the Panthers were a small grassroots organization with a few chapters and revolutionary action and rhetoric that was almost extinct within a year.

So how did it explode into an international movement, embraced by people of all ethnicities, class and beliefs? It captured the imagination of the general public. It engaged in high profile actions to force the media to pay attention. If the news wouldn't report on their rights being stripped away to defend themselves by any means necessary, then they would march right into the state capitol brandishing, legally, all their weapons. The Panthers were thrust into the spotlight, with the idea that their militaristic confrontations would shock and scare the public, which in turn would marginalize their cause even more. What happened was the opposite.

The public saw an international network of volunteers taking care of poor people, regardless of race, where the governments had failed. The Panthers opened schools to teach the history of oppressed people who had all but been erased from the annals otherwise. They published a nationally distributed newspaper to educate the public on their issues when they weren't being covered properly by the national media. They inoculated people from sickle cell anemia in Panther-run free clinics when the government would not. They clothes and fed breakfast to more school children with their food programs every morning than the U.S. government did. They helped community members avoid the pitfalls of alcohol, drugs, and gangs. And they patrolled their communities, legally armed, not only watching out for their neighbors, but also keeping abusive police in check.

Within a handful of years, the Black Panthers rose to fame and just as quickly were snuffed out by an organization working just as hard to suppress their beliefs - the U.S. government. Like all strong movements, the government came down on the Panthers hard, through a program called COINTELPRO. They used illegal tactics to misdirect and neutralize activists, including spying, infiltration, falsifying internal Panther communications, imprisonment, beatings, and even murder. But what they left behind was a legacy of amazing activism that was only limited by their own imagination, which anyone contemplating action should study. The principles they put into practice can still be utilized today if properly refined, and have been used to redefine modern day activism and what a relatively small group can accomplish with a little ingenuity.

The campaign to close Huntingdon Life Sciences is an international movement comprised of grassroots activists and the general public, which has embraced an "every tool in the toolbox" philosophy, and has utilized it successfully. It took off quite quickly and unexpectedly in the U.S. and left few industries untouched. It took the pharmaceutical and financial sectors and turned them on their heads, with just about every tactic imaginable, and then some. It broke down every barrier of protest through creative thinking, an abundance of energy and radical activism. The campaign even stretched the common definition of revolution by making swift change with radical action, while avoiding outright physical violence.

Huntingdon Life Sciences (HLS) is the third largest contract research organization in the world. As a laboratory, they are contracted as a third party to test a company's latest product on animals, to protect them from future litigation. HLS will perform toxicology tests on any and every species they can get their hands on, from wild-caught primates, dogs and cats, down to mice, rats, and fish. They kill at the rate of 500 animals a day, approximately 180,000 a year.

If the death rate wasn't egregious enough for another sweetener or oven cleaner, the animal cruelty and sloppy science would do it. Multiple undercover investigations by both activists and unbiased news reporters have pulled back the curtain on HLS' dirty business. Video footage revealed unsanitary conditions, animals with open sores, vivisectors throttling beagle puppies by the neck and punching them in the face, throwing animals around and cutting open a primate's rib cage while it was still conscious. Other documents revealed employees intoxicated and using illegal drugs while working, falsifying scientific data to make it appear tests were effective, trying to cover up multi-million dollar disasters, and eventually putting pharmaceutical drugs on to the market that have resulted in the loss of human life.

There was an international uproar to shut HLS down for good after the video footage appeared on national media outlets. But a multinational corporation got what they always get, a slap on the wrist. But what they needed was a smack across their smug faces to wake them up to reality - that they didn't just answer to a board of directors and shareholders. They answered to us.

In order to deliver such a blow, an all-volunteer, grassroots, no-nonsense movement was formed - Stop Huntingdon Animal Cruelty (SHAC). It spread from its roots in England over to the U.S., and then on to eighteen countries at its peak. Its coordinators studied what made a corporation tick, what its pillars of support were and what part of its foundation could be removed in order to make the whole structure topple. After years of campaigning against a multitude of targets, one thing was for sure - standing outside a building yelling at it was not going to make it come crashing down. What was of importance was, who was inside the building and what they needed to keep it a functional business. These people turned the keys, made the decisions, paid the bills, and kept the wheels in motion. They also were sort of like us - they had lives, jobs, homes, and a social life, and were desperate to keep work as separate as possible.

Additionally, it was noted that a business requires certain elements to stay operational. They needed a bank, an insurer, an auditor, shareholders and companies to facilitate the buying and selling of shares. They needed a market to do these transactions. They needed an internet provider and someone to pick up and cremate the 500 dead bodies they produced daily and the clients who paid them to do it. So what would happen if one by one, a pressure campaign removed each of these blocks? If, while the company scrambled to replace one block, another was already being pulled out from under them?

Over the course of several years, HLS was reduced to nothing, financially speaking, by removing these building blocks. Their share price dropped from over $30 to less than a penny at its lowest. They were unable to write a check to pay the rent because not a single bank in the world would give them a checking account. Their work and employees couldn't be insured because not a single insurance company in the world would provide them with coverage. (In an unprecedented move, the UK government stepped in and provided them with both). No one in the world would act as their auditor, sit on their board of directors, invest in the company or even provide them with paper towels for their bathrooms. What is often considered a very marginalized movement, the animal rights community stepped up to the plate and accomplished what very few had in the past - a very successful and unified stand against what was once considered untouchable.

The U.S. government thought by chopping off the head, the body would quickly die, and I suppose in certain respects, it did. But what they really didn't understand was what little we actually did. The prosecutors pointed their fingers at six people and an organization that were outspoken on their support of direct action, public protest and shutting down HLS, pushed aside the First Amendment and got guilty charges on all of us for nothing more than exercising free speech and our right to assemble. Who they failed to nab were the thousands of activists and everyday people who took to the internet, the streets and disappeared into the night. These were the folks who were getting the job done. The people who were inspired into action.

SHAC USA simply operated as a clearing house of sorts. We published newsletters and literature, posters and videos, available at no cost. We researched potential protest targets and campaign ideas. We operated a web page to not only allow the public to read about the issues, but to provide a forum for anybody to post their protest reports no matter what the scope of activity or legality was. Through our website and self-published magazines, we bypassed the national media and created our own. Eventually, the media couldn't ignore what was going on and they were clamoring for stories. What would transpire over the course of several years was that people from all walks of life became inspired by the creativity and abundance of action. While SHAC USA organized protests and speaking events, usually coordinating our actions with local law enforcement and keeping everything above board, thousands were taking their own lead. Letter writing campaigns and petitions, placards and bullhorns at business fronts, homes and social clubs, smashed windows, cars covered in paint stripper, and liberated beagles, ferrets, chicks, and other animals. The sky was the limit and everyone was trying to reach higher. Even to my own amazement, every tactic was successful when applied properly. And they were being applied by just about everyone. A year long campaign of relentless home demonstrations and never-ending underground direct action ended the world's largest insurer's contract with HLS. But it was the mountains of letters generated by a group of retired women in Florida, and nothing else, that made HLS' third largest investor sell all of its shares and write one of the most critical letters on HLS' animal cruelty and terrible financial sense. The sinking of a bank president's yacht by the Pirates for Animal Liberation, over-run internet servers from email attacks by Russian hackers and a stink bomb attack that cleared an entire high rise surely influenced a number of companies to sever all ties with HLS. But it was also the faxes, petitions, and phone calls that had a whole slew of them jumping ship. The campaign saw actions from grassroots activists, underground revolutionaries, welfarists, parents, school teachers, lawyers, vegans, vegetarians, carnivores, young, old - a true melting pot of our society. They were inspired by each other and their ability to achieve, on their own, what they once thought impossible, and what they were told was impossible by welfarists wanting their donations and governments afraid of actual accountability.

Their imagination had been captured. And in a major way. After four years, over 100 companies lay in our wake, including the biggest financial and pharmaceutical firms in the world. They were forced to change forever the way they do business. Who would be traded on the New York Stock Exchange was now being determined by grassroots activists. Companies were begging governments for legal relief and threatening to move their entire operations out of the country. They were so quickly challenged and with so much pressure, all they could do was succumb. And insist there be retaliation.

There's no bigger proponent of retaliation than the U.S. government. They are often methodical, play dirty and play to win. (Really, if we should emulate anyone's credo as revolutionaries, it's theirs). They raided our office and home, taking just about everything that wasn't nailed down. Conveniently, they waited until the day before we were to move, so practically the entire house was already boxed up for them by the front door. A year later they came again, this time for us. We were now deemed the biggest domestic terrorism threat to the U.S. (despite not hurting a single animal, human or otherwise) and would be put on trial. A little over two years later and after a lengthy jury trial, better described as railroading, we would all be in federal prisons serving a variety of sentences.

The immediate response by many will be *you didn't succeed. You didn't achieve your goals. It's not quite the blueprint for a revolution you proclaimed it to be.* But I disagree. Yes, HLS is still operational. It's hanging on, but so are the thousands of activists who were inspired to fight that fight. Actions still continue on to this day. But more importantly, a seed has been planted. Ideas and strategies that had not yet been utilized were now proven effective even against the strongest of foes. A once unstoppable industry is now capable of teetering. Now, it's just a question of how hard we want to push. Are we willing to recognize the sacrifice that will be required? Are we willing to accept tactics and ideas that might not be appealing to us but might to others? Are we ready to stop talking and theorizing and ready to take action to make lasting change?

I've seen these tactics studied and emulated in other movements around the world, quite successfully. A friend went to an organizer's conference to talk about the campaign and the ideas. She met a woman who came from South America who was sent to the conference to learn about "SHAC tactics." They were living under an oppressive local government and they were confident that a similar campaign would be the only way to take back their communities. When I heard that, I realized that whatever the end held in store for our campaign, we had already won. The people's imagination had been captured, and there was no turning back. Real change could be ours, regardless of how big our opponent was. It was just a matter of our choice of unconventional tactics and how hard we push them.

I don't write. When making a list of my strengths, writing doesn't even come close to making the list. It amazes me that I'd be included among this list of authors, some of which I've been reading for 15 years. They are much more qualified to argue the necessities for revolution in the world today. I've been hugely inspired by them and the actions they write about. At the same time, I found them to be somewhat depressing. Up until recently I felt hopeless, that the struggles they envisioned were just that, visions.

However, my hopelessness was really just a reaction from my own inability to choose a new path of action. To recognize that the old way wasn't working and that we needed to venture down unexplored avenues. I can now say definitely that a revolution is not only something we so desperately need on many fronts, it's something we can achieve. It may not be the traditional view of balaclavas and bullets, but it's a modern day activism that is unrelenting, unapologetic, and a force to be reckoned with. I've lived it for a number of years and can attest to its rate of success. If a small group of us can pull it together, so can you. Just make sure you do it quicker and better. For in today's world, there's no time to waste.

ABOUT THE AUTHOR

Jake Conroy has been active since 1995 in a wide variety of struggles, including environmental, Native American, anti-death penalty, civil rights, LBGT rights, and animal liberation, which he focuses most of his efforts on. He has organized on a local, regional and national level, forging successful campaigns against a variety of animal abuse industries in the Northwest, co-coordinated the first ever whale hunt sab in coastal U.S. waters and organized with the Stop Huntingdon Animal Cruelty campaign.

He is a member of the SHAC7 and is currently housed in a federal prison in southern California, serving a 48-month sentence for his role in SHAC USA. Jake is anxiously awaiting his late 2009 release to return to the relative normalcy of family, friends, and activism.

Recognizing he is way out of his league, Jake would encourage you to check out these proper works of prose to supplement his own attempts:

The Stop Huntingdon Cruelty Campaign and the SHAC 7:
• InsideHLS.com
• SHAC.net
• SHAC7.com
• SupportJake.org, SupportLauren.com, JoshHarper.org

Radical Activism and the Government's Response:
• *The COINTELPRO Papers: Documents from the secret wars against dissent in the United States*, by Ward Churchill.
• *Revolutionary Suicide* by Huey P. Newton
• *Seize the Time* by Bobby Seale
• *From Dusk til Dawn* by Keith Mann
• *Free the Animals* by Ingrid Newkirk
• *Earth Liberation Front, 1997-2002*, by Leslie James Pickering
• *Bite Back Magazine*/directaction.info

CHAPTER TWELVE

THIS COUNTRY MUST CHANGE

THE MYTH OF DEMOCRACY
IN THE UNITED STATES

CRAIG ROSEBRAUGH

CRAIG ROSEBRAUGH

> *In a time of universal deceit,*
> *telling the truth becomes a revolutionary act.*

- George Orwell

Is It All A Dream?

Imagine waking up tomorrow morning and stepping outside your door only to realize everything has changed. As you begin walking, it becomes evident you are in a different place, a different country, far from anything you had ever imagined. This country isn't like the one you remember growing up in, nor does it resemble that in which you reside. Convinced you are at home, sound asleep in the midst of an adventurous dream, you continue on your journey – a quest if you will – to learn about this new land.

Pleasantly enough, you find yourself in a lush, green meadow. The warm spring sun envelops your body and soul as the sound of chirping birds mingles with a light wind blowing through the grass. Walking along toward a hillside, this new country appears and feels much like a remarkable utopia.

Approaching the top of the hillside, you begin to see distant clouds of smoke and with each step, a faint sound – one creating a most unpleasant juxtaposition to the song of the birds and grass – but nonetheless, a peculiar, unfamiliar sound grows stronger. Irregular pounding... *Are those fireworks off in the distance?* You wonder. *Or maybe thunder?*

And then, just as quickly as the beauty of this dream world hit you, the reality of what lies beyond the hill comes sharply into view. Reaching the peak of the hillside, your eyes feast upon what appears to be a city, or the remains of one, off in the distant valley. Plumes of billowing smoke from factories joins that from what appear to be some sort of explosions, creating a thick haze shadowing the metropolis.

And now the sound becomes recognizable, vividly recognizable. Gunshots ring out fiercely from afar – an unforgettable sound, familiar to you from watching action dramas on television. You are stunned, not only from the unrest that appears ahead, but perhaps more so from this disturbance disrupting your utopian dream. *Within all this beauty and tranquility, how can such war, unrest, and evil exist?* You wonder.

Curious to learn more, you begin making your way down the hill toward the valley below and the approaching city. Descending rapidly with your eyes focused on the battle-zone, you feel your legs give way and your body slamming against the dry, craggy ground.

Awakening minutes later, you find yourself lying in a ditch down at the base of the hillside. With the side of your head pounding profusely, you realize you tripped, knocking your head against a rock, a fall that proceeded to send you tumbling down the hill unconscious. Lying in the ditch in pain, with gun battles blazing in the near distance, you feel something sharp under your back. Reaching underneath, you pull out an old, worn and decrepit book.

Aching from the fall, you sit up, grabbing the book to see just what it was stabbing you in the back. The hardcover is tattered and aged to the point the title is indiscernible. Opening the front cover, the bold black title sits as if imbedded upon hundreds of layers of sun-yellowed sheeting. **"STATEMENT OF THE REVOLUTIONARY FORCES FOR FREEDOM"** the title reads. You assume from this title that the book is likely a historical account of struggles for democracy that occurred in many of the developing countries – countries that sought to free themselves from the bondages of dictatorships, oligarchies and corrupt governments.

Fighter jets and helicopters begin flying overhead, roaring over you toward the city, trembling the ground and your entire body. Sore and discombobulated, you glance through this book only to quickly find that it was not written about a historical conflict in some far off land, but rather about the revolutionary movement occurring directly in front of your very own eyes! With exceptional interest, you begin reading about the revolutionary forces and the country you are visiting.

According to the book, the battle began only two years before after a large percentage of the population tired of living under tyrannical and unjust conditions. As the nearby city appeared – at least from a distance – to be very much a part of the "civilized" and modern world, you wonder just what sort of injustice prevailed in this land. *What was so treacherous and oppressive that drove people to rebel?*

In the context of world history, this country appeared

relatively new, having been established just a few hundred years ago by settlers fighting off a foreign imperialist power that had been tightening its proverbial belt increasingly around its colony. Taking a political methodology of governing from ancient Athens, the victorious settlers set out to create a new country ruled by a concept referred to as *democracy* – from the Greek *demokratia* or government by the people. They drafted their founding documents declaring liberty and equality and began building their own version of utopia.

Sounding oddly familiar, you read on with a growing interest.

On the surface, it appeared as though this new country had all the makings of a true democracy, granting freedom and equality to all. And yet, it became quickly apparent that there was never any honest intention within this new land to grant liberty and equality to all, but rather to maintain it only for a select minority at the expense of the majority of the population. In fact, according to this book, from the day this new country originated the only members of this society to experience any form of democracy were those from a particular race, gender, and class – coincidentally, the same race, gender, and class of those who ruled the recently defeated colonial power. The local indigenous populations, poor whites, blacks, and women had few, if any, real rights under this new "democracy."

Slowly over the years, some of the groups listed above, began to experience some progress, making incremental steps toward being included amongst those privileged enough to fall under the reigns of this political doctrine. These minute steps were not voluntarily granted by the powers that be, but were only agreed to after long, arduous campaigns by the oppressed populations. Yet, never to this date, were any of the excluded groups granted full participatory and coverage rights under this democratic system. The same race, gender, and class of individual continued to maintain full power and control of the country, and still at the expense of the majority.

Perhaps the most ingenious aspect of this whole government, you learn, was that from day one through to the beginning of the current rebellion, the policy makers and rulers of this country were able to convince large portions of this society that they did in fact live in a democracy. Somehow, in some manner or form, even many of those excluded from liberty and equality in this country were able to be continually convinced that this was a democracy – a free country ruled by and for the people. They were convinced that this was the greatest, freest nation of all and went as far as to espouse patriotic tendencies.

Each and every time a war was fought overseas by this country, the government convinced its people the war was for democracy and freedom and to preserve the liberty and equality that makes this nation so special. Convinced of this mission, the *excluded* (as you begin to refer to them) either volunteer or are drafted to go fight the battles started by the rulers – the battles occurring allegedly to defend freedom.

Within the country the "*included*" (those who created and chiefly benefit from the democracy) do a marvelous and skilled job of increasing their power and control over the population, while continuing to keep the population tucked in nicely under the blanket of democracy. Anytime someone attempts to leave the bed and remove the cover of this phenomenon, they are labeled an enemy of the country, a threat to democracy, a threat to freedom and equality and liberty. As a result they are killed, jailed, or otherwise silenced and stuffed back underneath that blanket.

The *included* rule the schools and educational system in the country, producing their own textbooks and teaching materials, ensuring a dominance over what is learned. They run and control the various modes of media within the country, ensuring that whatever is distributed to the minds of the public is precisely what is engineered and manufactured as a means of strict obedience. The newspapers, the television news and entertainment, the magazines, the radio, the movies all are controlled chiefly by the rulers with the result being the creation and maintenance of public opinion.

The rulers of this land even go a step further and orchestrate a mandatory adherence to labor, making the *excluded* employees of the perceived democratic state. The *excluded* employees are forced into labor to pay for their very necessities of life – food, water and shelter. Beyond that, the *included* implemented an ingenious taxation program designed to raise revenue for the rulers while preoccupying the underprivileged by forcing them to work even harder, longer hours to not only simply live, but to pay the constantly increasing income, property, and even sales taxes. A nation of employees is therefore created, employees that do not have the ability and privilege to see the true fruits of their own labor, but who are forced to engage in labor that produces wealth for the rulers and just enough for the *excluded* to keep returning to work the next day.

As you flip through page after page of this book in disbelief, you wonder how this country's government even continued unchallenged during the last few hundred years. And the damning evidence of injustice only deepens with each page turned.

You would think that if the *included* went to the trouble of creating a nation of obedient employees under the guise of democracy, there would be a vested interest in the health and well being of the people. If the workers are not taken care of then it is likely they will not produce as much monetary reward for the rulers. Yet, according to the book, the *included*, not only have never offered nor allowed the *excluded* any resemblance of democratic representation or governing, but they have instead viewed the *excluded* as expendable commodities, mere pawns or even tools in the almighty quest for further financial gain and power.

During the many wars that have been fought by the *excluded* on behalf of the *included* to protect and expand its revenue possibilities, over one million of the *excluded* soldiers have lost their lives. They died fighting for the cause of democracy, having been repeatedly told that their very freedom – the freedom they truly had yet to ever obtain – was being threatened. Millions more have been slaughtered around the world by the rulers or the *excluded* acting on their behalf. Fair governments have been destroyed, leaders murdered and puppet regimes instituted in their places in the attempt to build the *included* a colonial regime for further economic acquisitions. And similar to inside the *included's* homeland, in the international community, when individuals or governments have raised their voices in objection to the unjust policies of the rulers in this country, they have been silenced one way or another.

With the sounds of gunshots still piercing your ears, you sit back against the hill, pondering this book, and allowing the sun to once again beat down upon your face. Your utopian dream has developed into a nightmare and you find yourself desiring to awaken, to be back at home in your bed, where everything is safe and back to normal. But your eyes continue to seek information and answers within the weathered book.

As further evidence of the lack of representation or even concern for the *excluded*, the rulers have purposely used biological and chemical weapons on them, they have contaminated the food supply with illness-causing chemicals, and the ruler's enterprises have poisoned the water, air and even soil resulting in thousands of *excluded* deaths. And when the sick and dying members of the *excluded* majority seek medical assistance to remedy their illness, they have little or no healthcare, as the *included* have made medical treatment too costly for most to receive proper attention.

The open and fair democratic elections that the rulers so fondly boast about are neither open, fair or even slightly democratic. When the majority is even allowed to vote, they are able to cast their ballots and choose between yet another one of two *included* candidates vying for each position. And nearly without exception, the candidate among the rulers that has the highest degree of monetary wealth and power wins. Campaign promises of fairness, of change, of improvements become lost in the business as usual policy of ruling the *excluded* with the goal being the increase of the empire's power and wealth.

In this supposed freest land of all, in this alleged democratic nation of liberty and equality, why is it, you wonder, *why is it that this country has never allowed the "excluded" to be an equal part of society? Why is it that this country,* according to the book, *has the highest rate of incarceration per capita of any country in the world? Why is it that this government and the ruling members of the country make up only a small minority that obtain and maintain their power and wealth at the expense of the "excluded" majority?*

In a country so ripe with corruption and oppression... you wonder, *in a country whose government has lied to them from day one and continues the purposeful daily deceit, why did it take so long for the "excluded" to rebel?*

In a state of pondering confusion, you set the book down and stare out at the fires burning from buildings in the distance. With the warm sun maintaining its glowing presence, you lie back closing your eyes, allowing the sounds of the now distant birds and blowing grass to once again transform your soul. Among the gunfire, aircraft overhead, and looming uncertainty you fall asleep confident you will awaken in the morning back in your warm bed, in your safe home, and within your truly democratic country.

The Greatest Myth

By far, the greatest myth ever forced upon the American people, is that the United States is a democracy. From 1776 through to the current day, in times of peril and anguish as well as prosperity, this one belief has stood as the backbone of American society. It is this very belief that has continuously rallied the nation into a frenzy of flag waving patriotism – either on the sacred July 4th Independence Day or anytime a real or perceived threat to the country becomes apparent. This *rally-round-the-flag-boys* mentality has shaped every generation in the United States, producing an unquestionable pride in the liberty, freedom, and justice for which our founding fathers fought so diligently.

We are raised in the United States to believe that this country is the freest, most opportunistic, and democratic nation in the world. It is, after all, the nation that boasts the American Dream - where after a slice of apple pie, baseball game and Fourth of July celebration, any one of us can work hard and reap the benefits of financial success.

Believing in the American Dream is akin to a religious devotion, where by following certain prescribed guidelines and social norms we expect to prosper and be saved. Under this mythology, Americans have believed wholeheartedly that the political structure itself is sound and just and fundamentally democratic, it simply needs some fine tuning, and some reformist conditioning from time to time.

Within the mythology of the American Dream, it becomes easy to forget, or even easier to never acknowledge that this country was never a democracy and has always served the interests of only a minority of the population. It is well known that the original founding documents of the country set out to serve a single white male minority interest and therefore the only notion of democracy pertained exclusively to the privileged white man. Women, Native Americans, African Americans and even poor whites were purposely not included within these agreements. After all, these minority groups were not who the American Revolution was fought for in the first place. Fleeing religious persecution and desiring to rid themselves of the taxation and colonization of England, the privileged white male settlers formed a new country they would govern by and for themselves. And any of the neglected and excluded minorities would have to fight like hell to acquire even a hint of the most basic human rights.

Craig Rosebraugh

It is a grim history that begs the pertinent question of whether a country that has its very foundations based on extreme genocide, on slavery, on theft and robbery, and on subjugating women, Africans, Native Americans, and poor whites can provide a fair and just political structure for all of its people. Judging from the intent of the Founding Fathers, their originating documentation, and the history of exclusion and oppression that has been present throughout U.S. history, the answer demonstrates a most certain impossibility.

From 1776 through to the current day, the governing apparatus of the U.S. has been more akin to a plutocratic oligarchy than a democracy. Where a democracy requires government by the people and for the people, an oligarchy vests all power within a few, a dominant class or a clique. It is a government by the few, benefiting the few, precisely what our Founding Father's agreed upon in drafting the Bill of Rights and the Constitution. So when our Presidents have calmly addressed the nation, telling the public that our women and men in uniform are overseas protecting the democracy and freedom of the United States during a time of war, military action, or police action, in actuality, it is the oligarchy of the U.S. that is being protected. This oligarchy consists of the corporate elite and the individuals used as pawns within government.

Corporate influence and control over the political process in the United States has further strengthened the reality of the oligarch structure. Political campaigns are being won, not out of honest competition, not out of an honest, inclusive political process, but are being won by special interest groups, industry lobbyists, and corporate donors. It is increasingly the case that whoever spends the most money - or is able to raise the most money from corporate sponsors - has the highest chance of being elected. Is it any wonder the United States entered into a war in Iraq and Afghanistan when energy companies and defense contractors fund so much of U.S. politics?

Observing the problems associated with the U.S. oligarchy is simplistic, if one has the desire to open their eyes and think about something other than the new reality television program or who won American Idol, whether one should buy the silver or gold SUV, whether one should sport the new designer fashions, what type of fat, sodium, and chemical laced and animal based food to devour, or what type of mind-deadening device to use as a distraction from reality - crack, heroine, alcohol, or just

222

television.

In 2007, over 37 million people within the United States lived below the mockery of the federally created poverty line. The U.S. continues to have one of the highest rates of poverty among minors of any nation globally. As of 2008, over 47 million people in the U.S. were entirely without healthcare, which included nearly 12 percent of all children below the age of 18.

As a nation we are becoming sicker and dumber. The U.S. consistently ranks below 2/3 of all industrialized countries in teenage testing in science, mathematics, and reading. In less than 30 years, the U.S. has gone from a worldwide leader in education to the back end of the industrialized world. The failure of schools to keep up with advancing technologies, the lowering of education standards, drug and alcohol abuse all play a part in this, but the primary reason for this decline in educational competency is the limiting of educational access by the reduction of funds from the federal level. During Bush Jr.'s Administration, the federal budget allocation for education was a mere 4%, compared with 21% of the federal budget going for military, defense, and security.

Not only is there not a priority on education in the U.S., but health and nutrition have also been severely neglected. Our global food supply has been thoroughly contaminated with chemicals and genetically modified organisms, thanks to corporate giants such as Monsanto and an ineffective Food and Drug Administration. Our children are growing up sicker and malnourished as a result of a reliance upon junk food based around the sugar, salt, fat addiction. The Surgeon General in the U.S. has estimated that by the year 2015, 75% of adults and 24% of children and adolescents in this country will be overweight or obese. This often contributes to an increased risk of heart disease, high blood pressure, diabetes, breathing problems and more. There has, and continues to be, an economic incentive and a societal pressure through the media to forgo a diet and lifestyle of health for one of convenience and addiction.

Global warming has evolved from a theoretical perspective to a very dangerous reality. The U.S. has certainly done its part, being the number one polluter per capita of carbon dioxide (CO_2) in the world. The G8 (the world's wealthiest nations) are responsible for over 80% of the climate change we are experiencing today. As a further step in the wrong direction, the U.S. refused to sign the Kyoto Protocol - the first international agreement to fight global warming. It was signed by 141 nations, including all European and other developed industrial nations, except for the U.S. and Australia. President Obama, who campaigned on promises of environmental protection, only set targeted fuel emissions standards for cars in the U.S. at 35 m.p.g. by 2016, demonstrating once again to the world that the U.S. does not take the threat of global warming seriously.

As of 2009, our war economy and foreign policy in the U.S. has left a documented estimate of over 100,000 Iraqi civilians killed since the beginning of the war. Added to this number are the well over 500,000 Iraqi children who were killed during the 1990s as a result of U.S. sanctions. As of May 20, 2009, some 4,298 U.S. troops have been killed in Iraq along with significant numbers of both civilians and troops killed in Afghanistan. Between 2001 and 2009, the U.S. spent over $850 billion on the *War on Terror*, money that should have been spent elsewhere. For example, $500 billion could have helped fund employer-based health insurance for some 107.5 million Americans.

And what for? Why are we in Iraq? Weapons of mass destruction? To liberate and free the Iraqi people? A freedom somehow acquired through the annihilation of their country? Saddam Hussein was charged with killing 500,000 people and in the 1990s, as a result of U.S.-imposed sanctions, the U.S. had already killed the same number of Iraqis. Add to that the constantly increasing number of civilians killed from the U.S. military invasion after post 9/11, and the U.S. has far surpassed the evil-doings of Saddam. And where Saddam received a hanging for his criminal acts, former President Bush received a healthy retirement package. The U.S. War on Terror has been yet another in the long line of U.S. military actions and occupations designed to protect the corporate and political oligarchy that runs the country. Of course, this was once again disguised as spreading democracy while protecting the freedoms of the U.S. The only freedom this War on Terror has protected is that of the U.S. corporate elite and its freedom to seize and extract any and all resources it desires around the globe for financial gain. While this elite attempt to hide behind their rhetoric of humanitarianism, the people of Rwanda and Darfur wonder if they too had sizable reserves of oil beneath their lands, would they have been "saved"?

Over two million people now reside within U.S. prisons and the U.S. incarcerates more people per capita than any country in the world. Under apartheid, South Africa was internationally condemned as a racist society, jailing 850 per 100,000 black males. The U.S., as of 2008, imprisons 4,789 per 100,000 black males. The U.S. locks up black men at a rate 5.8 times higher than the openly racist South Africa under apartheid in 1993.

With all of the problems attributed to the U.S. political structure and its methodology of governing, why is it then we allow the oligarchy to continue? From the general distrust of the government stemming from occurrences such as the Iraq invasion and failed 9/11 and New Orleans flood responses, to the large gathering of protesters at the World Trade Organization (WTO) and International Monetary Fund (IMF) meetings and Republican and Democratic National Conventions, to the general increase in anger, crime, and disillusionment with the United States, to the record number of voters who turned out to the polls to elect the nation's first African American President in 2008, it is clear the public at large realizes something is wrong. So why do we as a nation allow this to continue? Why do we allow the wars, the corrupt taxation, environmental destruction, animal exploitation, violence and injustice to continue? Why do we continue to allow ourselves to live under the myth of democracy in the United States?

Manufacturing consent. With all of this injustice, one would assume that people would be in the streets demanding justice, demanding change from the government that is supposed to represent them. Perhaps the public rallying behind the Obama Presidential campaign was just that, a cry for change. And yet, just as Malcolm would greet church-goers with a dose of reality after they stepped out from their Sunday sermons expecting to find utopia, the door opening after Obama's election revealed another politician, representing one of the two pre-determined political parties, failing to live up to campaign promises of closing Guantanamo, of environmental protection, of ending the War on Terror and of providing the kind of change truly sought by the American people. More utopian dreams quashed by the oligarchy.

In this society structured upon violence and injustice, one would assume that the military would need to be deployed constantly on the streets to maintain law and order - to "keep the peace" from the masses who would be rising up to demand justice and change. But that is not the case. U.S. corporations and the federal government have a far greater control mechanism in place designed to maintain law and order through the manufacture of consent, desire, and life. *They have the media.*

One wonders, with the amount of advertising that a person in the U.S. is exposed to each and every day, with the news media being yet another form of advertisement for corporate and government agendas, one wonders how much of our own thoughts, opinions, and desires are actually are own? The manufacture of life is a means of taming and configuring the population through corporate control.

Corporate media continually shapes the manner in which we think, what we eat, wear, our appearances, our thoughts, our activities and lives. And yet rarely is that control ever realized or questioned. Too often the word of corporate media is taken as the world of God. The ingenious nature of corporate media is that while all of this injustice is occurring in this country, while all of this bloodshed and violence is occurring overseas in Iraq and Afghanistan, overwhelming proportions of us, from the old to the young, from the rich to the poor, from the sick to the healthy, women, men of all races and origins are conditioned to desire the same thing - a life built around the desire for consumerist goods that we have been convinced we want and need. The new SUV, the new cell phones, the new trendy clothes, the on-demand television, the perfect house in the suburbs, the ideal life - we see all of this on television, in magazines and newspapers. We hear about it on the radio and through ingenious marketing campaigns, which delve heavily into the field of psychology, we are conditioned to believe we want things too. No, we don't just want these things, we *need* them.

So much of our time is spent in constant pursuit of consumer goods - working ourselves to death not just to survive, but to survive in a world where we are able to have our desired consumerist goods and the bills that accompany them. We are so fundamentally caught up in a consumerist culture that the idea of justice, of right and wrong, becomes an abstract. It is something that unfortunately only may come up when one is personally affected by something. Or rather, when one actually feels personally affected. The rest of the time we, as a society, are living our lives in a business as usual manner, immune to the effects our actions or inactions are having on one another and the rest of the world. We are immune to the reality that our inability or refusal to confront injustice in the U.S. is only allowing a heightened degree of violence and injustice to exist.

As we are caught up in consumer culture, our limited intake of any possible rationality comes from the corporate media who line for line accept precisely what the U.S. government and corporations want them to report. *Sure there were weapons of mass destruction, that's why we invaded Iraq, right? Sure, the Iraqis love us there, the locals toppled the giant statue of Saddam shortly after the takeover of Baghdad. We saw it on television. That wasn't staged, that was reality, right? I am positive we are getting all of the news about Iraq and the War in Terror. I mean I see it on television and in the papers every day, right? Certainly, there must be no truth to the fact that nearly 100% of all westernized media stories about the war in Iraq are only stories that the Pentagon approves and wants released. Certainly, there is no truth to the fact that all reporters covering the war in Iraq are kept on a secure compound and restricted from any free travel and movement. The only information they acquire is from the daily Pentagon briefings on site in the compound and from pre-approved excursions with military units. Sure the new wonder drug will cure you from a lifestyle consisting of no exercise, a high fat, sugar, salt, alcohol, and drug diet, right? I saw it on the news, so it must be true.*

When we mix two factors, a manufactured lifestyle with a devotion to consumerist goods and a news media that is manufacturing that very lifestyle, it is no wonder why there is not any significant change in this country. It is no wonder why injustice and violence continue to be prevalent in the U.S. It is no wonder why the myth of democracy continues to prosper, alongside that of the American dream.

So how then do we go about changing this country? How do we go about stopping the injustice and violence that plagues our society and is causing bloodshed around the world? Though it is a matter of simplicity to identify existing and historical problems within the U.S., the difficulty has been suggesting positive, feasible and concrete plans for change. While reformists often still believe that the encompassing political structure is sound, just in need of minor repair (as prominently evidenced with the active and vocal support of the Obama campaign in 2008) this analysis fails to consider that the structure itself is based on a fraudulent and hypocritical notion of democracy. Thus, even if minor repairs are made, the overall structure - the one created in 1776 - will remain the same.

On the opposite end of the spectrum are idealists who, while often having admirable visions of utopia, typically demonstrate little connection to reality and the major complexities in considering the implementation of those dreams. Rarely are there feasible roadmaps offered on how society will transform into these utopian states.

So the difficulty lies not in identifying the problems, but rather in coming up with realistic solutions and a map of how to get there. *So, how do we do it? How do we get to the point of a society that allows for freedom, equality, health, sustainability, peace, and justice? What do we do?* If you're like me and ponder this question daily, a question that has haunted me for many years, you naturally come to the conclusion that what we as a society are doing, what we have done so far to alter or fundamentally change the oligarchy in the U.S. is not working. The same single minority interest is still being served today, as was the case in 1776. This means that our social and political movements, while making fruitful steps in the right direction, have still failed overall in creating the fundamental change necessary to rid the country of its unjust structure. *So where then does the answer lie?*

So often we search externally for answers that we don't feel we are able to answer ourselves. We look to religion, to family, to peers, to friends, to mentors, and even to the myth of democracy and the American Dream. But indeed, our first and most crucial answers must come from within our own hearts. We must look deep within ourselves first and ask ourselves what are we willing to do to create a just, free and sustainable society? What are we willing to give up? What type of devotion are we willing to have? What in our lives are we willing to sacrifice in order for the violence and injustice to end? Are we willing to sacrifice ourselves and devote our lives to creating a peaceful and just society? Only you can answer these questions. Only you have the ability to draw on your compassion, to draw upon the love in your heart, to draw upon your concern for the well being of others, and figure out on your own what you are willing to do.

So often we tell ourselves that we are doing all we can. Yet, there is a significant different between doing all that one is comfortable with, and doing all one can and is able to do. In order for the possibility of fundamental political and social change to ever come to the United States, we all have the responsibility to do not just what we are comfortable with, but all we can do. No change has ever occurred from people restricting their activity to that which is only comfortable.

The motivation is endless. Think of the millions of animals killed every year for food, for clothing, for entertainment, for research. Think of the clear cutting of forests in the Pacific Northwest, or the pollution of waterways in the East, or the rampant urban sprawl all across the country. Think of the polar bear becoming extinct due to warming temperatures melting ice caps and glaciers and the industrial pollution of its habitat. Think of the millions of people and animals that will be displaced and killed as a result of global warming and the rising of global sea levels. Think of the foreign policy atrocities of the U.S. that have resulted in the institution of corporate puppet regimes and the murder of millions of people globally. Think of the lack of healthcare, the poor nutrition, the ailing economy, the failed New Orleans flood response, the daily deceit used by politicians to justify their corporate wars and domestic oppression. Think of the prison population, or better put, the modern day slave plantations and concentration camps, in which more people are incarcerated per capita than in any other country. Think of all the political prisoners in the U.S. that have sacrificed their lives and freedom in pursuit of positive change. And perhaps most of all, think of the myth of democracy, a myth that has been forced onto the American people since 1776. Are you going to continue to believe in the myth and in the American Dream or are you going to do something about it?

A new movement needs to be born, unlike one ever to live in the United States, that uses creativity, that is innovative, that engages the masses, that empowers people, that draws on all of the population, one that is truly based upon the concern we have for one another, animals and our environment, a movement based upon health and longevity, and one that is uncompromising in its pursuit of justice, equality, sustainability and peace. Maybe you will play a part in this movement. Maybe your life will be dedicated towards reaching these goals. Maybe we will all join together one day in the future, breathing deeply in happiness, as we celebrate the success in creating a new society we can be proud of. Only you can answer this. Only you can create your own potential. Once our individual power and commitment are realized, our capabilities are endless.

To continue this dialogue, or if you're interested in getting involved in creating a revolutionary movement in the United States, contact:

USrevolutionarymovement@gmail.com

(Assume all correspondence is monitored).

ABOUT THE AUTHOR

A political activist since the early 1990s when he opposed the Gulf War, Craig Rosebraugh is best known for his role as the national spokesperson for the Earth Liberation Front and Animal Liberation Front. From 1997 through 2001, Craig was the public face of the Earth Liberation Front, representing the group to the international news media and public. He was the co-founder of the North American Earth Liberation Front Press Office (NAELFPO) in 2000. Despite being threatened with imprisonment, two raids by federal authorities on his homes and businesses, eight federal grand jury investigations, a forced appearance in front of U.S. Congress, FBI and ATF questioning, and hundreds of death threats, he did not reveal the identities of members of the movements.

In addition to his work as a spokesperson for direct action movements, Craig was a volunteer organizer for People for Animal Rights (Portland), co-founded and served as Executive Director for the Liberation Collective organization (Portland), has co-organized two national conferences against animal experimentation, was the National Organizer for the 1997 Regional Tour of the Seven Regional Primate Research Centers, was the National Organizer for the 1999 Primate Freedom Tour (a three-month caravan protesting primate research centers across the U.S.), organized marches, protests and benefits in support of political prisoners and against police brutality, participated in a dozen civil disobedience actions nationwide in support of human, environmental and animal liberation, drafted legislation to change post-conviction relief laws in Arizona, owned and operated an organic vegan restaurant, and is the founder and Managing Editor of Arissa Media Group.

Craig has been featured in hundreds of news media stories, including: New York Times and NY Times Sunday Magazine, National Geographic, Inc. Magazine, Los Angeles Times, Denver Post, Seattle Times, Maxim, Details, Rolling Stone, The Guardian, Christian Science Monitor, USA Today, Time, Newsweek, Village Voice, Outside Magazine, National Public Radio, 60 Minutes, 20/20, The Today Show, Court TV, CBS/NBC/ABC Evening News, Fox News, PBS Nova/Frontline, and Dateline Australia. He has lectured on environmental protection, animal liberation and the necessity of a revolution in the United States at dozens of locations across the United States, including: National Conference on Organized Resistance (Washington, DC), World Congress on

Animal Rights (Washington, DC), Land, Air, Water Environmental Law Conference (Eugene, OR), Animal Law Conference (Lewis & Clark College, Portland, OR), Fresno State University (CA), University of Arizona (Tucson), Vassar College (NY), Virginia Tech (VA) , University of Pennsylvania (Philadelphia), Reed College (OR), Oregon State University (Corvallis), University of Wisconsin (Madison), Portland State University (OR), University of Oregon (Eugene), Pacific University (OR), and the Evergreen State College (WA).

Craig is the author of *Burning Rage of a Dying Planet: Speaking for the Earth Liberation Front* and *The Logic of Political Violence: Lessons in Reform and Revolution.* Additionally, he has written articles for the *Earth First! Journal, No Compromise* magazine and *Toward Freedom,* in addition to a feature-length screenplay, *One Earth,* based on the Earth Liberation Front.

Craig holds both a bachelor of arts and a master of arts in political science and is currently working toward a law degree. He may be contacted directly through his website at: www.craigrosebraugh.com.

Links
www.resistancemagazine.org
www.elfpressoffice.org
www.directaction.info
www.finalnail.com
www.animalliberationfront.com
www.ecoprisoners.org
www.thejerichomovement.com
www.indymedia.org
www.arissamediagroup.com